Collins

French

with Audio

AQA GCSE

Revision Guide

vision

ch

Karine Harrington,
and Vanessa Salter

D0183131

Contents

Contents

Key Stage 3 Concepts

1 **Copiez les mots ci-dessous dans la bonne espace dans les trois listes.** Copy out the words below into the correct space in the three lists.

juillet | hiver | dimanche | printemps | août | mardi | avril | vendredi | mercredi | janvier

Les saisons (seasons)	Les mois (months)		Les jours de la semaine (days of the week)
le *printemps*	janvier	*juillet*	lundi
l'été	février	*août*	*mardi*
l'automne	mars	septembre	*mercredi*
l' *hiver*	*avril*	octobre	jeudi
	mai	novembre	*vendredi*
	juin	décembre	samedi
			dimanche

[10 marks]

2 **Reliez les dates et les fêtes**. Match up the dates and the festivals.

le premier avril	le Jour de Noël
le quatorze février	Halloween
le vingt-cinq décembre	le Jour de l'An
le trente-et-un octobre	la Saint-Valentin
le premier janvier	April Fool's Day
le cinq novembre	Bonfire Night

[6 marks]

3 **Répondez aux questions suivantes en français.** Answer these questions in French.

a) **Comment t'appelles-tu?**
   Je m'appelle Zarina.

b) **Quel âge as-tu?**
   J'ai quatorze ans.

c) **Quelle est la date de ton anniversaire?**
   La date de mon anniversaire est vingt-six juillet deux mille et trois.

d) **Où habites-tu?**
   J'habite en London, Wembley.

e) **As-tu des frères ou des sœurs?**
   Non, je n'ai pas des frères ou des sœurs.

f) **As-tu un animal à la maison?**
   Non, je n'ai pas un animal à la maison.

[6 marks]

4 **Recopiez chaque groupe de nombres en changeant les mots en chiffres.** Copy each group of numbers, changing the words into numerals.

a) **dix** 10   **deux** 2   **douze** 12

b) **quatre** 14   **quarante** 40   **quatorze** 14 .

c) **quinze** 15   **cinquante-cinq** 55   **cinq** 5

d) **trente** 30   **treize** 13   **trois** 3

e) **soixante** 60   **soixante-dix** 70   **seize** 16

f) **vingt-quatre** 24   **quatre-vingts** 80   **quatre-vingt-dix** 90

[18 marks]

5 **Écrivez ces nombres en mots français.** Write these numerals as French words.

a) 32   b) 53   c) 46   d) 65   e) 74   f) 82   g) 93

a) trente-deux   b) cinquante-trois   c) quarante-six   d) soixante-cinq
   e) soixante-dix-quatre   f) quatre-vingt-deux   g) quatre-vingt-dix-trois

[7 marks]

6 **Reliez l'heure à la bonne phrase.** Match the time to the correct sentence.

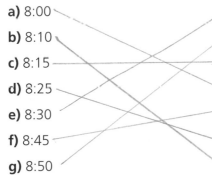

a) 8:00   Il est huit heures et demie.
b) 8:10   Il est neuf heures moins dix.
c) 8:15   Il est huit heures et quart.
d) 8:25   Il est huit heures.
e) 8:30   Il est neuf heures moins le quart.
f) 8:45   Il est huit heures vingt-cinq.
g) 8:50   Il est huit heures dix.

[7 marks]

7 **Écrivez une phrase pour chaque heure. Pour vous aider, utilisez l'exercice 6.** Write a sentence for each time. Use exercise 6 to help you.

a) 7:30   b) 2:15   c) 5:20   d) 9:45   e) 10:00

a) Il est sept heures et demie. b) Il est deux heures et quart.

c) Il est cinq heures vingt. d) Il est dix heures moins le quart.

e) Il est dix heures.

[5 marks]

My Family

You must be able to:

- Describe appearance and personality
- Say how well you get on with family members
- Make adjectives agree correctly.

Family Members

- **mon (beau-) père** — my (step-) father
  mon grand-père — my grandfather
  mon (demi-) frère — my (step/half-) brother
  mon frère aîné / cadet — my older / younger brother
  mon beau-frère — my brother-in-law
  mon oncle — my uncle
  mon neveu — my nephew
  ma (belle-) mère — my (step-) mother
  ma grand-mère — my grandmother
  ma (demi-) sœur — my (step/half-) sister
  ma sœur aînée / cadette — my older / younger sister
  ma belle-sœur — my sister-in-law
  ma tante — my aunt
  ma nièce — my niece
  mes parents — my parents
  mes grands-parents — my grandparents

> ### Key Point
>
> Remember, there are three words for 'my':
>
> Masculine singular **mon**
> Feminine singular **ma**
> Plural **mes**

Describing Appearance

- **Il / Elle est…** — He / She is…
- **Ils / Elles sont…** — They are…

  assez / un peu — quite / a bit
  très / trop — very / too

> ### Key Vocab
>
> | | |
> |---|---|
> | **Il / Elle est** | He / She is |
> | **Ils / Elles sont** | They are |

	masculine singular	feminine singular	masculine plural	feminine plural
big / tall	**grand**	**grande**	**grands**	**grandes**
small	**petit**	**petite**	**petits**	**petites**
pretty	**joli**	**jolie**	**jolis**	**jolies**
ugly	**laid**	**laide**	**laids**	**laides**
slim	**mince**	**mince**	**minces**	**minces**
thin	**maigre**	**maigre**	**maigres**	**maigres**
young	**jeune**	**jeune**	**jeunes**	**jeunes**
fat	**gros**	**grosse**	**gros**	**grosses**
old	**vieux**	**vieille**	**vieux**	**vieilles**
beautiful / good-looking	**beau**	**belle**	**beaux**	**belles**

> ### Key Point
>
> Adjectives must agree with the noun they describe. Most adjectives add **–e** in the feminine singular, **–s** in the masculine plural and **–es** in the feminine plural.
>
> If the adjective already ends in **–e** (e.g. **mince**) it stays the same in the feminine.
>
> A few adjectives, like **beau** and **vieux**, are irregular.

- **Mon grand-père est assez vieux et un peu gros. Il a une barbe blanche.**
  My grandfather is quite old and a bit fat. He has a white beard.
- **Ma belle-sœur est petite, mince et très jolie.**
  My sister-in-law is small, slim and very pretty.
- **Mes parents sont assez grands et maigres.**
  My parents are quite tall and thin.

Relationships

- **Je m'entends bien avec**…   I get on well with…
- **Je ne m'entends pas très bien avec**…   I don't get on very well with…
- **Je me dispute avec**…   I argue with…
- **On se dispute.**   We argue.
- **Je me fâche contre**…   I get angry with…
- **Il / Elle se fâche contre moi.**   He / She gets angry with me.

Adjectives of Personality

aimable	nice	**agaçant(e)**	annoying
généreux / généreuse	generous	**bavard(e)**	talkative
		bête	stupid
gentil / gentille	kind	**égoïste**	selfish
heureux / heureuse	happy	**méchant(e)**	naughty
		paresseux / paresseuse	lazy
sage	good, well-behaved		
sympa	nice, kind	**pénible**	a pain
tranquille	quiet, calm	**sévère**	strict
travailleur / travailleuse	hard-working	**têtu(e)**	stubborn
		triste	sad

- **Je m'entends bien avec ma grand-mère parce qu'elle est toujours très gentille.**
  I get on well with my grandmother because she is always very kind.
- **Mais je me dispute tout le temps avec mon frère aîné car il est trop égoïste.**
  But I argue all the time with my older brother because he is too selfish.

> **Key Point**
>
> Use expressions of frequency, to add detail:
> **toujours**   always
> **souvent**   often
> **tout le temps**   all the time
> **quelquefois**   sometimes
> **rarement**   rarely
> **de temps en temps**   from time to time

> **Quick Test**
>
> 1. Translate into English:
>   **Je m'entends très bien avec mon oncle. Il est assez vieux et maigre, mais il est toujours heureux et aimable.**
> 2. Translate into French:
>   I don't get on very well with my younger sister. She is slim and pretty, but very lazy and badly behaved. We argue all the time.
> 3. Write a description of a family member. Describe his / her appearance and say whether you get on well with him / her, giving reasons.

> **Key Vocab**
>
> **Je m'entends bien avec**…
> I get on well with…
> **Je ne m'entends pas très bien avec**…
> I don't get on very well with…

My Friends

You must be able to:

- Describe a friend's appearance
- Explain why you are friends
- Use **on** and **nous** correctly.

Describing a Friend's Appearance

Mon meilleur ami / copain...	My best friend (male)...
Ma meilleure amie / copine...	My best friend (female)...
s'appelle...	is called...
Il / Elle a...	He / She has...
les yeux bleus	blue eyes
... **gris**	grey
... **verts**	green
... **marron**	brown
... **noisette**	hazel
les cheveux bruns	brown hair
... **noirs**	black
... **blonds**	blond
... **roux**	red / ginger
... **longs**	long
... **courts**	short
... **mi-longs**	medium-length
... **bouclés / frisés**	curly
... **raides**	straight

- **Il / Elle porte des lunettes.**   He / She wears glasses.
- **Il / Elle est plus / moins grand(e) que moi.**   He / She is taller / shorter than me.
- **Il / Elle est de taille moyenne.**   He / She is of medium height.
- **On se connaît depuis ... ans.**   We have known each other for ... years.

- **Mon meilleur ami s'appelle Tom. Il a les yeux noisette et les cheveux courts, noirs et bouclés. On se connaît depuis cinq ans.**
  My best friend is called Tom. He has hazel eyes and short, black, curly hair. We have known each other for five years.

- **Ma meilleure copine s'appelle Chloé. Elle porte des lunettes et elle a les cheveux roux, mi-longs et raides. Elle est un peu plus grande que moi.**
  My best friend is called Chloé. She wears glasses and has red, medium-length, straight hair. She is a bit taller than me.

The Qualities of a Friend

Il / Elle est...	He / She is...
fidèle	faithful, loyal
honnête	honest
intelligent(e)	intelligent / clever

Key Point

Adjectives of colour always come *after* the noun.
e.g. **les yeux bleus**.

A small number of adjectives are invariable (do not agree). e.g. **marron**, **noisette**.

NB 'Brown' = **marron** with eyes, but **bruns** with hair.

sportif / sportive	sporty
timide	shy
toujours de bonne humeur	always in a good mood

- **Il / Elle me fait rire.** — He / She makes me laugh.
- **Il / Elle n'est jamais…** — He / She is never…

fâché(e)	angry, cross
jaloux / jalouse	jealous
de mauvaise humeur	in a bad mood

What You Have in Common

- **Nous avons / On a beaucoup de choses en commun.** — We have a lot in common.
- **Nous avons / On a le même sens de l'humour.** — We have the same sense of humour.
- **Nous aimons / On aime…** — We like…

la même musique	the same music
la même équipe de foot	the same football team
les mêmes sports	the same sports
les mêmes émissions de télé	the same TV programmes

What You Do Together

- **On se retrouve tous les week-ends.** — We meet up every weekend.
- **On s'envoie des SMS tous les soirs.** — We text each other every evening.
- **On fait les magasins ensemble.** — We go shopping together.
- **On va au cinéma ensemble.** — We go to the cinema together.
- **On joue à des jeux vidéo ensemble.** — We play video games together.
- **On écoute de la musique ensemble.** — We listen to music together.

- **Mon meilleur copain, Sayed, est fidèle et assez timide. Il est toujours de bonne humeur et il me fait beaucoup rire.**
  My best friend Sayed is loyal and quite shy. He is always in a good mood and makes me laugh a lot.
- **Ma meilleure amie, Sophie, n'est jamais jalouse. Nous aimons la même musique. On se retrouve tous les week-ends et on fait les magasins ensemble.**
  My best friend Sophie is never jealous. We like the same music. We meet up every weekend and go shopping together.

Revise

Key Point

même (same) is an important little word which often crops up in exams. The same… =
le même… (followed by a masculine singular noun)
la même… (followed by a feminine singular noun)
les mêmes… (followed by a plural noun)

Key Point

Remember, '**on**' and '**nous**' can both be used to mean 'we'. Take care to use the correct verb ending with each one.
In the present tense:
- Most verbs end in **–ons** in the **nous**-form.
- Regular **–er** verbs end in **–e** in the **on**-form, but irregular verb endings can vary.

Key Vocab

Mon meilleur ami / copain…
My best friend (male)…
Ma meilleure amie / copine…
My best friend (female)…
Il / Elle a…
He / She has…
Nous avons / On a…
We have…
Nous aimons / On aime…
We like…

Quick Test

1. Say or write in French: My best friend (female) has green eyes and long, blond, curly hair. She is quite sporty.
2. Choose the correct word: **Il n'est jamais de mauvaise humeur / humour.**
3. Choose the correct words, then translate the sentence: **Nous aimons le / la / les même / mêmes musique et le / la / les même / mêmes sports.**
4. Describe your best friend: say what he / she looks like, what his / her qualities are and what you have in common or do together.

Marriage and Partnerships

You must be able to:

- Describe people's marital status
- Say whether you want to get married
- Use **depuis** with the present tense.

Marital Status

- **la situation de famille** — marital status
  l'amour — love
  célibataire — single (not married)
  le petit ami — boyfriend
  la petite amie — girlfriend
  le mariage — marriage / wedding
  le mari / la femme — husband / wife
  le / la partenaire — partner
  le fils / la fille — son / daughter
  le fils / la fille unique — only child
  le fiancé / la fiancée — fiancé / fiancée
  HT l'anniversaire de mariage — wedding anniversary

- **habiter ensemble** — to live together
  être marié(e) — to be married
  se marier — to get married
  être divorcé(e) / séparé(e) — to be divorced / separated
  avoir un bébé / des enfants — to have a baby / children
  naître — to be born
  mourir / décéder — to die
  HT tomber amoureux / amoureuse — to fall in love
  se fiancer — to get engaged
  se pacser — to become civil partners

- **Mon oncle est célibataire.** — My uncle is single.
- **Mon grand-père est mort.** — My grandfather is dead.
- **Mes parents sont divorcés depuis deux ans.** — My parents have been divorced for two years.

> ### Key Point
>
> **Depuis** means 'since'.
>
> Use it with *the present tense*, to say how long something has been going on.
>
> **Ma sœur est mariée depuis six mois.**
> My sister has been married for six months.

> ### HT Key Point
>
> Make sure you know how to use reflexive verbs in other tenses:
> - **Ma cousine va se marier en juin.**
>   My cousin is going to get married in June.
> - **Mon frère s'est fiancé la semaine dernière.**
>   My brother got engaged last week.

Do You Want to Get Married?

- **Tu voudrais te marier?** — Would you like to get married?
  Je voudrais me marier un jour. — I'd like to get married one day.
  Je ne voudrais pas me marier. — I wouldn't like to get married.
  Je préférerais rester célibataire. — I'd prefer to stay single.
  J'aimerais avoir des enfants. — I'd like to have children.
  Je ne sais pas encore. — I don't know yet.

> ### Key Point
>
> Use the conditional to say what you would / would not like to do:
> **Je voudrais / J'aimerais / Je ne voudrais pas / Je n'aimerais pas** (+ an infinitive).

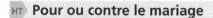 **Pour ou contre le mariage** — For and against marriage

Pour	Contre
C'est une preuve d'amour. It's proof of love.	**C'est complètement démodé.** It's completely outdated.
C'est mieux pour les enfants. It's better for children.	**Il vaut mieux habiter ensemble.** It's better to live together.
C'est plus sécurisant que simplement habiter ensemble. It's more secure than simply living together.	**Le mariage se termine souvent par un divorce.** Marriage often ends in divorce.

D'un côté, le mariage, c'est une preuve d'amour. D'un autre côté, beaucoup de mariages se terminent par un divorce.
On the one hand, marriage is proof of love. On the other hand, lots of marriages end in divorce.

> ### Key Vocab
>
> **être marié(e)**
> to be married
> **être divorcé(e) / séparé(e)**
> to be divorced / separated
> **célibataire**
> single, not married
> **depuis**
> since, for
> **Je voudrais me marier.**
> I'd like to get married.
> **Je ne voudrais pas me marier.**
> I wouldn't like to get married.

> ## Quick Test
>
> 1. Give the French for these words:
>   married divorced separated to be born
>   to die to have children
> 2. Translate into English:
>   a) **Je crois que je ne voudrais pas me marier. Je préférerais rester célibataire.**
>   b) **Mes grands-parents sont mariés depuis trente ans.**
> 3. Say or write whether you would like to get married one day.
>   Give a reason.

Social Media

You must be able to:

- Talk about computers and the internet
- Discuss how you use social media
- Use **il faut**.

Computers and the Internet

- **l'ordinateur** (m)   computer
  l'ordinateur portable (m)   laptop
  la tablette   tablet
  le réseau social   social network
  le clavier   keyboard
  le forum   chat room
  le mail / le courrier électronique / le mél   email
  le site web / internet   website
  la souris   mouse
  la touche   key
  l'écran (m)   screen
  l'imprimante (f)   printer
  la page d'accueil   homepage
  HT **la clé USB**   memory stick

Online Activities

- **les activités en ligne**   online activities
  aller en ligne   to go online
  chercher   to search
  cliquer   to click
  envoyer   to send
  imprimer   to print
  mettre en ligne   to upload
  recevoir   to receive, get
  surfer (sur internet)   to surf (the net)
  taper   to type / key in
  tchatter (en ligne)   to chat online
  télécharger   to download
  HT **mettre à jour**   to update

- **Je passe beaucoup de temps en ligne.**   I spend a lot of time online.
- **Chaque jour, je vais sur mes sites web préférés.**   Every day, I go on to my favourite sites.
- **J'envoie et je reçois des messages.**   I send and receive messages.

> ### Key Point
>
> The verbs **aller**, **envoyer**, **mettre** and **recevoir** are irregular: **je vais** (I go), **j'envoie** (I send), **je mets** (I put), **je reçois** (I receive)

Protecting Yourself Online

- **se protéger en ligne** — protecting yourself online

Il faut… You should / have to / must…	**Il ne faut jamais**… You should / must never…
installer un logiciel anti-virus install anti-virus software	**révéler son mot de passe** reveal your password
changer régulièrement son mot de passe change your password regularly	**partager ses détails personnels** share your personal details
	communiquer avec des inconnus communicate with strangers

Key Point

Il faut… means 'you / we / one must or should…' It is followed by a verb in the infinitive.

Social Networks

- **les réseaux sociaux** — social networks
- **J'utilise les réseaux sociaux pour**… — I use social media for…
  rester en contact avec mes copains. — staying in touch with my friends.
  poster des messages. — posting messages.
  partager des photos, des vidéos et des liens. — sharing photos, videos and links.

HT Advantages and Disadvantages

- **les avantages et les inconvénients** — advantages and disadvantages
- **La meilleure chose, c'est qu'on peut rester en contact avec les autres.** — The best thing is that you can stay in touch with other people.
- **La pire, c'est le cyberharcèlement.** — The worst thing is cyber bullying.

Key Vocab

l'ordinateur (m) computer
le site web / internet website
le réseau social social network
aller en ligne to go online
rester en contact avec mes copains to stay in touch with my friends
Il faut… You / we / one must…

Quick Test

1. Name four pieces of computer equipment, in French.
2. Correct the following advice about using the internet:
   a) **Il faut partager son mot de passe.**
   b) **Il ne faut jamais installer un logiciel anti-virus.**
3. Complete the following sentence about yourself. Mention at least two things.
   J'utilise les réseaux sociaux pour…

Mobile Technology

You must be able to:

- Talk about what you use your mobile for
- Give opinions about mobile technology
- Use adverbs.

Using a Mobile Phone

- **Utiliser son portable** — Using a mobile phone
  J'envoie des SMS. — I send texts / I text.
  Je téléphone à mes amis. — I call my friends.
  Je parle avec mes copains / copines. — I talk to my friends.
  Je fais des achats en ligne. — I shop online.
  J'écoute de la musique. — I listen to music.
  Je télécharge des applis et des sonneries. — I download apps and ringtones.
  Je joue à des jeux. — I play games.
  Je lis mes messages. — I read my messages.
  Je fais des recherches pour mes devoirs. — I do research for my homework.
  Je prends des photos. — I take photos.

Giving Opinions

- **À mon avis, c'est**… — In my opinion, it is…

  Je trouve ça… — I find it…

amusant	amusing
drôle / marrant	funny
génial	great
pratique	practical / handy
rapide	fast
rigolo	a laugh / funny
utile	useful

affreux / horrible	horrible, terrible
barbant / ennuyeux	boring
ridicule	ridiculous
trop cher	too expensive

- **Je télécharge de la musique sur mon portable, parce que je trouve ça rapide et moins cher.**
  I download music on my mobile, because it's fast and less expensive.

> ### Key Point
> Look back at the expressions of frequency on page 7. Use these to say how often you do things on your mobile.

> ### Key Point
> Make sure you know these irregular verbs:
> **faire** (to do) – **je fais**
> **lire** (to read) – **je lis**
> **prendre** (to take) –
> **je prends**

HT Advantages and Disadvantages of Mobile Technology

les avantages de la technologie portable	the advantages of mobile technology
• **On peut**…	You / One can…
communiquer facilement avec les gens	communicate easily with people
contacter quelqu'un en cas d'urgence	contact someone in an emergency
se tenir toujours au courant	always keep up to date
trouver rapidement des informations	find information quickly
organiser des sorties et des rendez-vous	organise going out and getting together

HT **les problèmes de la technologie portable**	the problems with mobile technology
• **Parfois, il n'y a pas de réseau.**	Sometimes, there is no signal.
• **Il faut recharger régulièrement son portable.**	You have to charge your mobile regularly.
• **La technologie change trop vite.**	The technology changes too fast.
• **Ça coûte cher d'acheter la dernière version.**	It's expensive to buy the latest upgrade.
• **Certaines personnes passent trop de temps sur leur portable.**	Some people spend too much time on their mobile.

Key Point

Use adverbs to say **how** you do something. Most adverbs end in **–ment**:

facilement (easily)

rapidement (quickly)

régulièrement (regularly)

Key Vocab

Je parle
I talk / speak
J'écoute
I listen to
Je fais
I do
Je lis
I read
Je prends
I take
À mon avis, c'est…
In my opinion, it is…
Je trouve ça…
I find it…

Quick Test

1. Which is the odd verb out and why?
   je parle   je prends   je joue   je télécharge   j'écoute
2. Translate these adverbs into English:
   rapidement   facilement   régulièrement
3. Translate into French:
   In my opinion, mobile technology is useful and fun, but it's too expensive.

Music

You must be able to:

- Discuss musical interests and preferences
- Give your opinions on different types of music and songs
- Talk about a favourite musician or music event you've been to.

Musical Interests and Preferences

- **la musique pop**   pop music
  la musique classique   classical music
  l'électro   electronic music
  le hip-hop   hip hop
  le jazz   jazz
  le rap   rap
  le reggae   reggae
  le (vieux) rock   rock music

- **l'artiste** (m, f)   artist
  le chanteur   (male) singer
  la chanteuse   (female) singer
  le groupe   group
  HT la chorale   choir

- **aimer**   to like
  aimer mieux   to prefer
  adorer   to adore
  préférer   to prefer
  être fana de   to be a fan of
  chanter   to sing
  écouter   to listen to
  jouer (du piano / de la guitare) to play (the piano / the guitar)
  s'intéresser à   to be interested in
  télécharger   to download

Talking about Music

- **On discute la musique**   Talking about music
  Je m'intéresse beaucoup à la musique. I'm very interested in music.
  Je télécharge les chansons et j'écoute de la musique sur mon iPod tous les jours.
  I download songs and listen to music on my iPod every day.

- **Quel genre de musique préfères-tu?** What sort of music do you prefer?
  Je préfère…   I prefer…
  Ma famille préfère…   My family prefers…
  Nous préférons…   We prefer…
  Mes parents préfèrent…   My parents prefer…

- **Je préfère le rock.**   I prefer rock.
- **Ma famille préfère écouter de la musique classique.**
  My family prefers listening to classical music.

Key Vocab

l'artiste	artist
le chanteur	singer (m)
la chanteuse	singer (f)
le groupe	group
le tube	hit

Key Vocab

Je préfère I prefer
mon chanteur préféré
my favourite singer
Je préfère écouter
I prefer to listen to / I prefer listening to
que j'aime le plus / le moins
(that) I like most / least

Key Point

Remember not to pronounce the '**–ent**' ending: '**préfère**' and '**préfèrent**' sound the same!

- **Le genre de musique que j'aime le plus / le moins, c'est** …
  The type of music (that) I like most / least is…

- **As-tu un chanteur ou une chanteuse préféré(e)?**
  Do you have a favourite singer?
- **Mon chanteur préféré s'appelle**… My favourite singer is…

- **le rythme** the rhythm
  la voix voice
  HT **la mélodie** melody
  les paroles (f) the words

- **ça me plaît** I like it
  ça m'énerve it gets on my nerves
  ça me détend it relaxes me
  ça me fait sourire it makes me smile
  ça me rend triste it makes me sad

- **Sa chanson me fait sourire à cause des paroles romantiques**.
  His / Her song makes me smile because of the romantic words.
- **La mélodie me détend et me rend heureux.**
  The melody relaxes me and makes me happy.

HT Opinions using the Perfect Tense

- **J'ai toujours écouté du rap même si mes copains ne l'aiment pas.**
  I've always listened to rap even if my friends don't like it.
- **Je n'ai jamais écouté de jazz parce que ça ne me plaît pas.**
  I've never listened to jazz because I don't like it.

Describe a Music Event

- **le concert** concert
  les émissions de musique music TV programmes
  la Fête de la Musique World Music Day (annual festival 21 June)
  le festival (de musique) music festival
  le tube hit
  la vedette star
  HT **la tournée** tour

- **L'année dernière je suis allé(e) au festival de Glastonbury où j'ai vu tous mes groupes préférés.**
  Last year I went to Glastonbury where I saw all my favourite groups.

Key Point

Always use de after a negative phrase, e.g. **Il n'a jamais écouté de hip-hop.** He has never listened to hip hop.

Key Vocab

toujours	always
ne…**jamais**	never
parce que	because
à cause de	because of
même si	even if / even though
Je suis allé(e)	I went
J'ai vu	I saw

Quick Test

1. How do you pronounce **'Mes parents préfèrent le jazz'**?
2. What is the difference between **'je préfère'** and **'mon chanteur préféré'**? Say them out loud!
3. Translate into English:
   Le genre de musique que j'aime le plus c'est le hip-hop.
   La chanson me fait sourire.
4. Translate into French:
   I've always listened to reggae music.

Cinema and TV

You must be able to:

- Describe a film or TV programme
- Discuss whether you prefer going to the cinema or watching TV
- Use verbs followed by the infinitive.

Describing a Film or TV Programme

- **décris un film ou une émission** — describe a film or TV programme

- **les actualités / les informations** (f) — the news
  le dessin animé — cartoon
  le feuilleton — soap
  le film de guerre — war film
  le jeu télévisé — game show
  la série — series
  la télé réalité — reality TV

- **un film policier** — detective film
  une émission de télé réalité — a reality TV programme
  une histoire — a story

- **Ça / Il me fait rire.** — It makes me laugh.
- **Ça / Il me fait pleurer.** — It makes me cry.
- **Ça / Il me fait peur.** — It frightens me.
- **qui** — which
- **HT avoir lieu** — to take place

- **C'est une histoire d'amour émouvante qui a lieu en Afrique pendant la guerre.**
  It's a moving love story which takes place in Africa during the war.
- **C'est un dessin animé amusant qui me fait rire.**
  It's a funny cartoon which makes me laugh.

- **De quoi s'agit-il?** — What's it about?
- **Il s'agit de…** — It's about…
- **qui** — who

- **Il s'agit d'un ado qui sauve la planète.**
  It's about a teenager who saves the planet.
- **Il s'agit d'une fille qui recherche sa famille.**
  It's about a girl who is looking for her family.
- **Il s'agit de soldats qui éliminent leurs adversaires.**
  It's about soldiers who eliminate their enemies.

Go to the Cinema or Watch TV?

- **Aller au cinéma ou regarder la télé?** — Go to the cinema or watch TV?

- **le billet** — ticket
  le grand écran — the big screen
  la publicité — adverts

Key Vocab

De quoi s'agit-il?
What's it about?
Il s'agit de…   It's about…
qui   who / which

Key Point

Remember to change **de** to **d'** before a word beginning with a vowel and with words beginning with a silent 'h' BUT **qui** is never shortened.

le siège	seat
la séance	performance
le son surround	surround sound
la vedette (de cinéma)	(film) star
HT les effets spéciaux	special effects

- **Je préfère regarder les films chez moi.**
  I prefer to watch films at home.
- **Mes copines adorent aller au cinéma.**
  My (girl)friends love to go to the cinema.
- **Nous aimons mieux télécharger les films.**
  We prefer to download films.

Making Comparisons

- **pourquoi?**   why?

- **Les effets spéciaux sont meilleurs sur le grand écran.**
  The special effects are better on the big screen.
- **Les sièges sont plus confortables.**
  (The) seats are more comfortable.
- **Les séances sont moins fréquentes.**
  (The) showings are less frequent.
- **Les billets deviennent de plus en plus chers.**
  Tickets are becoming more and more expensive.

Key Vocab

meilleur(e)(s)	better
plus	more
moins	less
de plus en plus	
more and more	

HT Justifying your Argument

- **On doit**…   You must…
- **Il faut**…   You have to…
- **On peut**…   You can…
- **On veut**…   You want to…
- **Il vaut mieux**…   It's better to…

- **Il faut regarder toute la publicité.**   You have to watch all the adverts.
- **On doit payer les billets.**   You must (have to) pay for tickets.
- **Selon ma mère, il vaut mieux rester chez nous parce qu'on peut regarder le film quand on veut. Si on va au cinéma, on doit payer les billets et en plus il faut regarder toute la publicité.**
  According to my mother, it's better to stay at home because you can watch the film when you want to. If you go to the cinema, you must pay for tickets and what's more you have to watch all the adverts.

- Make some sentences negative.
  - **On ne doit jamais payer les billets.**
    You never have to pay for tickets.

Key Point

The following verbs are all followed by an infinitive:
j'aime, j'aime mieux, j'adore, je préfère, on doit, on peut, on veut, il faut, il vaut mieux.

Key Vocab

On doit…	You must…
Il faut…	You have to…
On peut…	You can…
On veut…	You want to…
Il vaut mieux…	
It's better to…	

Quick Test

1. What does the question **'De quoi s'agit-il?'** mean?
2. Translate into English: **Il s'agit d'un homme qui doit sauver la planète.**
3. Translate into French:
   a) I prefer watching television at home.
   b) You never have to pay for tickets.

Food

You must be able to:

- Buy food in France
- Discuss what you and your family eat at mealtimes
- Use negatives.

Quantities

la boîte	box, tin, can
la bouteille	bottle
500 grammes	500 grams
le kilo	kilo
le morceau	piece
le paquet	packet
la tranche	slice

Shopping at a French Market

- **Je voudrais un kilo de framboises, s'il vous plaît.** — I would like a kilo of raspberries, please.
- **Bien sûr. Je vais les peser.** — Of course. I'll weigh them.
- **Avez-vous des ananas?** — Do you have any pineapples?
- **Combien en voulez-vous?** — How many would you like?
- **Et avec ça?** — Anything else?
- **Voilà. C'est tout?** — There you are. Is that everything?
- **Oui merci. C'est combien?** — Yes, thank you. How much is that?
- **Ça fait neuf euros cinquante.** — That's € 9,50.

Meals

le petit-déjeuner	breakfast		**le dîner**	dinner, evening meal
le déjeuner	lunch		**le repas**	meal
le goûter	afternoon snack			

Verbs

manger	to eat		**dîner**	to have dinner (evening meal)
prendre	to have (take)		**déjeuner**	to have lunch
boire	to drink		**goûter**	to taste / sample

How Often?

tous les jours	every day		**une fois par semaine**	once a week
normalement	normally		**de temps en temps**	from time to time
d'habitude	usually			
souvent	often		**rarement**	rarely
quelquefois	sometimes			

- **D'habitude pour le petit-déjeuner mon frère mange un œuf à la coque et boit du chocolat chaud.**
  Usually for breakfast my brother eats a boiled egg and drinks hot chocolate.
- **Nous dînons chez ma grand-mère deux fois par semaine.**
  We have dinner with my grandmother twice a week.

Describing Food and Taste

- **amer / amère** — sour
  bien cuit — well done
  la cuisine — cookery / cooking
  épicé(e) — spicy
  le goût — the taste
  gras(se) — fatty
  la nourriture — food

  l'odeur (f) — the smell
  piquant(e) — spicy
  poivré(e) — peppered
  salé(e) — salty
  sucré(e) — sweet
  trop — too
  végétarien(ne) — vegetarian

- **C'est trop piquant.** — It's too spicy.
- **Les frites sont trop salées.** — The chips are too salty.

Using Negatives

- **Je ne prends rien.**
  I have nothing / I don't have anything. (i.e. to eat)

- **Je ne mange plus de pamplemousse parce que c'est trop amer.**
  I don't eat grapefruit any longer because it's too sour.

- **Ma sœur ne mange jamais de poisson parce qu'elle ne peut pas supporter l'odeur.**
  My sister never eats fish because she can't stand the smell.

- **Mes parents ne mangent ni canard ni dinde parce qu'ils sont végétariens.**
  My parents eat neither duck nor turkey because they are vegetarian.

- **Je n'ai jamais goûté d'escargots.**
  I've never tasted snails.

- **Il n'a pas goûté à la cuisine thaïlandaise.**
  He hasn't tasted Thai cooking.

Quick Test

1. How do you ask for: a slice of ham? a kilo of raspberries? a tin of plums?
2. What do the following words mean in French: **souvent**; **quelquefois**; **d'habitude**?
3. Translate into English: '**il ne mange rien**', '**elle ne mange plus de viande**', '**ils ne mangent ni fruits ni légumes**'.
4. Translate into French: 'I've never tasted duck'.

Eating Out

You must be able to:

- Understand a French menu
- Order a meal in a restaurant in France
- Describe a visit to a restaurant.

The Menu

la carte	menu	**le plat principal**	main course
les hors-d'œuvre (m)	starters	**la viande**	meat
les crudités (f)	raw chopped vegetables	**l'agneau** (m)	lamb
		le bœuf	beef
l'escargot (m)	snail	**le canard**	duck
le potage	soup	**la dinde**	turkey
les fruits de mer (m)	seafood	**le poulet**	chicken
le saumon	salmon	**le steak haché**	burger
le thon	tuna		
la truite	trout		

les légumes (m) **du jour**	vegetables of the day
les pâtes (f)	pasta
le plateau de fromages	cheese board
la crêpe	pancake
la glace	ice cream
la pâtisserie maison	home-made cakes / pastries
la tarte aux cerises	cherry tart

HT	**le veau**	veal
HT	**l'ail** (m)	garlic
HT	**l'ananas** (m)	pineapple
HT	**la noix**	walnut
HT	**le pamplemousse**	grapefruit
HT	**la prune**	plum

Ordering a Meal

une table pour quatre personnes	a table for four people
dans le coin / à la terrasse	in the corner / on the patio
Comme entrée je voudrais…	As a starter, I'd like…
Pour commencer je voudrais…	To start, I'd like…
Comme plat principal je prendrai…	As a main course, I'll have…
Comme dessert je vais prendre…	As a dessert, I'm going to have…
Comme boisson nous voudrions…	As a drink, we'd like…
Qu'est-ce que vous avez comme légumes?	What sort of vegetables do you have?
Qu'est-ce que c'est, le…?	What is…?
Un peu plus de pain, s'il vous plaît.	Some more bread, please.
la cuillère	spoon
la tasse	cup
le verre	glass

Key Vocab

la carte	menu
les hors-d'œuvre (m)	starters
le plat principal	main course
la viande	meat
les legumes (m)	vegetables
l'addition	the bill

Key Vocab

je voudrais
I would like
nous voudrions
we would like
comme dessert
as a dessert
pour commencer
to start

- **l'addition** (f)   bill
- **compris**   included
- **hors (taxes)**   without (taxes), excluding
- **le pourboire**   tip
- **la TVA (taxe sur la valeur ajoutée)**   VAT (value added tax)
- **le serveur**   waiter
- **la serveuse**   waitress
- **Je n'ai pas de**…   I don't have a…
  le couteau   knife
  la fourchette   fork

Describing a Visit to a Restaurant

To describe an event in the past, use the perfect tense:

- <u>Regular –er verbs</u> follow this pattern:

  j'ai mangé   I ate
  on a mangé   one / we ate
  nous avons mangé   we ate
  ils ont mangé   they ate
  - **commander**   – to order
  - **visiter**   – to visit
  - **réserver**   – to reserve
  - **commencer**   – to start
  - **goûter**   – to taste / sample
  - **dîner**   – to have dinner (evening meal)
  - **coûter**   – to cost
  - **payer**   – to pay for

- <u>Regular –**ir** verbs follow</u> this pattern:
  j'ai choisi   I chose
  on a choisi   one / we chose
  nous avons choisi   we chose
  ils ont choisi   they chose

- <u>Some are irregular</u> and need to be learned separately:
  J'ai bu   I drank
  J'ai pris   I had (took)

- **Nous avons dîné dans un grand restaurant français où nous avons commandé des plats traditionnels.**
  We had dinner in a big French restaurant where we ordered traditional dishes.

- To express your opinion, use the imperfect tense:
  C'était parfait.   It was perfect.
  Le potage était froid.   The soup was cold.

> **Key Point**
>
> Use '**de**' to say you don't have something:
> **Je n'ai pas de fourchette.**
> I don't have a fork.

> **Key Point**
>
> To describe the event, use the perfect tense:
> **J'ai mangé**… I ate…
> To describe opinions, use the imperfect tense:
> **C'était**… It was…

> **Quick Test**
>
> 1. Name two types of fish and three types of meat in French.
> 2. Translate into English:
>   '**Comme plat principal je voudrais l'agneau.**'
>   '**Qu'est-ce que vous avez comme légumes?**'
> 3. Translate into French:
>   We had lunch in a French restaurant.
>   It was perfect.

Sport

You must be able to:

- Discuss which sports and activities you used to do
- Compare past and present activities
- Talk about activities you would like to try in the future.

Sporting Activities

les activités sportives	sporting activities	**l'escalade** (f)	climbing
jouer	to play	**la natation**	swimming
le basket	basketball	**la planche à voile**	wind-surfing
le volley	volleyball	**le VTT (vélo tout-terrain)**	mountain biking
les échecs	chess	**la voile**	sailing
– **Je joue au basket.**	I play basketball.	**la promenade (à vélo)**	walk (bike ride)
faire	to do	**la randonnée**	walking
le patinage à glace	ice-skating	**la pétanque**	bowls
le skate	skate boarding	– **Je fais du ski**.	I go skiing.
		aller	to go
le ski nautique	water-skiing	**à la pêche**	fishing
l'équitation (f)	horseriding	– **Je vais à la pêche**.	I go fishing.

Key Vocab

jouer	to play
faire	to do
aller	to go

Key Point

jouer à + sport = to play a sport; **faire de** = to do an activity:
jouer au basket (m),
jouer à la pétanque (f),
jouer aux échecs (plural),
faire du skate (m), **faire de l'équitation**, **faire de la voile** (f), **faire des randonnées** (plural)

To say *what you used to do*, use the *imperfect* tense:

- **Quand j'étais plus jeune, je jouais au foot tous les jours.**
  When I was younger, I used to play football every day.
- **Je faisais du skate tous les week-ends.** I used to skateboard every weekend.

Places

le centre sportif	sports centre
le club des jeunes	youth club
la montagne	the mountain
la patinoire	ice rink
la piscine	swimming pool
la plage	beach
le stade	stadium
HT **la course**	race
HT **le tournoi**	tournament

To say *where you used to go*, use the *imperfect* tense:

- **Quand j'avais onze ans, j'allais à la patinoire trois fois par semaine.**
  When I was 11, I used to go to the ice rink three times a week.

Comparing Now and Then

Useful Verbs

avoir envie de	to want to
avoir horreur de	to hate
avoir peur de	to be frightened of

HT avoir le vertige	to be afraid of heights
HT avoir le mal de mer	to be sea-sick
courir	to run
débuter	to start
être fana de	to be a fan of
être amateur de	to be an enthusiast of
espérer	to hope to
essayer	to try
nager	to swim
patiner	to skate
pouvoir	to be able to
s'intéresser à	to be interested in
se passionner pour	to love
vouloir	to want to
HT marquer (un but)	to score (a goal)

Useful Connectives and Phrases

avant	before	**quand**	when
maintenant	now	**mais**	but
il y a … ans	…years ago	**cependant**	however
en ce moment	at the moment	**donc**	therefore
auparavant	in the past	**même si**	even if
de nos jours	nowadays	**puis**	then

HT **Avant je nageais tout le temps, mais maintenant je suis plutôt fana de voile.**
Before I used to swim all the time, but now I'm more of a fan of sailing.

- **Il y a cinq ans j'avais le vertige, cependant de nos jours je me passionne pour l'escalade.**
Five years ago I was afraid of heights, however nowadays I love climbing.

Types of Sports to Try

- **les sports d'équipe** — team sports
les sports d'hiver — winter sports
les sports extrêmes — extreme sports
les sports individuels — individual sports
les sports nautiques — water sports

- **J'ai envie d'essayer les sports nautiques.** I want to try water sports.
- **Je voudrais essayer la planche à voile.** I would like to try wind-surfing.

Key Vocab

je jouais	I used to play
je faisais	I used to do
j'étais	I was
j'avais	I had (but 'I was' when talking about your age)
j'allais	I used to go

Key Vocab

| **J'ai envie de** | I want to |
| **Je voudrais** | I would like to |

Quick Test

1. How do you say 'I play volleyball' in French?
2. What is the difference between '**je fais du ski**' and '**je faisais du ski**'?
3. Translate into English: '**Je jouais au basket**'.
4. Translate into French: 'I used to go to the ice rink.'
5. Translate into English: '**Je voudrais essayer les sports nautiques**'.

Customs and Festivals

You must be able to:

- Know main festivals and celebrations in France and French-speaking countries
- Describe how you spend public holidays
- Explain why you think they are important – or not.

Festivals

- **les fêtes** — festivals
- **la fête des mères** — Mother's Day
- **la fête des rois** — Epiphany (6 January)
- **la fête du travail** — May Day
- **la fête nationale** — Bastille Day
- **le Jour de l'An** — New Year's Day
- **Mardi Gras** — Shrove Tuesday
- **Noël** — Christmas
- **Pâques** — Easter
- **la Pâque juive** — Passover
- **le premier avril** — April Fool's Day
- **poisson d'avril!** — April Fool!
- **le Ramadan** — Ramadan
- **la Saint-Sylvestre** — New Year's Eve
- **la Saint-Valentin** — St Valentine's Day
- **la Toussaint** — All Saints' Day
- **la veille de Noël** — Christmas Eve
- HT **la messe** — mass

- **Yom Kippur** — Yom Kippur
- HT **la Pentecôte** — Whitsun

- **le cadeau** — present
- **la coutume** — custom
- **juif / juive** — Jewish
- **musulman / musulmane** — Muslim
- **religieux / religieuse** — religious
- **traditionnel / traditionnelle** — traditional
- **la tradition** — tradition

- **l'église** (f) — church
- **la mosquée** — mosque
- **le mariage** — wedding
- **les noces** (f) — wedding ceremony

- **Félicitations!** — Congratulations!
- **Bonne Année!** — Happy New Year!
- **Joyeux Noël!** — Merry Christmas!
- **Bon Anniversaire!** — Happy Birthday!
- **Bonne Chance!** — Good Luck!
- **Meilleurs Vœux** — Best Wishes

Key Vocab

- **la fête** — festival
- **le jour férié** — public holiday
- **fêter** — to celebrate
- **religieux / religieuse** — religious
- **traditionnel / traditionnelle** — traditional

How do you Spend Public Holidays?

- **Comment passer les jours fériés** — How to spend public holidays
- **le feu d'artifice** — firework display
- HT **le jour férié** — public holiday
- HT **le défilé** — procession
- HT **le patrimoine** — heritage
- HT **la réunion** — meeting

Useful Verbs

- **célébrer** — to celebrate
- **chanter** — to sing
- **conserver** — to keep, conserve
- **danser** — to dance

- **donner** — to give
- **épouser** — to marry
- **fêter** — to celebrate
- **perdre** — to lose

recevoir	to receive		rire	to laugh
réunir	to bring together (also: to have friends round)		HT **féliciter**	to congratulate

Tout le monde passe la journée à manger, à chanter et à danser.
Everyone spends the day eating, singing and dancing.

Are Traditional Festivals Important Or Not?

- **Les fêtes traditionnelles, sont-elles importantes?**
  Are traditional festivals important?

pour moi	for me
pour ceux qui…	for those who…
à mon avis	in my opinion
selon eux	according to them
selon certains	according to some

il est important de	it is important to
l'essentiel est	the most important thing is
il faut	it is necessary to (we must)
on doit	one (we) must
il ne faut pas	one (we) must not
on ne doit jamais	one (we) must never
HT **on devrait**	one (we) should (ought to)
HT **on pourrait**	one (we) could

je pense que	I think
HT **certains croient que**	some believe
HT **beaucoup de gens estiment que**	lots of people consider (that)
HT **d'un côté**	on the one hand
HT **d'un autre côté**	on the other hand

- **Pour moi les coutumes sont fascinantes car je m'intéresse à l'histoire.**
  For me customs are fascinating because I'm interested in history.

- HT **Pour ceux qui aiment les fêtes traditionnelles, il est important de conserver le patrimoine.**
  For those who love traditional festivals, it is important to conserve (their) heritage.

- HT **Selon certains, les fêtes sont démodées et on devrait célébrer notre vie moderne.**
  According to some, festivals are outdated and we should celebrate our modern life.

Practice Questions

My Family and Friends & Marriage and Partnerships

1 **Choisissez la forme correcte de l'adjectif pour compléter chaque phrase.** Choose the correct form of the adjective to complete each sentence.

    a) Ma tante est assez jeune / jeunes et très joli / jolie, mais un peu gros / grosse.   [3]

    b) Mon beau-père a une barbe noir / noire. Il est trop vieux / vieille et laid / laide.   [3]

    c) Mes frères sont petit / petits et très mince / minces. Ils sont assez beau / beaux.   [3]

    d) Ma sœur est très belle / belles. Elle est assez grand / grande et un peu maigre / maigres.   [3]

[Total: 12 marks]

2 **Trouvez la bonne fin de chaque phrase et traduisez les phrases complètes en anglais.**
Find the correct ending for each sentence and translate the complete sentences into English.

a) Je m'entends bien avec mon neveu, …	ma sœur aînée, car elle est agaçante et égoïste.
b) Je me dispute quelquefois avec ma mère…	il est rarement heureux et trop têtu.
c) Je ne m'entends pas très bien avec…	car il est toujours sage et très gentil.
d) Mon beau-père se fâche contre moi, parce qu'…	parce qu'elle est souvent trop sévère.

[Total 16 marks: 4 for matching, 12 for translation.]

3 **Complétez le texte, en utilisant les mots ci-dessous.** Complete the text, using the words below.

Samedi dernier, je suis allé au _____ de mon frère. Sa femme est très _____ Ma sœur est mariée aussi _____ deux ans. Mais mes parents sont _____ Je ne sais pas encore si je _____ me marier, ou si je préférerais rester _____ En ce moment, je n'ai pas de petite _____ Mais un jour, je voudrais avoir des _____

amie	célibataire	depuis	divorcés	enfants	gentille	mariage	voudrais

[8 marks]

Social Media & Mobile Technology

1 **Trouvez dix mots au sujet des ordinateurs ou de l'internet et traduisez-les en anglais.** Find ten words to do with computers or the internet and translate them into English.

l'ordinateurlasourislepagewebl'écranlatablettelelclavierl'imprimantelacléUSBlatoucheleréseausocial

[20 marks: 1 mark for each item found and copied out correctly, 1 mark for each correct translation]

2 **Mettez les mots dans le bon ordre pour décrire des activités sur un ordinateur ou sur un portable.** Unjumble the sentences to describe things you do on a computer or a phone.

a) SMS mes J'envoie tous amis des à

b) télécharge de musique la Je applis des et

c) beaucoup Je sur photos mon de prends portable

d) vais sur web Je mes préférés sites

e) recherches Je mes des pour devoirs fais

[5 marks]

3 **Chaque phrase est-elle un avantage ou un inconvénient de la technologie? Écrivez 'A' ou 'I'.** Is each sentence an advantage or a disadvantage of technology? Write 'A' or 'I'.

a) C'est rapide et très pratique.

b) On peut rester en contact avec les autres.

c) Le cyberharcèlement est affreux.

d) Parfois, il n'y a pas de réseau.

e) Il faut recharger régulièrement son portable.

f) On peut contacter quelqu'un en cas d'urgence.

[6 marks]

Practice Questions

Music & Cinema and TV

1 **C'est quel genre de musique?** What type of music is it?

a) le _ _ zz

b) l_ r_g_ _ e

c) le _ i e u _ _o _ k

d) l_ m _ _ i _ u e _ _a _ _ i q _ _   e) l_ h _ _ - h _ _

[5 marks]

2 *préfère* ou *préfèrent*? Remplissez les blancs. *préfère* or *préfèrent*? Fill in the gaps.

a) Mes parents .... le rock, mais ma sœur .... l'électro.

b) Je .... les paroles profondes, mais mes copains .... un bon rythme.

c) Ma famille .... regarder les feuilletons.

[5 marks]

3 **Reliez l'anglais au français.** Match up the English and French phrases.

ça me plaît	it makes me sad
ça m'énerve	it makes me cry
ça me détend	it makes me laugh
ça me fait sourire	it frightens me
ça me rend triste	it gets on my nerves
ça me fait rire	I like it
ça me fait pleurer	it relaxes me
ça me fait peur	it makes me smile

[8 marks]

4 **Comment dit-on en français...?** What's the French for…?

a) the news   b) a cartoon   c) a soap   d) a war film   e) reality TV

f) a TV programme   g) special effects   h) adverts   i) the performance   j) a ticket   [10 marks]

5 **Reliez les bouts de phrases.** Match the phrases to make sentences.

Je m'intéresse	allé au festival de musique
Je préfère	écouté la musique forte
J'ai toujours	à la musique pop
Je suis	écouter la musique en direct

[4 marks]

Food and Eating Out, Sport & Customs and Festivals

1 **Mettez les mots dans le bon ordre.** Put the words into the correct order to make sentences.

a) Je / plaît / carottes / un / vous / voudrais / de / kilo / s'il

b) fois / dînons / semaine /chez / Nous / par / grand-mère / deux / ma

c) pas / parce / trop / Je / c'est / de / chocolat / que / mange / sucré / ne

d) poisson / Mes / jamais / ne / parents / de / mangent   [4 marks]

2 **Traduisez les phrases de l'exercice 1 en anglais.** Translate the sentences in exercise 1 into English. [4 marks]

3 **Traduisez en français.** Translate into French.

a) As a starter, I'd like the soup, please.

b) What (sort of) vegetables do you have?

c) I don't have a knife.

d) It was delicious, thank you.   [4 marks]

4 **Remplissez les blancs.** Fill in the gaps.

| au   à la   du   de l'   de la   des |

a) Ma sœur aime faire _____ promenades.

b) Mon frère fait _____ équitation tous les samedis.

c) Je jouais   volley.

d) Mes copains vont souvent _____ pêche.

e) Avez-vous fait _____ planche à voile?   [5 marks]

5 **Comment dit-on en français…?** How do you say in French…? (Include the gender of nouns.)

a) present (gift)   b) public holiday   c) firework display   d) procession   e) mosque
f) a traditional festival   g) to celebrate   h) to marry   i) to keep   j) to give   [10 marks]

At Home

You must be able to:

- Describe your house and bedroom
- Say where things are in relation to each other
- Use prepositions.

My House

Features

- **la maison**   house
  - **individuelle**   – detached
  - **jumelée**   – semi-detached
  - **mitoyenne**   – terraced
  - **la pièce**   room
  - **le bâtiment**   building
  - **l'escalier** (m)   staircase
  - **l'étage** (m)   floor, storey
  - **le rez-de-chaussée**   ground floor
  - **le sous-sol**   basement
  - **le bricolage**   (DIY) Do it yourself
  - HT **le foyer**   home

- **J'habite dans une maison jumelée.**   I live in a semi-detached house.
- **Il y a huit pièces.**   There are eight rooms.
- **Au rez-de-chaussée il y a le salon et la cuisine. À l'étage se trouvent trois chambres et la salle de bains.**
  On the ground floor there is the living room and the kitchen. Upstairs there are three bedrooms and the bathroom.

Rooms

- **le bureau**   office, study
  la cave   cellar
  la chambre   bedroom
  le couloir   corridor
  la cuisine   kitchen
  la douche   shower
  l'entrée (f)   hallway
  le grenier   attic
  la salle à manger   dining room
  la salle de bains   bathroom
  le salon   living room
  le toilettes   toilet
  HT **la pelouse**   lawn

- Prepositions:

à côté de	next to	**entre**	between
en face de	opposite	**près de**	near
en	in		

> ### Key Point
>
> When describing your home use prepositions. But take care to adjust the **de** to agree with the gender of the word that follows:
> **La cuisine est en face de la salle à manger.**
> The kitchen is opposite the dining room.
> **Ma chambre est près du (de + le) bureau.**
> My bedroom is near to the office.
> **Le salon est à côté de l'entrée.**
> The living room is next to the entrance.

My Bedroom

- **le poster** — poster
  les meubles (m) — furniture
  l'armoire (f) — wardrobe
  le bureau — desk
  le mur — wall
  le lit — bed
  l'étagère (f) — shelf

  la commode — chest of drawers
  la fenêtre — the window
  nettoyer — to clean
  propre — neat / clean
  sale — untidy / dirty
  HT **la lumière** — light

- **Dans ma chambre j'ai une grande armoire et d'autres meubles. Il y a des posters au mur.**
  In my bedroom I have a big wardrobe and some other furniture. There are posters on the wall.

- **Ma chambre est toujours propre.** — My bedroom is always clean.

- **Je nettoie ma chambre chaque week-end.** — I clean my bedroom every weekend.

- More prepositions:

  au-dessous de, sous — beneath, below
  au-dessus de, sur — above, over
  derrière — behind
  devant — in front of

Quick Test

1. Translate into English:
   J'habite dans une petite maison mitoyenne. Il y a sept pièces. Au rez-de-chaussée il y a le salon, la salle à manger et la cuisine. À l'étage se trouvent trois chambres et la salle de bains.

2. Translate into French:
   I live in a semi-detached house. Upstairs there are four bedrooms. My bedroom is neat and there is a wardrobe next to the door. I have some posters on the wall. I clean my bedroom every week. On the other hand my brother's bedroom is untidy.

3. Write a description of your house including as many details as possible regarding the rooms and where they are in relation to each other. Then give a description of your room. Is there any furniture? Is it neat and tidy?

Where I Live

You must be able to:

- Describe your local town and its shops
- Say what there is, or isn't in your town
- Say what you did in town by using the perfect tense
- Use negatives, quantifiers, and the modal verb **pouvoir**.

In the Town

la bibliothèque	library
la boucherie	butcher's
la boulangerie	baker's
la bijouterie	jeweller's shop
le centre commercial	shopping centre
la charcuterie	delicatessen
le commissariat	police station
la gare	(train) station
la gare routière	coach station
l'hôtel de ville (m)	town hall
l'immeuble (m)	block of flats
la librairie	bookshop
la mairie	town hall
le marché	market
la pâtisserie	cake shop
la place	square
la poste	post office
le tabac	newsagent's
l'usine (f)	factory
HT **les distractions** (f)	things to do

Key Point

When using a negative such as '**ne…pas**', it must always be followed with '**de**', then you leave out the '**le**' '**la**' '**les**'. For example, **Il n'y a pas de bibliothèque**.

- **Les transports en commun sont assez fréquents.**
  The public transport is quite frequent.
- **Il n'y a pas beaucoup de circulation. / Il y a trop de circulation.**
  There is not much traffic. / There is too much traffic.
- **Il n'y a pas de station-service ni de cinéma.**
  There is no service-station or cinema.
- **On a besoin d'un centre commercial.**
  We need a shopping centre.
- **La gare routière se trouve près de la gare.**
  The coach station is right next to the station.

Key Point

When using quantities such as '**beaucoup de**', '**trop de**' leave out the '**le**' '**la**' '**les**' that would usually appear before the next word. For example, '**il y a trop de circulation**.'

Shopping

- **les soldes** — the sales
- **Ce magasin est très bon marché!** — This shop is very cheap!
- **le choix** — The choice
- **Le parking est gratuit.** — The car park is free.
- **On peut acheter un cadeau ici.** — You can buy a present here.
- **Je peux payer par carte bancaire?** — Can I pay by bank card?

HT **la fermeture**	closure / closing
HT **la grande surface**	superstore
HT **faire du lèche-vitrine**	go window shopping
HT **la marque**	make / label / brand
HT **le rayon**	department
HT **rembourser**	to reimburse

- **le vendeur / la vendeuse** — shopkeeper
  la caisse — till
  le portefeuille — wallet
  le porte-monnaie — purse

- **dépenser / dépensé** — to spend / spent
  perdre / perdu — to lose / lost
  vendre / vendu — to sell / sold
- **J'ai dépensé mon argent dans les soldes.** — I spent all my money in the sales.
- **J'ai perdu mon portefeuille.** — I've lost my wallet.

In the Clothes Shop

- **Je peux essayer cette robe?** — Can I try this dress on?
- **C'est très à la mode!** — It's very fashionable!

- **les vêtements** (m) — clothes
  le bijou — jewellery
  le blouson — jacket
  la ceinture — belt
  le chapeau — hat
  la chaussette — sock
  la chaussure — shoe
  la chemise — shirt
  la cravate — tie
  le gilet — waistcoat / cardigan
  la jupe — skirt
  le manteau — coat
  le pantalon — trousers
  la robe — dress
  la veste — jacket

HT **l'écharpe** (f)	scarf
HT **le foulard**	scarf
HT **le sweat à capuche**	hoodie

Key Point

Use your knowledge of the perfect tense to talk about things that you did. You will need to use the present tense of **avoir** followed by the past participle:

- **dépenser / dépensé**
  to spend / spent
- **perdre / perdu**
  to lose / lost
- **vendre / vendu**
  to sell / sold

Key Vocab

…**se trouve**…
…is found / is located…
Il n'y a pas de…
There is no…
Il y a trop de…
There are too many…
On a besoin de…
We need…
On peut acheter…
You can buy…
Je peux essayer…?
Can I try on…?
les magasins / les commerces the shops
J'ai perdu… I have lost…

Quick Test

1. Write what there is in your town, and what is lacking.
2. Jot down what clothes you most recently bought.
3. Translate the following sentences into English:
   En ville, il y a des commerces et un grand magasin où on peut acheter de beaux vêtements.
   Je peux essayer cette veste?
   Ma mère a payé par carte bancaire.

Town or Country?

You must be able to:

- Describe your surrounding area
- Compare living in a town with living in the countryside
- Use comparatives along with adjectives.

Town or Country?

Moi j'habite…	I live…
– **en ville**	– in town
– **à la campagne**	– in the country
– **à la montagne**	– in the mountains
Tu habites dans quel quartier?	Which part of town do you live in?
surchargé(e)(s)	overcrowded
HT l'endroit (m)	place

In the Town

J'adore vivre en ville.	I love living in town.
Mes parents travaillent en centre ville.	My parents work in the town centre.
Il y a beaucoup de choses à faire.	There is a good choice of things to do.
La ville est très animée!	The town is very lively!
On y trouve une zone piétonne.	There is a pedestrianised zone.
Il y a trop de circulation / de bruit.	There is too much traffic / noise.
La ville est très bruyante.	The town is very noisy.
Les rues sont sales.	The streets are dirty.
Le loyer est plus cher.	The rent is more expensive.

In the Countryside

La vie à la campagne est très calme.	Life in the countryside is very quiet.
J'habite dans une ferme.	I live on a farm.
Je voudrais déménager à la campagne!	I would like to move to the country!
Je peux faire du jardinage.	I can do gardening.
On voit des fleurs et des collines par la fenêtre.	You can see flowers and hills out of the window.
C'est un endroit très propre.	It's a very clean place.
Il n'y a pas de commerces tout près.	There are no shops nearby.
On doit se déplacer en voiture / prendre la voiture pour voir ses amis.	You have to travel by car to see friends.
Les transports en commun ne sont pas assez fréquents.	The public transport is not frequent enough.
On n'a pas de voisins.	We have no neighbours.

> ### Key Point
>
> Remember that when using a modal verb such as **devoir** or **pouvoir** the verb that follows should be in the infinitive, e.g.
> **On doit prendre le bus.**
> You have to take the bus.
> **Je peux me promener sur les collines.**
> I can walk in the hills.

- l'arbre (m) — tree
- le champ — field
- la colline — hill
- la fleur — flower
- la montagne — mountain
- la sécurité — safety
- **HT** l'embouteillage (m) — traffic jam

- Adjectives should agree with the noun they are describing. Sometimes the noun is not placed right next to the adjective in the sentence.
- Adjectives already ending in **–e** do not need a further **–e** in the feminine form.
- **La ville est très animée.** The town is very busy.
- **La campagne est calme.** The countryside is quiet.

- animé(e)(s) — busy, lively
- bruyant(e)(s) — noisy
- calme — quiet
- pauvre — poor
- propre — clean
- sale — dirty

Key Point

To compare two things use **plus / moins** + adjective **que** more / less + adjective than:
C'est plus propre à la campagne qu'en ville. It is cleaner in the country than in town.
Il y a moins de circulation à la campagne qu'en ville. There is less traffic in the countryside than in town.

Key Vocab

J'habite I live
en ville / à la campagne in town / in the country
Il y a / On trouve There is / You find
On doit You have to
Je peux I can
moins / plus less / more
vivre to live
déménager to move home

Quick Test

1. Can you say the following in French?
   There are lots of shops in town.
   Houses in the country are bigger than in the town.
2. Translate into English:
   J'adore vivre en ville parce que je peux aller à l'école à pied. Mon cousin habite à la campagne et il doit prendre le bus.
3. Do you live in the town or the country? Make a list of some benefits of living where you do.

Charity and Voluntary Work

You must be able to:

- Describe voluntary work
- Say what you do and what others do using **je** and **on**.
- Use **je voudrais** and an infinitive to say what you would like to do in the future.

Voluntary Work

- **Je fais du travail bénévole pour une association caritative.**
  I do voluntary work for a charity.
- **Je rends visite à des personnes exclues.**
  I visit vulnerable people.
- **On fait des excursions avec des personnes handicapées.**
  We go on outings with disabled people.
- **Je voudrais devenir médecin.**
  I would like to become a doctor.

- **l'aide** (f)   aid
  l'association caritative (f)   charity
  le travail bénévole   voluntary work

- **l'eau potable** (f)   drinking water
  le repas   meal
  le médecin   doctor
  le médicament   medicine
  malade   ill
  la maladie   illness
  HT **le soin**   care
  HT **agir (il s'agit de)**   to act (it's a question of)

- **J'aide des personnes malades.**
  I help people who are ill.
- **On distribue des repas et de l'eau potable aux SDF.**
  We distribute meals and drinking water to the homeless. (**SDF Sans domicile fixe** homeless)
- **Je fais des collectes d'argent.**
  I collect money.
- **Je livre des médicaments aux personnes âgées.**
  I deliver medicine to older people.
- HT **On aide aussi les personnes souffrant de dépression.**
  We also help people who are depressed.
- HT **Les dettes peuvent mener à la misère.**
  Debt can lead to misery.

> ### Key Point
>
> You can use **on** to mean 'we':
> **On a distribué des repas ce week-end**
> We gave out meals this weekend.
> It can also be used to say that things are done by others:
> **On adore les associations comme la Croix-Rouge.**
> Organisations such as the Red Cross are loved.

Verbs that Can Follow 'Je Voudrais'

- **Après le lycée je voudrais aller à l'université. Je voudrais devenir médecin.**
  After sixth form I would like to go to university. I would like to become a doctor.

HT Another option might be to substitute '**voudrais**' with '**aimerais**':
J'aimerais travailler avec des personnes défavorisées (f).
I would like to work with disadvantaged people.

Je voudrais (I would like)	aider (les SDF)	to help (the homeless)
	travailler (comme infirmière)	to work (as a nurse)
	faire (des collectes d'argent)	to make / do (money collections)
	livrer (des médicaments)	to deliver (medicines)
	distribuer (des repas et de l'eau potable)	to distribute (meals and drinking water)
	rendre visite (à des personnes âgées)	to visit (older people)
	devenir (médecin)	to become (a doctor)
	voyager (en Afrique pour y apporter mon aide)	to travel (to Africa to help over there)
	HT surveiller les enfants dans des clubs sportifs	run childrens' sports clubs

Key Point

HT Certain verbs are used almost exclusively in structures with '**il**' making them '**impersonal**' verbs.
falloir (to be necessary) – **il faut** (it is necessary / one must / we have to)
agir (to act) – **il s'agit de** (it's about)
valoir mieux (to be better) – **il vaut mieux** (it's better)
il vaut mieux aider une association caritative.
It's better to help a charity.

Quick Test

1. Translate into English:
   Je fais du travail bénévole. Je distribue de l'eau potable et des repas chauds aux SDF dans la rue.
2. Translate into French:
   I deliver medicine to older people. In the future I would like to be a nurse. I would like to work with disabled people.
3. Can you think of something that you currently do that might help you with your chosen career? Can you use the language in this unit to help you say it in French?

Key Vocab

l'association caritative charity	
le travail bénévole voluntary work	
J'aide	I help
Je voudrais	I would like
aider	to help
travailler	to work
visiter	to visit
devenir	to become

Healthy and Unhealthy Living

You must be able to:

- Describe your lifestyle choices
- Say whether you live healthily or not
- Use the future tense as well as **il faut**.

Fitness

aller bien	to be well	**la ligne**	figure
la forme	fitness	**l'habitude** (f)	habit
en forme	in good shape	**la santé**	health
en bonne santé	in good health	**se sentir**	to feel
fort(e)	strong	**le sommeil**	sleep

- **Je vais bien / j'ai de bonnes habitudes.**
  I feel well / I have good habits.
- **Je garde la forme parce que je fais beaucoup de sport.**
  I stay in good shape because I do lots of sport.
- **Je me sens bien dans ma peau.**
  I feel good about myself.
- **Je reste en bonne santé parce que je mange bien et je dors suffisamment.**
  I stay healthy because I eat well and I get enough sleep.

Meals and Diet

le repas	meal	**pressé(e)(s)**	busy
le déjeuner	lunch	**faire un régime**	to go on a diet
le dîner	dinner	**sain(e)(s)**	healthy
le petit-déjeuner	breakfast	**sainement**	healthily
HT **le casse-croûte**	snack	**sucré(e)(s)**	sweet(ened)
		les matières grasses	fatty products
l'alimentation (f)	food	HT **le conseil**	advice
gras(se)(s)	fatty	HT **s'enivrer**	to get drunk
manger équilibré	to eat a balanced diet	HT **le mannequin**	model
		HT **la nourriture bio**	organic food
malsain(e)(s)	unhealthy	HT **salé(e)(s)**	salted

- **Il faut manger sainement. / Il faut éviter les produits mauvais pour la santé.**
  It is necessary to eat well. / It is necessary to avoid unhealthy products.
- **Je fais / Je vais faire un régime.**
  I am on / I am going to go on a diet.
- **Je mange trop de matières grasses.**
  I eat too many fatty things.
- **Je vais essayer de manger plus sainement.**
  I am going to try to eat more healthily.
- **C'est ma faiblesse!**
  It's my weakness!

Key Point

Look at the way that you can adapt a word such as **la santé**:
Je suis en bonne santé.
I am in good *health – noun*
Je mange des produits sains.
I eat *healthy* products – *adjective*
Je mange sainement.
I eat *healthily – adverb*

Health

- **s'arrêter** — to stop
- **combattre** — to combat / fight
- **se détendre** — to relax
- **dormir** — to sleep
- **éviter** — to avoid
- **la fatigue** — tiredness
- **fumer** — to smoke
- **l'obésité** (f) — obesity
- **se relaxer** — to relax
- **réussir** — to succeed
- **le tabac** — tobacco

- **tuer** — to kill
- HT **accro** — addicted
- HT **dégoûtant(e)(s)** — disgusting
- HT **l'entraînement** (m) — training
- HT **épuiser** — to exhaust
- HT **essoufflé(e)(s)** — breathless
- HT **ivre** — drunk
- HT **la peau** — skin
- HT **quotidien(n)(e)(s)** — daily
- HT **le tabagisme** — addiction to smoking
- HT **le/la toxicomane** — drug addict

Key Point

Il faut is not easy to translate. It can mean 'it is necessary, one must, you should', etc. It is very useful because you just follow it with an infinitive:
Il faut éviter le gras.
It is necessary to avoid fat.

HT **Il faut suivre les conseils.**
We need to follow advice.

- **Mon père a arrêté de fumer.**
  My father has stopped smoking.
- **Le tabac peut tuer, et ça produit une mauvaise odeur.**
  Tobacco can kill and it produces a horrible smell.
- **Il faut se détendre pour éviter le stress.**
  It is necessary to relax to avoid stress.
- **J'ai réussi à combattre l'obésité.**
  I succeeded in beating obesity.
- HT **Je m'entraîne deux fois par semaine.**
  I train twice a week.
- HT **Respirer de l'air frais**
  To breathe some fresh air

- **le cabinet medical** — medical surgery
- **le médecin** — doctor
- **la maladie** — illness
- **vomir** — to vomit, to be sick
- **aller mieux** — to feel better
- HT **avoir sommeil** — to be sleepy
- HT **le cancer (du poumon)** — (lung) cancer
- HT **la crise cardiaque** — heart attack
- HT **la douleur** — pain
- HT **le foie** — liver
- HT **hors d'haleine** — out of breath
- HT **tousser** — to cough

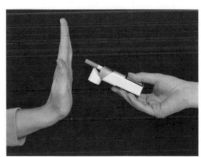

Key Vocab

Je fais / Je vais faire
I do / I am going to do
Il faut (+ infinitive)
It is necessary (+ infinitive)
éviter
to avoid
s'arrêter
to stop
la santé / sain(e)(s) / sainement
health / healthy / healthily
la forme
fitness

Quick Test

1. Describe what you currently do to be healthy. Now describe an intention of yours to be even healthier.
2. Come up with five sentences beginning with **Il faut**, relating to this topic.
3. Translate into French:
   I eat quite healthily but I do not do enough sport. I am going to play tennis and avoid fatty foods because it is necessary to remain in good health.

The Environment: Problems

You must be able to:

- Talk about environmental issues
- Express your opinion about the environment
- Use quantifiers.

Environmental Problems

les boîtes en carton (f)	cardboard boxes
les canettes (f) / **les boîtes** (f)	cans / tins
la circulation (f)	traffic
le chauffage central (m)	central heating
le déboisement (m)	deforestation
les déchets (m)	rubbish / waste
l'électricité (f)	electricity
l'emballage (m)	packaging
en danger	in danger
les espèces (f) **en voie de disparition** (f)	endangered species
l'environnement (m)	environment
les énergies renouvelables (f)	renewable energy
le gaspillage	waste
l'inondation (f)	flooding
le monde (m)	the world
les ordures (f)	rubbish
le papier (m)	paper
le pétrole (m)	oil
les pistes cyclables (f)	cycle lanes
le plastique (m)	plastic
pollué(e)(s)	polluted
la poubelle (f)	(dust-)bin
le réchauffement de la Terre / **le réchauffement climatique** (m)	global warming
le recyclage (m)	recycling
les ressources (f)	resources
les sacs (m) **en plastique**	plastic / carrier bags
les transports (m) **en commun**	public transport
le trou (m) **dans la couche d'ozone**	the hole in the ozone layer

Key Point

Expressing quantities:

trop de	too many / much
assez de	enough
beaucoup de	a lot of
autant de	as much / many
plus de	more
moins de	less

Which Do You Think are the Most Important Problems?

Je pense qu'il y a trop de déchets par terre.
I think that there is too much rubbish on the ground.
Pour moi le problème le plus important c'est qu'il n'y a pas assez de pistes cyclables.
For me the most important problem is that there aren't enough cycle tracks.
En ce qui me concerne le réchauffement climatique et la pollution sont très inquiétants.
As far as I am concerned global warming and pollution are very worrying.

Key Point

Remember when using quantifiers to use '**de**' when your quantifier is followed by a noun, e.g **trop de papier, plus de recyclage**.

À mon avis la planète est trop polluée et il y a aussi trop de circulation.
In my opinion the planet is too polluted and there is also too much traffic.

Useful Verbs

- | **allumer** | to turn on / to light |
consommer	to consume
détruire	to destroy
disparaître	to disappear
économiser	to save up
gaspiller	to waste
éteindre	to switch off
endommager	to damage
jeter	to throw away
polluer	to pollute
recycler	to recycle
trier	to sort out
menacer	to threaten
produire	to produce
protéger	to protect
sauver	to save
utiliser	to use

Key Point

Remember to change the ending of your verbs when using them with different persons (**je / on / nous**…). Check what type of verb it is and whether it is regular or irregular.

- Using verbs with different persons in the present tense:

on utilise	**nous utilisons**	**les gens utilisent**
(one uses)	(we use)	(people use)
on gaspille	**nous gaspillons**	**les gens gaspillent**
(one wastes)	(we waste)	(people waste)
on recycle	**nous recyclons**	**les gens recyclent**
(one recycles)	(we recycle)	(people recycle)

Key Point

Remember that you can use 'on' when you want to say 'we'.

- **Je trouve que je ne recycle pas assez et que les gens gaspillent trop.**
  I find that I do not recycle enough and people waste too much.
- **À mon avis on pollue trop notre environnement.**
  In my opinion we pollute our environment too much.
- **À mon avis on consomme trop d'énergie de nos jours.**
  In my opinion we consume too much energy nowadays.

> **HT** Show that you can use tenses confidently. So, for example, compare now and before, using the imperfect.
> - **Avant, on n'utilisait pas autant d'énergie, cependant de nos jours on gaspille tout!**
>   Before, we didn't use as much energy; however nowadays we waste everything!

Key Vocab

les déchets
rubbish / waste
le gaspillage
waste
le réchauffement de la Terre
global warming
économiser
to save up
gaspiller
to waste
Je pense que…
I think that…
En ce qui me concerne…
As far as I am concerned…
À mon avis…
In my opinion…

Quick Test

Translate the following sentences into English:
1. **Je pense qu'il y a trop de pollution.**
2. **Le problème le plus inquiétant, c'est qu'il y a trop d'emballages.**
Translate the following sentences into French:
3. As far as I am concerned people use too much electricity.
4. I think that I waste too much and I don't recycle enough.

The Environment: Solutions

You must be able to:

- Suggest solutions to environmental issues
- Use a range of modal verbs in the conditional
- Use verbal structures such as **pour + infinitive** (in order to), **en + –ant** (by doing).

What Should we do to Protect our Environment?

Useful Verbs

améliorer	to improve	**fournir**	to provide
conseiller	to advise	**gaspiller**	to waste
conserver	to preserve	**interdire**	to ban
construire	to build	**limiter**	to limit
créer	to create	**polluer**	to pollute
développer	to develop	**protéger**	to protect
économiser	to save up	**ramasser**	to pick up
encourager (à + inf)	to encourage (to do)	**recycler**	to recycle
		sauver	to save
endommager	to damage	**supprimer**	to abolish / get rid of
éteindre	to switch off		
essayer de	to try to	**trier**	to sort out
faire attention	to be careful	**utiliser**	to use

Modal Verbs in the Conditional Tense

Modal verbs are very useful to express what should / must be done. Here are some useful forms in the conditional tense:

On pourrait	One / We / You could / might
Je pourrais	I could / might
On devrait	One / We / You should / ought to
Je devrais	I should / ought to
Si je pouvais, je voudrais	If I could, I would like
Il faudrait	It would be necessary
Il vaudrait mieux	It would be worth

- **À mon avis on devrait faire plus attention à notre environnement local et on devrait également limiter le nombre de sacs en plastique disponibles dans les magasins.**

  In my opinion we should be more careful about our local environment and we should also limit the number of carrier bags available in shops.

- **À mon avis, il faudrait tout d'abord interdire les matériaux non-recyclables et conseiller aux gens de recycler plus.**

  In my opinion it would first of all be necessary to ban non-recyclable materials and advise people to recycle more.

- **Moi, je pense qu'il vaudrait mieux interdire les voitures dans le centre-ville et encourager les gens à utiliser les transports en commun.**

  I think that it would be worth banning cars from the town centre and encourage people to use public transport.

- **Personnellement, je sais que je devrais essayer de gaspiller moins d'énergie et que je devrais limiter ma consommation d'électricité. Je pense aussi que je pourrais marcher plus au lieu d'utiliser la voiture.**
  Personally I know that I should try to waste less energy and I should limit my electricity consumption. I also think that I should walk more instead of using the car.

Useful Grammatical Structures

These two structures are very useful for improving your French:

pour + infinitive	in order to
en + present participle (–ant)	by doing

- **pour** + infinitive — in order to
  pour protéger — in order to protect
  pour améliorer — in order to improve
  pour conserver — in order to preserve
  With a negative:
  pour ne pas détruire — in order not to destroy
  pour ne pas gaspiller — in order not to waste
  pour ne plus endommager — in order not to damage <u>any more / longer</u>

Key Point

Remember when you use two verbs together the second one is always in the infinitive form (the 'to do' form). The infinitive form will also be needed after certain prepositions such as **pour / à / de / sans**.

- **en** + present participle — by doing
  en gaspillant — by wasting
  en améliorant — by improving
  en créant — by creating
  en supprimant — by abolishing / by getting rid of
  With a negative:
  en n'augmentant pas — by not increasing
  en ne créant plus — by not creating any more

Key Point

Negatives go around a conjugated (changed) verb, e.g. **je ne gaspille pas / en ne gaspillant pas**, but go before an infinitive, e.g. **pour ne pas polluer** = in order not to pollute.

- using modal verbs, **pour** + infinitive, **en** + **–ant**, negatives and opinion phrases together

- **En ce qui me concerne, je pense que pour protéger l'environnement on devrait penser à notre attitude en limitant notre consommation d'énergie.**
  As far as I am concerned I think that in order to protect the environment we should think about our attitude by limiting our energy consumption.

- **Pour améliorer notre environnement je pense qu'on devrait conseiller aux gens de ne plus polluer en recyclant plus et en utilisant moins leur voiture.**
  In order to improve our environment I think that we should advise people not to pollute any more by recycling more and by using their cars less.

Key Vocab

améliorer
to improve
économiser
to save up
gaspiller
to waste
polluer
to pollute
on pourrait + infinitive
one could
je devrais + infinitive
I should
en + –ant
by doing

Quick Test

Unjumble the sentences and translate them:
1. devrait / recycler / on / je / qu' / pense / plus
2. pourrait / plus de / créer / on / pistes cyclables
3. il / protéger / en / l'environnement / faudrait / moins / gaspiller
   What is the French for:
4. by recycling? by improving? by not using? by not wasting?
5. in order to save? in order to improve? in order to encourage? in order not to pollute any more?

Poverty and Insecurity

You must be able to:

- Talk about the issues relating to poverty
- Talk about the consequences of these issues
- Share your concerns.

Social Problems

Useful Verbs

- **agresser** — to attack
  effrayer — to frighten
  harceler — to harass
  lutter — to struggle
  mentir — to lie
  se soucier de — to worry about
  supporter — to tolerate
  voler — to steal

Useful Nouns

- **une attaque / une agression** — an attack
  une bande (f) — a gang
  le chômage (m) — unemployment
  l'ennui (m) — boredom
  la guerre (f) — war
  le harcèlement (f) — harassment / bullying
  un(e) immigré(e) — immigrant
  une manifestation (f) — demonstration
  la paix (f) — peace
  la pauvreté (f) — poverty
  un(e) réfugié(e) — a refugee
  un(e) sans-abri — a homeless person
  un souci (m) — a worry
  un témoin (m) — a witness
  un voyou (m) — a yob / hooligan

Useful Adjectives

- **effrayant(e)(s)** — scary
  entouré(e)(s) — surrounded
  lourd(e)(s) / grave — serious
  pauvre — poor
  reconnaissant(e)(s) — grateful

Useful Phrases

- **de nos jours** — nowadays
  maintenant — now
  actuellement — currently
  depuis peu — recently

- **Il y a de plus en plus de**…
  There are more and more…
- **On voit une augmentation du nombre de**…
  We see an increase in the number of…
- **On parle souvent des problèmes de**…
  We often talk about the issues of…
- **On entend souvent parler de**…
  We often hear about…
- **Le problème le plus important / inquiétant c'est**…
  The most important / worrying problem is…

> **Key Point**

Use subordinate clauses to make your sentences longer; use **qui**.

Which are the Most Important Social Problems?

- **De nos jours il y a de plus en plus de chômage et de pauvreté dans le monde.**
  Nowadays there is more and more unemployment and poverty in the world.
- **Depuis peu on entend parler d'une augmentation du nombre de réfugiés.**
  Recently we have heard about an increase in the number of réfugees.

- **Il y a de plus en plus de personnes qui sont au chômage.**
  There are more and more people who are unemployed.

sont agressées	are attacked
volent	steal
harcèlent	harass
sont harcelées	are harassed
sont sans-abri	are homeless

Expressing Feelings about these Issues

- **Je me sens concerné(e) par**…   I am feeling concerned about…
- **Je me soucie de**…   I worry about…
- **Ce qui m'inquiète c'est**…   What worries me is…
- **Ce que je trouve effrayant c'est**…   What I find frightening is…

- **On devrait**…   We should…
- **On ne devrait pas**…   We shouldn't…
- **s'inquiéter de**   worry about
- **se soucier de**   worry about
- **se sentir concerné(e) par**   feel concerned about

- **Je me sens concerné(e) par le nombre de sans-abri dans nos villes.**
  I feel concerned about the number of homeless people in our towns.
- **Ce qui m'inquiète c'est que de plus en plus de personnes volent et agressent les autres.**
  What worries me is that more and more people steal and attack other people.
- **On devrait se soucier du nombre de personnes qui sont au chômage.**
  We should worry about the number of people who are unemployed.

> **Key Vocab**

le chômage
unemployment
la pauvreté
poverty
un(e) sans-abri
a homeless person
le problème le plus important
the most important problem
qui
who

> **Quick Test**

Translate into English:
1. Il y a beaucoup de sans-abris.
2. Le problème le plus important c'est le chômage.
3. Maintenant il y a trop de voyous.
4. On entend souvent parler de la guerre aux infos.
5. On devrait s'inquiéter du nombre de personnes qui sont pauvres.

Travel and Tourism 1

You must be able to:

- Give the main details about a holiday
- Use key verbs in the Present, Past and Future
- Use the prepositions **à / en / y**

Countries and Nationalities

Feminine Countries

L'Allemagne	Germany	**allemand / e**	German
La Belgique	Belgium	**belge**	Belgian
La Chine	China	**chinois / e**	Chinese
L'Écosse	Scotland	**écossais / e**	Scottish
L'Espagne	Spain	**espagnol / e**	Spanish
La France	France	**français / e**	French
La Grande-Bretagne	Great Britain	**britannique**	British
La Suisse	Switzerland	**suisse**	Swiss
La Tunisie	Tunisia	**tunisien / enne**	Tunisian

Masculine Countries

Le Canada	Canada	**canadien / enne**	Canadian
Les États-Unis	United-States	**américain / e**	American
Le Maroc	Morocco	**marocain / e**	Moroccan
Le pays de Galles	Wales	**gallois / e**	Welsh
Le Portugal	Portugal	**portugais / e**	Portuguese

- **L'année dernière je suis allé(e) en Suisse avec ma famille et j'ai pensé que les Suisses étaient très chaleureux.**
  Last year I went to Switzerland with my family and I thought that the Swiss were very warm people.

- **L'année prochaine j'irai aux États-Unis pendant quinze jours pour rendre visite à mes cousins qui y habitent depuis 2013.**
  Next year I will go to the USA for two weeks to visit my cousins who have been living there since 2013.

- **Normalement nous passons nos vacances au Portugal parce que la vie portugaise nous plaît bien.**
  Normally we spend our holidays in Portugal because we like the Portuguese way of life.

Useful Verbs

passer	je passe / nous passons	j'ai passé / nous avons passé	je passerai / nous passerons
visiter	je visite / nous visitons	j'ai visité / nous avons visité	je visiterai / nous visiterons
voyager	je voyage / nous voyageons	j'ai voyagé / nous avons voyagé	je voyagerai / nous voyagerons

Key Point

To say *in* or *to* a country, use **en** with feminine countries, use **au** with masculine countries, use **aux** with plural countries, and with the names of towns, cities and villages use **à**.

Key Point

'**Y**' means *there* and it goes before the verb.

loger	je loge / nous logeons	j'ai logé / nous avons logé	je logerai / nous logerons
aller	je vais / nous allons	je suis allé(e) / nous sommes allé(e)s	j'irai / nous irons
rester	je reste / nous restons	je suis resté(e) / nous sommes resté(e)s	je resterai / nous resterons

> **HT** It is important to use **a range of persons** in your work so check the endings for *he* or *she*, for instance if you want to talk about somebody else's holidays. You also need to try to include **a wider range of tenses**. Why not compare what *you used to do when you were younger* using the **imperfect** or where *you would go* using the **conditional tense**?

Key Point

Remember to check whether you need **être** or **avoir** in the perfect tense.

Transport

- **la voiture**   car
  l'autobus (m)   bus
  le car   coach
  le bateau   boat
  l'avion (m)   plane
  la moto   motorbike
  une croisière   a cruise
  l'aéroport (m)   the airport
  la gare   train station

- **Quand nous allons en vacances nous préférons voyager en train car mon père dit que c'est moins fatigant que conduire.**
  When we go on holiday we prefer travelling by train because my dad says it is less tiring than driving.
- **L'année prochaine nous irons en vacances en France et nous y irons en bateau.**
  Next year we will go on holiday to France and we will go there by boat.

Key Point

Remember to use **en + means of transport**, e.g. **Je suis allé(e) en vacances en avion.**

Key Vocab

à	at / to / in
en	to / in / at
aux	to / at / in
dans	in
y	there
aller	to go
Je vais	I go
J'irai	I will go
Je suis allé(e)	I went

Quick Test

1. Use the correct prepositions: **à**   **en**   **aux**
   Habituellement je passe mes vacances..........**France**..........**la campagne.**
   L'année dernière nous sommes allées.........**Maldives.**
2. Use the appropriate form of the verbs:
   L'été dernier nous..........................**dans une villa. (loger)**
   Je .... **mes prochaines vacances au Canada. (passer)**

Travel and Tourism 2

You must be able to:

- Describe your holiday activities
- Use the perfect and the imperfect tense
- Use **il y a**.

Types of Holidays

à la campagne	to / at the countryside	**dans un gîte**	in a cottage
à l'étranger	abroad	**sur une île**	on an island
au bord de la mer	to / at the seaside	**dans un hôtel**	in a hotel
en colonie de vacances	on a holiday camp	**dans une auberge de jeunesse**	to / in a youth hostel
à la montagne	to / at the mountains	**dans un hôtel 4 étoiles**	in a 4 star hotel
		dans un dortoir	in a dormitory
		dans un camping	in a campsite

- **L'année prochaine j'irai en vacances en Allemagne et nous logerons dans un gîte au bord de la mer.**
  Next year I will go on holiday in Germany and we will stay in a cottage at the seaside.
- **J'apprécie vraiment les vacances à la montagne puisqu'on peut y faire un tas d'activités.**
  I really like holidays in the mountains since one can do a lot of activities there.

Holiday Activities

aller dans des parcs d'attractions	to go to theme parks	**se promener**	to go for a walk
se baigner	to bathe	**marcher**	to walk
se lever	to get up	**s'habituer**	to get used to
bronzer	to sunbathe	**se réveiller**	to wake up
nager	to swim	**faire du camping**	to go camping
se coucher	to go to sleep	**faire des randonnées**	to go hiking
louer	to hire		
faire la grasse matinée	to have a lie in		

- **En vacances j'apprécie vraiment de nager et de me promener le long de la plage.**
  On holiday I really like swimming and going for walks along the beach.
- **Ce qui me plaît le plus pendant les vacances, c'est me coucher tard et me lever tard. J'adore faire la grasse matinée!**
  What I like the most on holiday is to go to bed late and to get up late. I love to have a lie-in!

Key Point

Use **dans** for accommodation.

Describing a Past Holiday

- If you want to describe a holiday in the past you will need to use the *perfect* and the *imperfect tense*.
- **L'année dernière je suis allé(e) en vacances en France au bord de la mer et tous les jours je me baignais.**
  Last year I went on holiday in France at the seaside and every day I would bathe.
- **L'année dernière, en vacances, pendant que mon frère faisait la grasse matinée, moi j'allais faire des randonnées avec ma mère.**
  Last year on holiday, while my brother was having a lie-in, I would go for walks with my mum.
- **Notre auberge de jeunesse était très confortable et il y avait trois grands dortoirs.**
  Our youth hostel was very comfortable and there were three large dormitories.
- **Pendant nos vacances en Espagne l'année dernière il y avait du soleil et il faisait très chaud.**
  On our holiday in Spain last year it was very sunny and very hot.
- **Il y a deux ans nous avons passé nos vacances au Canada en hiver et il neigeait tous les jours.**
  Two years ago we spent our holidays in Canada and it snowed every day.

Useful Phrase: il y a

- **'Il y a'** has different meanings: *there is / are* and *…ago*
- Two years ago   **Il y a deux ans**
- When using **il y a** to say there is / are remember that **avoir** is used and not **être** (to be). So if you are talking about the future you should say **il y aura** (**aura** is the future tense of **avoir**).

 To describe your holiday use the following two structures: **après avoir / être + past participle** (after doing) and **avant de + infinitive** (before doing).

- **Avant d'aller me coucher j'aime bien aller me promener sur la plage.**
  Before going to bed I like going for a walk on the beach.
- **Après être allé(e) à la plage et après avoir nagé, je suis allé(e) retrouver mes amis au club des jeunes.**
  After going to the beach and after swimming I went to meet my friends at the youth club.

Key Point

When using reflexive verbs in the infinitive remember to change **'se'** into the correct person. If you are talking about yourself, change **se** to **me**.

Key Point

When describing your holiday, try to give as much detail as possible (where / how long for / who with / when / how / opinion).

Key Point

Use the perfect for what you did and the imperfect to describe things, what you were doing and activities that you would regularly do.

Key Vocab

Perfect tense, e.g.
Je suis allé(e)   I went
J'ai fait   I did
Imperfect tense, e.g.
J'allais
I used to go / I was going
Je faisais
I used to do / I was doing
Il faisait chaud It was hot
Il y a
There is / are and …ago

Quick Test

What is the French for:
1. I travelled by train.
2. We spent two weeks there.
3. On holiday I like going for walks.
4. On holiday what I like the most is going to theme parks.
5. Three years ago I spent two weeks on an island.

Travel and Tourism 3

You must be able to:

- Organise your holiday
- Talk about problems
- Use key phrases.

Organising Accommodation

- **réserver son logement** — book your accommodation
  Je voudrais réserver… — I would like to book…
  Avez-vous / Est-ce que vous avez…? — Do you have…?
  J'ai réservé / J'ai une réservation — I have booked / I have a reservation
  Est-ce qu'il y a…? — Is / are there…?
  Est-ce qu'on peut…? — Can we…?
  Où est-ce qu'on peut…? — Where can we…?
  À quelle heure est…? — At what time is…?
  Où se trouve / se trouvent…? — Where is / are…?
  Où est / sont…? — Where is / are…?
  du…au — from…to
  jusqu'au — until

Key Point

Remember that there are different ways to ask a question in French: you can add **est-ce que** in your question, change the order (subject-verb) or raise your voice at the end of the question.

- **Bonjour, est-ce que vous avez une chambre double avec vue sur la mer pour cinq nuits, s'il vous plaît?**
  Hello, do you have a double bedroom with a sea view for five nights, please?
- **Bonsoir monsieur, j'ai une réservation au nom de**…
  Good evening Sir, I have a booking in the name of….
- **Bonjour, où est-ce qu'on peut garer notre voiture?**
  Hello, where can we park our car?

At the Hotel

à l'hôtel	at the hotel	**se garer**	to park
l'accueil	reception	**une nuit**	a night
l'ascenseur (m)	lift	**le premier étage**	first floor
une chambre double / familiale	a double / family bedroom	**le rez-de-chaussée**	ground floor
		le salon	lounge
un escalier	stairs	**la vue sur la mer**	a sea view

At the Travel Agent

- **demander des renseignements à l'agence de voyage**
  ask for information at the travel agency

la carte	map	**le plan de la ville**	street map
la carte postale	postcard	**le rendez-vous**	meeting
l'essence (f)	petrol	**le spectacle**	show
l'horaire (m)	timetable	**la visite guidée**	guided tour
la location de voiture	car hire	**le vol**	flight
louer	to hire		

- **Bonjour, le rendez-vous pour la visite guidée est à quelle heure, s'il vous plaît?**
  Hello, at what time are we meeting up for the guided tour, please?
- **Bonjour, je voudrais réserver deux places pour le spectacle de demain soir à vingt heures.**
  Hello, I would like to book two tickets for the show tomorrow evening at 8pm.

Problems on Holiday

- **…est cassé / sont cassé(e)s** …is / are broken
- **…est sale / sont sales** …is / are dirty
- **…ne marche pas / ne marchent pas** …doesn't / don't work
- **Il manque…** …is missing
- **J'ai oublié…** I have forgotten…
- **J'ai perdu…** I have lost…
- **J'ai laissé…** I have left…
- **Je n'ai pas de…** I don't have…
- **On m'a volé…** I have had…stolen
- **On est tombé en panne.** We have broken down.
- **mes bagages** my luggage
  la baignoire bath
  le bureau des objets trouvés lost property
  ma clé my key
  ma crème solaire my sun cream
  mes lunettes (f) **de soleil** my sunglasses
  mon maillot de bain my swimming costume
  ma pièce (f) **d'identité** my ID
  mon porte-monnaie my purse
  le robinet the tap
  la serviette the towel
  mon sac de couchage my sleeping bag
  un savon soap
  ma valise my suitcase
- **Oh non! Quel dommage! J'ai oublié ma crème solaire chez moi.**
  Oh no! What a shame! I have forgotten my sun cream at home.
- **Excusez-moi…dans ma chambre la télé ne marche pas, la douche est sale et il n'y a pas de serviettes.**
  Excuse-me…In my bedroom the television is not working, the shower is dirty and there aren't any towels.
- **Quelle catastrophe! Je crois qu'on m'a volé ma valise avec ma pièce d'identité dedans.**
  What a disaster! I think that I have had my suitcase stolen with my ID inside it.

Key Point

If you want to describe what happened during your last holiday use your verbs in the imperfect.
La télé ne marchait pas la douche était cassée

Key Vocab

réserver
to book
Je voudrais…
I would like…
Est-ce qu'il y a…?
Is there / Are there…?
J'ai perdu…
I have lost…
J'ai oublié…
I have forgotten…

Quick Test

Translate into English:
1. Bonsoir, j'ai une réservation pour une chambre familiale pour six nuits.
2. J'ai perdu ma clé.
3. Est-ce que vous avez un plan de la ville, s'il vous plaît?
Translate into French:
4. Hello, I would like to book a room for two people for two nights, please.
5. I have left my suitcase at the airport.

Review Questions

My Family and Friends & Marriage and Partnerships

1 **Complétez le texte, en utilisant les mots ci-dessous.** Complete the text, using the words below.

Ma .... copine s'appelle Yasmine. Elle a les yeux .... et les .... bruns, longs et frisés. Elle ..... des lunettes. Elle est un peu .... grande que moi. On se connaît .... six ans. Elle me fait .... et elle n'est .... de mauvaise humeur.

cheveux	porte	meilleure	jamais	depuis	rire	moins	marron

[8 marks]

2 **Lisez ces phrases sur l'amitié. Corrigez l'erreur dans chaque mot souligné.**
Read the sentences about friendship. Correct the mistake in the underlined words.

a) On <u>avons</u> beaucoup de choses en commun.

b) Nous <u>aime</u> la même équipe de foot.

c) <u>On</u> avons le même sens de l'humour.

d) On <u>aimons</u> les mêmes émissions de télé.

e) <u>Nous</u> va au cinéma ensemble.

f) On <u>écoutons</u> de la musique ensemble. [6 marks]

3 **Mettez les mots dans le bon ordre pour faire des phrases sur le mariage et traduisez-les.** Put the words into the correct order to make sentences about marriage and translate them.

a) habiter Il vaut ensemble mieux

b) divorce termine mariage Le se un souvent par

c) avoir enfants des J'aimerais

d) rester préférerais célibataire Je

e) complètement Le mariage démodé est

f) voudrais Je un me jour marier [12 marks: 6 for writing sentences correctly, 6 for translation.]

Social Media & Mobile Technology

1 **Complétez chaque phrase sur la technologie avec le bon verbe de la case.** Complete each sentence about technology with the correct verb from the box.

a) J'utilise mon portable pour .... en contact avec mes amis.

b) J'utilise mon imprimante pour .... des documents.

c) Je vais sur des sites web pour .... des recherches.

d) Je vais sur les sites de musique pour .... des chansons.

e) Pour se protéger en ligne, il faut .... un logiciel anti-virus.

f) Il ne faut jamais .... avec des inconnus.

communiquer	faire	imprimer	installer	rester	télécharger

[6 marks]

2 **Trouvez les dix adjectifs et copiez-les dans la bonne case.** Find the ten adjectives and copy them into the correct box.

utilearousantbarbantrapidegénialpratiquetropcherrigoloennuyeuxafreux

Adjectifs positifs	Adjectifs négatifs
utlle	

[10 marks]

3 **Complétez logiquement les phrases sur la technologie, en utilisant des adjectifs de l'exercice 2. Puis traduisez les phrases en anglais.** Complete the sentences about technology logically, using adjectives from exercise 2. Then translate the sentences into English.

a) Je passe beaucoup de temps en ligne, parce que c'est ....

b) Je ne joue pas à des jeux en ligne, parce que je trouve ça ....

c) Je prends beaucoup de photos sur mon portable, car c'est ....

d) Je déteste le cyberharcèlement: je trouve ça ....

e) Je fais tous mes achats en ligne, parce que c'est ....

f) J'aimerais acheter le dernier modèle de portable, mais c'est ....

[12 marks: 1 mark for each sentence completed logically and 1 mark for each correct translation.]

Review Questions

Music & Cinema and TV

1 **Écrivez les bonnes terminaisons pour les verbes suivants au présent.** Write the correct endings for these verbs in the present tense.

a) **Nous ador____** (we adore) b) **Elle écout__** (she listens to) c) **Ils télécharg___** (they download)

d) **Nous chant____** (we sing) e) **Elles s'intéress____** (they are interested in) [5 marks]

2 *J'ai* ou *Je suis*? *J'ai* or *Je suis*?

a) .... **fana de jazz.**

b) .... **téléchargé le nouvel album de Guizmo.**

c) .... **toujours aimé le vieux rock.**

d) .... **vu mes chanteurs préférés.**

e) .... **allé au dernier concert de Mustang.** [5 marks]

3 **Aller au cinéma ou regarder la télé?** Decide whether the following statements are about watching the television or going to the cinema:

	Télé	Cinéma

A **Les effets spéciaux sont meilleurs sur le grand écran.**

B **Les places deviennent de plus en plus chères.**

C **Pour moi, l'essentiel est le confort et on peut se détendre où on veut.**

D **Je préfère l'ambiance parce que le son surround est plus puissant.**

E **Il ne faut pas regarder toutes les publicités.**

F **On peut appuyer sur 'pause' et recommencer quand on veut.**

G **Tout le monde aime acheter le popcorn et les bonbons au kiosque!**

H **Il n'est pas nécessaire de garder le silence.** [8 marks]

4 **Traduisez les phrases de l'exercice 3 en anglais.** Translate the sentences in exercise 3 into English.

[8 marks]

Food and Eating Out, Sport & Customs and Festivals

1 **Complétez le menu.** Complete the menu.

hors d'œuvres	poissons	viandes	légumes	desserts

crudités; côtelette d'agneau; crêpes flambées; chou-fleur; tarte aux cerises; filet de veau; truite aux amandes; assiette de charcuterie; champignons; saumon fumé

[10 marks]

2 **Choisissez le verbe correcte pour remplir les blancs.** Choose the correct verb to fill the gaps.

je joue	je fais	je jouais	je faisais

a) Il y a a deux ans, ... au basket au club des jeunes.

b) En ce moment .... souvent des promenades à la campagne.

c) Maintenant .... au volley tous les samedis.

d) Quand j'étais plus jeune, ... de la natation trois fois par semaine. [4 marks]

3 **Trouvez les phrases.** Unscramble the sentences.

a) sports / voudrais / les / Je / nautiques / essayer

b) passionne / Je / l'escalade / pour / me

c) des / J'ai / sports / horreur / d'équipe

d) envie / J'ai / à /planche / d'essayer / voile / la [4 marks]

4 **Reliez les bouts de phrases et traduisez en anglais.** Match up and translate into English.

a) Les touristes regardent	i) à chanter les chansons traditionnelles
b) Beaucoup de gens mangent	ii) danse dans les rues
c) Tout le monde aime	iii) les défilés et les feux d'artifice
d) On passe la journée	iv) donner et recevoir les cadeaux
e) En fin de soirée on	v) les plats traditionnels

[5 marks]

Practice Questions

At Home, Where I Live & Town or Country?

1 **Choisissez les bons mots pour les espaces dans la description de la maison de Julien.** Choose the missing words to complete the description of Julien's home.

J'habite dans une maison .... Il y a neuf pièces. Au .... il y a la cuisine et .... salle à manger. Le salon est .... de l'entrée. À l'étage il y a trois .... et une salle de bains. Ma chambre est à côté de la .... de ma sœur.

près	chambres	la	individuelle	rez-de-chaussée	chambre

[6 marks]

2 **Écrivez une description en utilisant l'exemple de l'exercice 1.** Write your own description based on the example given in exercise 1.

[8 marks]

3 **Formez des phrases en reliant les éléments des deux colonnes.** Match the sentence parts together.

a) On peut acheter…	…mon portefeuille.

b) Je peux …	…circulation dans cette ville.

c) On a besoin…	…du pain ici.

d) Il y a trop de…	…essayer cette chemise?

e) Les transports en commun…	…d'un cinéma.

f) J'ai perdu…	…sont très fréquents.

[6 marks]

Charity and Voluntary Work & Healthy and Unhealthy Living

1 **Faites correspondre le nom de chaque personne et leurs citations.** Read the quotes and decide which person each quote belongs to by writing their name alongside the English question.

Je livre des médicaments aux personnes âgées. Luc, 18 ans

Moi, je fais des collectes d'argent à l'école. Delphine, 15 ans

Je voudrais devenir médecin. Henri, 15 ans

Je distribue des repas chauds aux SDF dans la rue. Nadia, 17 ans

Je voudrais travailler comme infirmière. Rachel, 15 ans

a) Who wants to be a doctor?

b) Who works with homeless people?

c) Who wants to help the lives of old people?

d) Who collects money?

e) Who would like to work as a nurse?

[5 marks]

2 **Mettez les mots dans le bon ordre pour traduire les phrases anglaises.** Rearrange the words to make the following sentences when translated.

a) faut / produits / gras / éviter / Il / les You must avoid fatty products.

b) en / bonne / très / Je / suis / santé – I am in very good health.

c) faut / stress / le / pour / éviter / se détendre / Il – It is necessary to relax to avoid stress.

d) mère / fumer / a / de / arrêté / Ma – My mother stopped smoking.

e) de / suivre / un / essayer / régime / vais / Je – I am going to try to follow a diet.   [5 marks]

3 **Écrivez les phrases dans le futur.** Put the following sentences into the future tense.

a) Je mange sainement.

b) J'évite les matières grasses.

c) Je m'entraîne trois fois par semaine.

d) Louis va au centre sportif.

[4 marks]

Practice Questions

The Environment & Poverty and Insecurity

1 **Comment dit-on en français…?** What is the French for…?

a) to waste   b) one should   c) global warming   d) a bin   e) one could

f) flooding   g) I should   h) we must   i) greenhouse effect   j) to damage

[10 marks]

2 **Remplissez les blancs avec les bons mots.** Fill in the gaps with the correct quantifiers.

beaucoup	trop	assez	trop	assez

Je pense qu'il y a [1] .... de pollution de nos jours et à mon avis on ne recycle pas [2] ....
nos déchets. Les gens jettent [3] .... de papier par terre et n'utilisent pas [4] .... les
poubelles et les centres de tri. Aussi je pense qu'il y a [5] .... d'animaux en danger.   [5 marks]

3 **Remettez les phrases dans le bon ordre et traduisez-les en anglais.** Unjumble the sentences and translate
into English.

a) devrait / protéger / on / en / plus / l'environnement / recyclant

b) pourrait / gaspiller / mon / on / avis / moins / à

c) respecter / autant / la planète / je / en / pas / ne / devrais / polluant

d) il / faut / pas / gaspiller / ne / autant

e) sauver / nos ressources / on / la Terre / ne / doit / en / gaspillant / pas /

[10 marks: 5 marks for correct ordering and 5 marks for translation]

4 **Comment dit-on en anglais…?** What is the English for…?

a) effrayer   b) voler   c) le chômage   d) la guerre   e) la pauvreté

f) un sans-abri   g) un voyou   h) pauvre   i) reconnaissant   j) un souci

[10 marks]

Travel and Tourism

1 **Choisissez la bonne préposition pour chaque phrase et expliquez pourquoi. Puis traduisez les phrases en anglais.** Choose the correct preposition for each sentence and explain why. Then translate the sentences into English.

a) L'année prochaine je passerai mes vacances <u>en / au</u> Italie.

b) J'aimerais bien aller en vacances <u>à / au</u> Pékin <u>en / au</u> Chine.

c) Normalement nous allons en vacances <u>en / par</u> voiture car mon père aime conduire.

d) Il y a trois ans j'ai passé mes vacances <u>aux / au</u> États-Unis.

[8 marks: 4 marks for correct choice and explanation and 4 marks for translation]

2 **Choisissez la forme correcte du verbe pour chaque phrase.** Choose the correct verb for each sentence.

j'allais	je passerai	je passais	j'ai passé	nous passons

a) Tous les ans .... nos vacances au bord de la mer en France.

b) L'année dernière pendant mes vacances .... à la plage tous les jours.

c) Il y a deux ans .... quinze jours en Égypte avec ma famille.

d) Je pense que .... mes prochaines vacances dans un gîte à la campagne pour me détendre.

e) Quand j'étais petite, ... mes vacances à la montagne chez ma tante qui habite dans les Alpes.

[5 marks]

3 **Regardez les situations ci-dessous. Que diriez-vous à la personne à la réception de votre hôtel?**
Look at the situations below. What would you say to the person at the reception of your hotel?

a) The bath in your room is dirty.

b) You have been given a single room instead of a double room.

c) You would like to know at what time breakfast is.

d) You have just realised that you do not have your ID on you any more.

e) You don't have a towel in your bedroom.

[5 marks]

My Studies

You must be able to:

- Name your school subjects
- Say what you study and what you like and dislike and why
- Use quantifiers to be precise about what you are good at, and not so good at.

School

• l'instituteur	primary school teacher (male)
l'institutrice	primary school teacher (female)
le professeur	teacher
le cahier	exercise book
le livre	book
la trousse	pencil case
la salle de classe	classroom
la journée scolaire	school day
la cour	playground
le brevet	GCSE (equivalent)
le baccalauréat / le bac	A-levels (equivalent)
HT le proviseur / le directeur (la directrice)	head teacher

School Subjects

• l'allemand (m)	German	l'informatique (f)	IT
l'anglais (m)	English	les langues (f)	languages
la biologie	biology	les mathématiques (f)	mathematics
la chimie	chemistry	la matière	subject
le dessin	art	la physique	physics
la technologie	technology	la religion	RE
l'espagnol (m)	Spanish	HT la couture	textiles
l'EPS (f)	PE	HT les langues	modern
le français	French	vivantes (f)	languages
l'histoire-géo (f)	history and geography	HT l'instruction civique (f)	citizenship

- **J'étudie l'espagnol et l'anglais.** — I study Spanish and English.
- **Je fais de l'EPS le lundi et le jeudi.** — I do PE on a Monday and a Thursday / on Mondays and Thursdays.

- **être fort(e) en** — to be good at
- **être faible en** — to be weak in
- **être nul(le) en** — to be rubbish at

- **Je suis fort(e) en mathématiques mais je suis faible en dessin.**
  I am good at Maths but weak in Art.
- HT **Elle est douée en EPS.** — She is gifted at PE.

Quantifiers

- **très** — very
- **assez** — quite
- **un peu** — a bit

- Quantifiers help give the language a bit more depth and detail. You can be more precise too:
- **Je suis très fort en histoire-géo, mais je suis plutôt nul en maths.**
  I am very good at History and Geography but I am a bit rubbish at Maths.

Likes and Dislikes

- **Ma matière préférée c'est**…   My favourite subject is…

J'adore	I love	**facile**	easy
J'aime (bien)	I (quite) like	**formidable**	great
Je n'aime pas (du tout)	I don't (at all) like	**génial(e)(s)**	great
		intéressant(e)(s)	interesting
Je déteste	I hate	**inutile**	useless
		nul(le)(s)	rubbish
amusant(e)(s)	funny	**pratique**	practical
barbant(e)(s)	boring	**rigolo**	funny
chouette	great	**utile**	useful
embêtant(e)(s)	annoying		
ennuyeux / ennuyeuse	boring		

- **Ma matière préférée, c'est la technologie parce que j'adore travailler avec mes mains.**
  My favourite subject is technology because I love working with my hands.
- **J'adore l'EPS parce que je suis très sportif mais je n'aime pas la religion parce que le professeur est sévère!**
  I love PE because I am very sporty but I don't like RE because the teacher is strict.

affreux / affreuse	awful
casse-pieds	annoying
content(e)(s)	happy
désagréable	unpleasant
drôle	funny
grave	serious
habile	clever, skilful
marrant(e)(s)	funny
sévère	strict

- **Mon prof d'espagnol est très content.** My Spanish teacher is very happy.
- **En général elle est assez marrante.** In general she is quite funny.

Quick Test

1. Jot down in French some sentences about which school subjects you are good at and those you are not so good at. Use quantifiers to add detail.
2. Can you name each of these subjects in English?
   l'histoire-géo, la chimie, l'EPS, l'allemand, la technologie, le dessin
   Could you say how good you are at each, and perhaps whether you like them or not?
3. Translate the following into English:
   En ce moment j'étudie pour le brevet. J'adore les langues, surtout l'espagnol parce que le prof est marrant et intéressant. Je suis fort en EPS parce que je suis assez sportif, mais je suis très faible en mathématiques.

Key Point

Remember to always justify your opinions. Use a connective such as **parce que** or **car**, both of which mean 'because':
J'adore la religion car c'est intéressant. – I love RE because it's interesting.

Key Point

Remember that adjectives always need to be agreed according to gender. But if the adjective already ends in an 'e' there is no need to add a further one.

Key Vocab

Ma matière préférée
My favourite subject
Je suis fort(e) / faible en
I am good at / not good at
J'adore
I love
J'aime / je n'aime pas
I like / I don't like
Je déteste
I hate
intéressant(e)(s)
interesting
ennuyeux(euse) boring
drôle funny
sévère strict

Life at School 1

You must be able to:

- Describe school in France
- Say what your school day is like
- Use the imperative to understand instructions, use key irregular verbs in the present tense to describe routine.

School

- **le collège**   secondary school
  le lycée   sixth form college / grammar school
  l'école primaire (f)   primary school
  l'école secondaire (f)   secondary school
  l'élève (m,f)   pupil
  l'étudiant(e)   student
  le professeur   teacher
  le directeur   headmaster
  la directrice   headmistress
  le diplôme   qualification
  en seconde   in year 11

- **Je vais au collège.**   I go to secondary school.
- **Je suis en seconde.**   I'm in year 11.
- **Il y a 1 200 élèves.**   There are 1,200 pupils.
- **La directrice s'appelle Madame Martin.**   The headmistress is called Mrs Martin.

In the Classroom

- **la salle de classe**   classroom
  le terrain de sport   sports field
  le tableau   board

- **Il y a 60 salles de classe.**   There are 60 classrooms.
- **On a un tableau dans chaque salle de classe.**   We have a whiteboard in every classroom.
- **Il faut avoir une calculette.**   You have to have a calculator with you.

The School Day

- **la journée scolaire**   the school day

- **l'emploi du temps** (m)   timetable
  le cours   lesson
  la leçon   lesson
  la pause (déjeuner)   lunch break
  la recré(ation)   break
  la rentrée   return to school
  le trimestre   term
  HT **le car de ramassage scolaire**   school bus

Key Point

Le collège: pupils aged 11–14 years old
Le lycée: pupils aged 15–18 years old

Key Point

When describing something which is routine, use the present tense. Often the verbs you need to use will be irregular so know these well:

Je vais	I go
Je suis	I am
Je fais	I do
J'ai	I have

- **Il y a cinq cours par jour.** — There are five lessons per day.
- **On commence à huit heures et quart.** — We start at a quarter past eight.
- **Le dernière cours se termine à cinq heures moins le quart.** — The last lesson finishes at a quarter to five.
- **La pause déjeuner est à une heure. Elle dure une heure et demie.** — The lunch break is at one o'clock. It lasts an hour and a half.

- **discuter** — to discuss
  distribuer — to distribute / give out
  faire attention — to pay attention
  oublier — to forget
  répéter — to repeat
  trouver — to find

- **Soyez attentifs!** — Pay attention!
- **N'oubliez pas vos devoirs.** — Don't forget your homework.
- **Répétez s'il vous plaît, toute la classe!** — Repeat please, (the whole) class!
- HT **Ne courez pas dans le couloir!** — Don't run in the corridor!

Quick Test

1. Try and talk for 30 seconds about your school. Include the type of school and information about it, such as number of pupils and name of the headteacher.
2. Complete these instructions by putting the infinitives into imperatives.
   é.g. Écouter, **toute la classe** – Écoutez, **toute la classe**
   Répéter le vocabulaire –
   Distribuer les livres –
   N'*oublier* pas vos cahiers! –
3. Translate these sentences into French:
   I go to secondary school.
   There are 800 pupils, 38 teachers and 29 classrooms.
   We start at 8.45, finish at 3.15 and lessons are an hour long.

Key Vocab

Je vais à	I go to
Je suis en	I am in
Il y a / On a	There is
l'élève	student
le professeur	teacher
le cours	lesson

Life at School 2

You must be able to:

- Describe your school day and other aspects of school
- Say what you have to do in school
- Use **devoir** to indicate school rules and school expectations.

My Studies

les études (f)	studies	**penser**	to think
apprendre	to learn	**réfléchir**	to consider / think about
comprendre	to understand		
demander	to ask	**savoir**	to know
le cours	lesson	**le travail scolaire**	school work
les devoirs (m)	homework	**la lecture**	reading
lire	to read	HT **enseigner**	to teach

> ### Key Point
>
> Make sure that you pay close attention to nouns that link to verbs but do not necessarily look alike.
> **lire** = to read,
> **la lecture** = reading
> **nager** = to swim,
> **la natation** = swimming

- **Pour les devoirs je dois apprendre du vocabulaire.**
  For homework I have to learn some vocabulary.
- **À l'école j'adore la lecture.**
  At school I love reading.
- **J'aime lire.**
  I like to read / reading.
- **Si on ne comprend pas, il faut demander au prof.**
  If you don't understand you must ask the teacher.
- **Lui, il enseigne les maths.**
  He teaches maths.

Lunch break

la pause déjeuner	lunch break
le restaurant	restaurant
la restauration	catering
la cantine / le self	the canteen
le panier-repas	packed lunch
le plat	dish
le sandwich	sandwich

- **Moi, je mange à la cantine le midi.** — I eat in the canteen at midday.
- **Je rentre à la maison pour déjeuner.** — I go home to eat.
- **J'apporte un panier-repas / mon propre repas / un sandwich.** — I bring a packed lunch / my own food / a sandwich.

School rules

- **la règle** — rule
- **le règlement intérieur** — school rules
- **le maquillage** — make-up
- **permettre** — to allow, permit
- **porter** — to wear, carry
- **le droit** — right
- **l'uniforme scolaire** (m) — school uniform

- **interdit(e)(s)** — forbidden
- **bien équipé(e)(s)** — well equipped
- **mal équipé(e)(s)** — badly equipped
- **les incivilités** — rudeness
- **l'injure** (f) — insult, term of abuse

- **avoir le droit** — to be allowed
- **être permis / interdit** — to be permitted / forbidden

- **Le maquillage n'est pas permis / autorisé.**
  Make-up is not permitted.
- **On doit porter l'uniforme scolaire.**
  School uniform has to be worn.
- **On n'a pas le droit d'avoir son téléphone portable allumé en cours.**
  You are not allowed to have your mobile switched on in lessons.
- **Le chewing-gum est interdit.**
  Chewing gum is forbidden.

Exams

- **l'examen** (m) — exam
- **la note** — mark
- **la pression** — pressure
- **la réponse** — reply / answer (to a question)
- **passer un examen** — to sit an exam
- **le redoublement** — repetition of school year

- **réussir un examen** — to pass an exam
- **le résultat** — result
- **redoubler** — to repeat the year

- **le bulletin scolaire** — school report
- **échouer** — to fail
- **la retenue** — detention

- **Olivia doit redoubler.** — Olivia has to repeat the year.
- **J'ai reçu une bonne note.** — I got a good mark.
- **Il y a trop de pression sur les élèves.** — There is too much pressure on pupils.

Key Point

Devoir
As well as being a noun (**les devoirs** = homework), and a straightforward verb (**devoir** = to owe), **devoir** is also a useful modal verb. It can be used interchangeably with **il faut** to say what is necessary, but can be conjugated fully. When used in this way it must be followed by an infinitive.
Je dois finir mes devoirs.
I must finish my homework.
Patrice doit refaire l'exercice. – Patrice has to redo the exercise.

Key Point

Remember the difference between:
Je vais passer un examen.
I am going to sit an exam. (future tense)
J'ai passé un examen.
I sat an exam (perfect tense)

Key Vocab

devoir
to have to
je dois + infinitive
I must + infinitive
il faut + infinitive
It is necessary + infinitive
lire
to read
la lecture
reading (noun)
avoir le droit
to be allowed
être permis / interdit
to be permitted / forbidden

Quick Test

1. Translate these rules into French:
   Mobile phones are not permitted.
   You are not allowed to talk in lessons.
2. Give the associated verb for each of these nouns. What does each mean?
   e.g. **jeu – jouer** (game / to play)
   écriture –   **voyage** –
   redoublement –   **lecture** –
   réponse –
3. Match the French words to their English translation:
la note	to learn
réussir un examen	lesson
apprendre	to sit an exam
le cours	mark
passer un examen	to pass an exam
interdit(e)	forbidden

Education Post-16

You must be able to:

- Describe further studies or other intentions
- Say what you would like to do, or intend to do
- Use **avoir** constructions to give information about your future.

At College

- **le lycée** — sixth form college, grammar school
- **le baccalauréat (le bac)** — A-level(s) equivalent
- **le BT (brevet de technicien)** — technical qualification
- **étudier / faire des études** — to study
- **se spécialiser** — to specialise
- **en seconde** — in year 11
- **en première** — in year 12
- **en terminale** — in year 13
- **laisser tomber** — to drop
- **l'université** (f) — university
- **la faculté / la fac** — university
- **continuer** — to continue
- **quitter** — to leave
- **mes études** (f) — my studies
- **l'interrogation** (f) / **le contrôle** — test
- **l'interne** (m, f) — boarder
- **l'internat** (m) — boarding (school)
- **la mention** — merit, distinction
- **l'examen écrit** (m) — written exam
- **l'examen oral** (m) — oral exam
- **la licence** — degree
- HT **le conseiller d'orientation** — careers adviser
- HT **l'épreuve** (f) — test
- HT **l'établissement scolaire** (m) — school

- **Cette année je suis en première.** — This year I am in year 12.
- **Je prepare mon bac.** — I am studying for my bac.
- **J'ai laissé tomber l'histoire-géo.** — I dropped History-Geography.
- **Je suis interne et je rentre chez moi le week-end.** — I am a boarder and I go home at the weekends.
- **L'année prochaine je vais continuer mes études.** — Next year I am going to carry on with my studies.
- **L'année prochaine je vais quitter l'école.** — Next year I am going to leave school.
- **Plus tard, je voudrais aller à la fac.** — I would like to go to university later.

 Key Point

When talking about where you are with your studies, you might want to say what you have just done. You can do this by using the present tense of **venir** + **de** + **the infinitive**.
Je viens de passer mes examens (or **mon brevet**).
I have just sat my exams.
Mon frère vient de commencer au lycée.
My brother has just started Sixth Form / college.

 Key Point

There are several ways of talking about your future.
If you want to give an indication of your intentions you can use:
Je vais + infinitive
I am going + infinitive
Je vais aller au lycée.
I am going to go to sixth form college.
Je voudrais + infinitive
I would like + infinitive
Je voudrais étudier les langues.
I would like to study languages.

After School

- **l'avenir** (m) — future
  l'idée (f) — idea
  avoir envie de — to want to
  avoir l'intention de — to intend to
  voyager — to travel
  faire un voyage — to go on a trip
  HT aller à la fac(ulté) — to go to university

- **Je vais voyager en Asie.** — I am going to travel in Asia.
- **Je n'ai aucune idée de ce que je veux faire!** — I have no idea what I want to do!
- **À l'avenir j'ai l'intention de gagner beaucoup d'argent.** — In the future I intend to earn lots of money.
- **J'ai vraiment envie de quitter l'école et de travailler.** — I really want to leave school and work.

- **un stage** — work experience
  une année sabbatique — a gap year
  l'apprenti(e) — apprentice
  faire un apprentissage — do an apprenticeship
  la liberté — freedom
  mettre de l'argent de côté — save money
  un petit job — part-time job
  HT former — to train

- **J'ai fait un stage en entreprise en tant que mécanicienne.** — I've done work experience as a mechanic.
- **Après une année sabbatique je vais faire un apprentissage.** — After a gap year I am going to do an apprenticeship.
- **J'ai besoin de liberté!** — I need freedom!

Quick Test

1. Put these sentences into the correct order:
   a) mes   continuer   l'intention   J'   de   ai   études.
   b) veux   Je   que   aucune   ce   ai   n'   idée   je   de   faire.
   c) être   terminale   en   année   vais   L'   je   prochaine.
2. Write a sentence or two about what your intentions are after finishing your GCSEs.
3. Translate the following into English:
   L'année prochaine j'ai l'intention de continuer mes études. J'ai envie d'étudier la physique et la chimie parce que je voudrais aller à la fac. À l'avenir, j'ai envie de gagner beaucoup d'argent.

Career Choices and Ambitions

You must be able to:

- Describe the job that you would like to do in the future
- Say what your aims are in life
- Use the future tense to detail your intentions.

Jobs

l'agent de police (m)	police officer
le boucher / la bouchère	butcher
le boulanger / la boulangère	baker
le coiffeur / la coiffeuse	hairdresser
le facteur / la factrice	postman / postwoman
le fermier / la fermière	farmer
l'infirmier / l'infirmière	nurse
l'informaticien / l'informaticienne	IT technician
l'ingénieur (m)	engineer
le maçon	builder
le mécanicien / la mécanicienne	mechanic
le patron / la patronne	boss
le plombier	plumber
le professeur	teacher
HT **l'avocat** (m) / **l'avocate** (f)	lawyer
HT **le (la) comptable**	accountant
HT **le dessinateur de mode / la dessinatrice de mode**	fashion designer

- **À l'avenir je voudrais devenir**… — In the future I would like to become…
- **Je compte travailler comme**… — I intend to work as…
- **Je vais être**… — I am going to be…

The Future

l'avenir (m)	future
le boulot	job
la candidature	application
l'employé(e)	employee
l'employeur (m)	employer
espérer	to hope
gagner	to earn / win
la livre	pound sterling
mettre de l'argent de côté	to put money aside
le petit job	part-time or holiday job
le rêve	dream
varié(e)(s)	varied
travailler à son compte	to be self-employed
travailler à mi-temps	to work part-time
HT **disponible**	available
HT **l'entreprise** (f)	firm / enterprise

Key Point

Notice how some jobs are different when describing male or female people, but some always remain the same:
Elle est professeur.
She is a teacher.
Elle est mécanicienne.
She is a mechanic.

Key Point

When saying what job you do or someone else does, you do not need to include the article in the sentence.
Mon père est policier.
My father is a policeman.
Je veux être vétérinaire.
I want to be a vet.

HT	**l'entretien** (m)	interview
HT	**enrichissant(e)(s)**	enriching / rewarding
HT	**l'espoir** (m)	hope
HT	**l'outil** (m)	tool

- **Je rêve d'avoir un boulot varié.** — I dream of having a varied job.
- **Elle gagne beaucoup d'argent.** — She earns lots of money.
- **Je veux travailler à mon compte.** — I want to be self-employed.
- **J'espère voyager pour mon métier.** — I hope to travel for my job.

HT	**Je ne veux pas travailler debout toute la journée.**	I don't want to work standing up all day long.

Future Prospects

- **Je gagnerai quarante mille livres par an.** — I'll earn forty thousand pounds a year.
- **J'aurai une voiture chère et je voyagerai partout dans le monde.** — I will have an expensive car and I will travel around the world.
- **Je resterai à la maison.** — I will stay at home.
- **J'aimerais avoir une grande famille.** — I would like to have a big family.

Future Tense Formation

- **Je**... — I...
  serai — will be
  ferai — will do
  gagnerai — will earn

- **J'**... — I...
  aurai — will have
  irai — will go
  habiterai — will live

- **Je serai riche.** — I will be rich.
- **J'habiterai au Brésil.** — I will live in Brazil.

HT	**Chaque année, je ferai des croisières aux Caraïbes.**	I'll go on cruises to the Caribbean every year.

> ### Key Point
>
> To form the future tense, you need to add these endings to the infinitive of a verb.
> **–ai, –as, –a, –ons, –ez, –ont**
> There are however a good number of verbs that are irregular, and the future stems for these need to be learned. These are very common and important verbs.
> **avoir aur– être ser–**
> **aller ir– faire fer–**
> **pouvoir pourr–**
> **devoir devr–**
> **vouloir voudr–**

> ### Key Vocab
>
> **À l'avenir**
> In the future
> **le boulot**
> job
> **le rêve**
> dream
> **j'espère** + infinitive
> I hope (to...)
> **Je vais** + infinitive
> I am going (to...)
> **Je serai**
> I will be
> **Je ferai**
> I will do / make
> **J'aurai**
> I will have
> **J'irai**
> I will go

> ### Quick Test
>
> 1. Jot down as many jobs in French as you can in 60 seconds. Review your list and correct any errors. Try it again. Can you name more this time?
> 2. Translate the following into French:
>   I am going to be a police officer.
>   My mother is a teacher.
>   I dream of having a big car.
> 3. Put the following sentences into the future tense in good French:
>   I live in a big house.
>   This year I am travelling.
>   I earn thirty thousand pounds.

Gender, Plurals and Articles

You must be able to:

- Use the correct gender of nouns
- Make nouns plural
- Use definite, indefinite and partitive articles.

Gender

- All nouns in French are either masculine or feminine.

- **Masculine:**

un homme	a man
un marché	a market
un chapeau	a hat

- **Feminine:**

une femme	a woman
une piscine	a swimming pool
une chemise	a shirt

Rules and Exceptions

- Words ending in **–age**, **–ège**, **–eau**, **–isme**, and **–ment** are *usually* masculine.

  Some exceptions:

une plage	a beach
une eau minérale	a mineral water

- Words ending in **–ée**, **–ie**, **–ine**, **–tion** and **–ence** are *usually* feminine.

  Some exceptions:

un musée	a museum
un magazine	a magazine

Plurals

- To make most nouns plural, you add **–s**.

une maison	a house
des maisons	houses

- Words ending in **–eau** add **–x**.

un oiseau	a bird
des oiseaux	birds

- Words ending in **–al** change to **–aux**.

un journal	a newspaper
des journaux	newspapers

- Words ending in **–s** or **–z** stay the same.

une souris	a mouse
des souris	mice

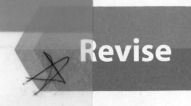
The Indefinite Article

- The indefinite article means 'a' or 'an'.

- Use **un** for masculine nouns.
- Use **une** for feminine nouns.
- Use **des** for plural nouns.

- **un ordinateur**   a computer
  une console de jeux   a games console
  des jeux vidéo   video games

- When referring to jobs, you do not need a word for 'a' in French:
- **Ma sœur est coiffeuse.** My sister is a hairdresser.
- **Je voudrais être fermier.** I'd like to be a farmer.

The Definite Article

- The definite article means 'the'. There are four forms of the definite article in French:

Masculine singular	Feminine singular	Before a vowel or silent 'h'	Plural
le	la	l'	les
le château (the castle)	la poste (the post office)	l'église (the church)	les magasins (the shops)

The Partitive Article

- The partitive article means 'some'. There are four forms of the partitive article in French:

Masculine singular	Feminine singular	Before a vowel or silent 'h'	Plural
du	de la	de l'	des
du fromage (some cheese)	de la salade (some salad)	de l'eau (some water)	des bananes (some bananas)

Quick Test

1. Masculine or feminine? Write **un** or **une** in front of these words.
   a) usine b) bureau c) lycée d) sortie
2. Make these nouns plural.
   a) **une pomme** b) **un ananas** c) **un cheval** d) **un château**
3. Write these words out, using the correct definite article (m = masculine, f = feminine). Watch out for plurals and words that start with a vowel!
   a) **patinoire** (f) b) **lycée** (m) c) **enfant** (m) d) **livres** (m)
4. Translate into French, using the correct partitive article:
   a) some bread b) some jam c) some water d) some sweets

Adjectives

You must be able to:

- Make adjectives agree correctly
- Know whether an adjective goes before or after the noun
- Use comparative, superlative, possessive and demonstrative adjectives.

Adjectival Agreement

- In French, most adjectives change their ending, depending on whether the noun they describe is masculine or feminine, singular or plural. This is called 'agreement'.

Patterns of Agreement

- The most common pattern is:

- Add nothing for a masculine singular noun.
  un tee-shirt vert   a green T-shirt

- Add **–e** for a feminine singular noun.
  une jupe verte   a green skirt

- Add **–s** for a masculine plural noun.
  des gants verts   green gloves

- Add **–es** for a feminine plural noun.
  des chaussettes vertes   green socks

- If an adjective already ends in **–e** in the masculine singular, don't add anything in the feminine singular.
  un film triste   a sad film
  une histoire triste   a sad story

Some Other Patterns of Agreement

Masculine singular	Feminine singular	Masculine plural	Feminine plural
heureux (happy)	**heureuse**	**heureux**	**heureuses**
travailleur (hard-working)	**travailleuse**	**travailleurs**	**travailleuses**
sportif (sporty)	**sportive**	**sportifs**	**sportives**
gentil (kind)	**gentille**	**gentils**	**gentilles**

Irregular Adjectives

Masculine singular	Feminine singular	Masculine plural	Feminine plural
beau (beautiful / good-looking)	**belle**	**beaux**	**belles**
vieux (old)	**vieille**	**vieux**	**vieilles**
blanc (white)	**blanche**	**blancs**	**blanches**

- **marron** (brown) and **noisette** (hazel) never change.

Key Point

Most adjectives go *after* the noun they describe.

une maison moderne
a modern house
des baskets blanches
white trainers

But the following go *before* the noun:

grand   (big, tall)
petit   (small)
beau   (beautiful)
joli   (pretty)
vieux   (old)
jeune   (young)

Adjectives

Comparative Adjectives

- To compare two people or things, use:

plus (+ adjective) **que**…	more (+ adjective) than…
moins (+ adjective) **que**…	less (+ adjective) than…
aussi (+ adjective) **que**…	as (+ adjective) as…

- **Les sciences sont aussi difficiles que les maths.**
  Science is as difficult as maths.

Superlative Adjectives

- Use the superlative to say 'the most…', or 'the least…':

le / la / les plus (+ adjective)	the most (+ adjective)
le / la / les moins (+ adjective)	the least (+ adjective)

- **Elle est la plus intelligente de la classe.**
  She is the most intelligent in the class.

Possessive Adjectives

	Masculine singular	Feminine singular	Plural
my	**mon**	ma	mes
your	**ton**	ta	tes
his / her / its	**son**	sa	ses
our	**notre**	notre	nos
your	**votre**	votre	vos
their	**leur**	leur	leurs

- **Leur chat est plus grand que notre chien!**
  Their cat is bigger than our dog!

Demonstrative Adjectives

'This', 'these', 'that' or 'those'.

Masculine singular	Feminine singular	Before a vowel or silent 'h'	Plural
ce	cette	cet	ces

> ### Key Point
>
> Better than… =
> **meilleur(e) que**…
> Worse than… =
> **plus mauvais(e) que**… (or)
> **pire que**
>
> The best… =
> **le (la) meilleur(e)** …
> The worst…= **le (la) plus mauvais(e)** … (or)
> **le (la) pire**

> ### Key Point
>
> 'His' and 'her' are the same in French.
>
> **Sa maison est grande**
> = 'His house is big' or 'Her house is big'.

Quick Test

1. Choose the correct form of the adjective:
   a) **un tee-shirt noir / noire**
   b) **une joli / jolie maison**
   c) **des enfants sportif / sportifs**
2. Put the adjective in the correct position.
   a) **un film (vieux)**   b) **une fille (sympa)**   c) **un chat (beau)**
3. Translate into French:
   a) He is taller than me. He is the tallest in the class.
   b) My house is less modern than his house.
   c) I am going to wear this tee-shirt and these trainers.

Adverbs and Expressions of Time and Place

You must be able to:

- Use regular and irregular adverbs
- Use comparative and superlative adverbs
- Use adverbs of time and place and qualifiers / intensifiers.

Adverbs

- Adverbs describe *how* you do something (quietly, slowly, etc.).
- To form most adverbs, take the feminine form of an adjective and add –**ment**:

  tranquille (quiet) → **tranquillement** (quietly)

Other Useful Adverbs

actuellement	currently	**normalement**	normally
évidemment	obviously	**rarement**	rarely
heureusement	fortunately, luckily	**récemment**	recently
lentement	slowly	**seulement**	only
malheureusement	unfortunately		

- **Malheureusement, j'ai seulement cinq euros.**
  Unfortunately, I only have five euros.

- The following adverbs are irregular:

bien	well
fort	loudly
mal	badly
vite	quickly, fast (you can also say **rapidement**)

- **Il chante mal et trop fort!**   He sings badly and too loudly!

Comparative and Superlative Adverbs

- These work like comparative and superlative adjectives (see page 75).
- **Il court plus vite que toi.**   He runs more quickly than you.
- **Tu cours le plus lentement.**   You run the most slowly.

- Note the comparative and superlative of these adverbs

adverb	comparative form	superlative form
bien (well)	**mieux** (better)	**le mieux** (the best)
mal (badly)	**plus mal** (worse)	**le plus mal** (the worst)

- **Ça va mieux maintenant? Non, ça va encore plus mal.**
  Are you better now? No, I'm worse.

Interrogative Adverbs

- These can be followed by '**est-ce que**', or you can use inversion (swap the pronoun and verb around).

combien (de)?	how much? how many?
comment?	how? in what way?
où?	where?
pourquoi?	why?
quand?	when?

- **Combien de cerises voulez-vous?** — How many cherries do you want?
- **Quand est-ce que tu pars?** — When are you leaving?

Adverbs of Time and Frequency

- Time:

aujourd'hui	today	**de bonne**	early
(avant-) hier	(the day before) yesterday	**heure / tôt**	
		tard	late
(après-) demain	(the day after) tomorrow	**maintenant**	now
		soudain / tout	suddenly
bientôt	soon	**à coup**	
déjà	already	**tout de suite**	straight away

- Frequency:

de temps	from time	**toujours**	always
en temps	to time	**tout le temps**	all the time
quelquefois /	sometimes	**tous les ans /**	every year / day /
parfois		**jours / mois / soirs**	month / evening
souvent	often	**toutes les semaines**	every week

Key Point

Another word for 'every' or 'each' is **chaque**:

chaque jour	every day
chaque année	every year

Adverbs of Place and Distance

à côté de	next to	**là(-bas)**	(over) there
en bas	down(stairs)	**loin**	far
en haut	up(stairs)	**près**	near
en face	opposite	**par**	by
ici	here	**partout**	everywhere

Qualifiers and Intensifiers

assez	quite, fairly	**si / tellement**	so
peu	not very	**très**	very
un peu	a little bit	**trop**	too
plutôt	rather		

Quick Test

1. Translate these pairs of adverbs into French:
   quickly / slowly   well / badly   better / worse   near / far   early / late
2. Translate into English:
   J'ai cherché mon portable partout – ici, là, en haut et en bas.
3. Complete the sentences with an adverb of frequency:
   a) **Je me douche**.......   b) **Je vais en ville**.......   c) **Je lis un livre**.....

Regular Verbs and the Present Tense

You must be able to:

- Use regular and reflexive verbs
- Use **depuis** + the present tense
- Use the imperative.

Regular Verbs

- There are three types of regular verb in French: **–er**, **–ir** and **–re**.
- The form of the verb with **–er**, **–ir** or **–re** on the end is called the infinitive.

	–er verbs	–ir verbs	–re verbs
Example:	**regarder** (to watch)	**finir** (to finish)	**vendre** (to sell)

The Present Tense of –er Verbs

- There are many regular **–er** verbs.
- In the present tense, they work like this:

je regarde	I watch / am watching
tu regardes	you watch / are watching
il / elle / on regarde	he / she / one watches / is watching
nous regardons	we watch / are watching
vous regardez	you watch / are watching
ils / elles regardent	they watch / are watching

- You learned many regular **–er** verbs at Key Stage 3, e.g. **chanter**, **danser**, **écouter**, **habiter**, **jouer** and **manger**. Here are some more useful **–er** verbs:

aider	to help
chercher	to look for
donner	to give
penser	to think
porter	to carry, wear
quitter	to leave (+ a noun)
travailler	to work
visiter	to visit (a place)

Key Point

There is only one present tense in French.
e.g. **Je regarde** = 'I watch' or 'I am watching'.
Be careful of this when translating from English. Don't try to translate 'am / is / are… –ing'.

Regular –ir and –re Verbs

- Useful **–ir** verbs: **choisir** (to choose), **finir** (to finish).
- Useful **–re** verbs: **attendre** (to wait), **perdre** (to lose), **répondre** (to answer, reply), **vendre** (to sell).

- They work like this in the present tense:

je finis (I finish)	**je vends** (I sell)
tu finis (you finish)	**tu vends** (you sell)
il / elle / on finit (he / she / one finishes)	**il / elle / on vend** (he / she / one sells)
nous finissons (we finish)	**nous vendons** (we sell)
vous finissez (you finish)	**vous vendez** (you sell)
ils / elles finissent (they finish)	**ils / elles vendent** (they sell)

Reflexive Verbs

- Reflexive verbs include a reflexive pronoun (**me**, **te**, **se**, etc.).
- These shorten to '**m**', '**t**' and '**s**' before a vowel or silent '**h**'.

se **coucher**	to go to bed
je me couche	I go / am going to bed
tu te couches	you go / are going to bed
il / elle / on se couche	he / she / one goes / is going to bed
nous nous couchons	we go / are going to bed
vous vous couchez	you go / are going to bed
ils / elles se couchent	they go / are going to bed

These are some useful reflexive verbs:

s'amuser	to have fun
se doucher	to have a shower
se disputer	to argue
s'ennuyer	to be / get bored
s'entendre	to get on
se fâcher	to get angry
s'habiller	to get dressed
se lever	to get up
se réveiller	to wake up

The Imperative

- You use the imperative to give instructions or orders.
- Take the **tu** or **vous** form of the verb and drop the pronoun (**–er** verbs lose the **–s** from the **tu** form).

Mange tes légumes!	Eat your vegetables!
Tournez à gauche.	Turn left.

Key Point

Some **–er** verbs add a grave accent to the stem in the following forms of the verb:
j'achète
je me lève
tu achètes
tu te lèves
il / elle / on achète
il / elle / on se lève
ils / elles achètent
ils / elles se lèvent

The **nous** and **vous** forms don't add an accent:

nous achetons
nous nous levons
vous achetez
vous vous levez

Key Point

Put '**ne … pas**' around the verb to make it negative. Shorten '**ne**' to '**n**' before a vowel or silent '**h**':
Il n'aide pas ses parents.
He doesn't help his parents

If the verb is reflexive, put '**ne**' before the reflexive pronoun:
Je ne me lave pas.
I don't have a wash.

Key Point

- Use **depuis** + the present tense to say how long you have been doing something:
- **J'habite ici depuis cinq ans.**
  I have been living here for five years.

Quick Test

1. Put the correct present tense ending on the verbs. Then give two possible translations of each verb.
   a) **je travaill_**   b) **nous attend_**   c) **elle choisi_**   d) **ils achèt_**
2. Put the correct reflexive pronoun before each verb. Then translate them.
   a) **je _ lève**   b) **il _ douche**   c) **vous _ amusez**
   d) **elles _ disputent**
3. Translate into French:
   a) I have been working here for three years.
   b) i) Finish your breakfast! (**tu** form)
      ii) Buy some bread. (**vous** form)

At Home, Where I Live & Town or Country?

1 **Choisissez le bon verbe de la case pour compléter les phrases.** Choose the correct verb from the box to complete the sentences.

a) J' .... une maison jumelée à la campagne.

b) Je .... ma chambre tous les week-ends.

c) Dans ma chambre j' .... une grande armoire et une commode.

d) Je voudrais .... à la campagne.

e) Les transports en commun .... très fréquents.

f) La bibliothèque .... près de la gare.

g) On .... faire des promenades sur les collines.

h) Ma mère .... en centre-ville.

peut
sont
ai
habite
se trouve
déménager
nettoie
travaille

[8 marks]

2 **Cochez les phrases qui suggèrent qu'il est mieux d'habiter en ville qu'à la campagne.**
Tick the sentences that suggest living in town is better than living in the countryside.

a) La ville est très animée. ☐

b) Les loyers sont plus chers. ☐

c) Je voudrais déménager à la campagne. ☐

d) Il n'y a pas de commerces tout près. ☐

e) J'adore le calme ici. ☐

f) Il y a un bon choix de choses à faire. ☐

g) Les rues sont surchargées. ☐

h) On doit se rendre en voiture chez ses copains. ☐

[4 marks]

3 **Complétez la description de la maison de Zara en mettant la version correcte de *du / de la / des / de l'*.**
Complete the description of Zara's house by inserting the correct version of *du / de la / des / de l'*.

J'habite une maison jumelée en centre-ville près .... gare routière. Il y a neuf pièces en tout, y compris trois chambres.

Au rez-de-chaussée il y a le salon à côté .... cuisine. Nous avons un des toilettes qui se trouvent en face .... entrée, et près .... escalier.

À l'étage il y a trois chambres. Ma chambre est en face .... chambre de mes parents et à côté .... bureau.

[6 marks]

Charity and Voluntary Work & Healthy and Unhealthy Living

1 **Choisissez le bon mot pour chaque trou.** Choose the correct word to fill the gap in each sentence.

a) **Je suis allé au** _____ [*maladie / cabinet médical / fatigue*] **parce que j'étais malade.**

b) **Je vais beaucoup** _____ [*mieux / grand / accro*], **merci beaucoup.**

c) **Le tabac peut** _____ [*éviter / réussir / tuer*].

d) **Je** _____ [*suis / mange / vais*] **faire plus de sport.**

e) **J'ai réussi à** _____ [*respirer / se relaxer / combattre*] **l'obésité.**

f) **Il faut suivre** _____ [*les conseils / matières grasses / faiblesses*]. [6 marks]

2 **Vous recevez un e-mail d'un ami en France. Répondez aux questions suivantes.** You receive an email from a friend in France. Answer the multiple choice questions that follow.

Salut Sam

Tu as demandé si je suis en forme? Alors oui, dans ma famille on mange bien. Par exemple on évite les choses sucrées et on boit de l'eau minérale. On ne boit pas de sodas et mes parents ne fument pas. Je dors assez et je joue au foot trois fois par semaine donc je suis en bonne forme.

Mon père mange trop de produits gras et ne fait pas assez d'exercice. Il a dit que cette année il va faire un régime, et il va jouer au badminton avec ma mère!

À bientôt

Éric

a) Which of these health habits does Eric *not* mention in the email? *not smoking / relaxing / exercising*

b) What does Eric's family tend to drink? *soft drinks / tea and coffee / mineral water*

c) How often does Eric play football? *three times a month / three times a day / three times a week*

d) What is Eric's father going to do this year? *go on a diet / stop smoking / eat more fatty foods*

e) Who is Eric's father going to exercise with? *Eric / Eric's brother / Eric's mother* [5 marks]

Review Questions

The Environment & Poverty and Insecurity

1 **Comment dit-on en français…?** What is the French for…?

    a) bin   **b)** waste   **c)** flooding   **d)** the hole in the ozone layer   **e)** deforestation

    f) one could   **g)** I could   **h)** we mustn't   **i)** one can   **j)** we have to

    [10 marks]

2 **Comment dit-on en français…?** What is the French for…?

    a) by recycling   **b)** by consuming   **c)** by not polluting   **d)** by avoiding   **e)** by wasting

    [5 marks]

3 **Reliez les parties de phrases et traduisez en anglais.** Match up and translate into English.

a)	**On doit recycler**	**i)**	**doit pas gaspiller l'énergie**
b)	**On ne**	**ii)**	**consommer trop d'électricité**
c)	**On ne devrait**	**iii)**	**réduire notre consommation**
d)	**Il ne faut pas**	**iv)**	**plus**
e)	**On pourrait**	**v)**	**pas polluer autant notre environnement**

    [10 marks: 5 marks for correct matching and 5 marks for translation]

4 **Transformez les phrases avec la conjonction 'qui' et en ajoutant un adverbe de quantité et une opinion. Traduisez les phrases en anglais.** Change the sentences with the conjunction **'qui'** and add a quantifier and an opinion. Translate into English.

    Exemple: **Les gens sont agressés**   <u>**Je pense qu'** il y a beaucoup de gens **qui** sont agressés</u>

    a) **Les personnes sont sans-abri**   [opinion] **il y a** [quantifier] **personnes qui** _____

    b) **Les jeunes sont au chômage**   [opinion] **il y a** [quantifier] **jeunes qui** _____

    c) **Les ados sont harcelés**   [opinion] **il y a** [quantifier] **ados qui** _____

    d) **Les voyous volent**   [opinion] **il y a** [quantifier] **voyous qui** _____

    e) **Les bandes sont effrayantes**   [opinion] **il y a** [quantifier] **bandes qui** _____

    [10 marks: 5 marks for correct sentences and 5 marks for translation]

Travel and Tourism

1 **Comment dit-on en français…?** What is the French for…?

a) Switzerland   **b)** a cottage   **c)** a key   **d)** Wales   **e)** first floor

f) a lift   **g)** a flight   **h)** ground floor   **i)** an island   **j)** abroad

[10 marks]

2 **Réécrivez les phrases en utilisant 'y' pour remplacer les mots soulignés et traduisez les nouvelles phrases en anglais.** Rewrite the sentences using 'y' to replace the underlined words and then translate the new sentences into English.

a) **Quand nous étions <u>en Australie</u> nous sommes tombés en panne dans le désert.**

b) **J'aime bien passer mes vacances <u>en France</u> avec ma famille.**

c) **J'aimerais aller un jour <u>aux États-Unis</u> pour rendre visite à ma tante.**

[6 marks: 3 marks for correct sentences and 3 marks for translation]

3 **Changez les phrases suivantes dans le temps donné entre parenthèses. Il faut aussi utiliser le mot entre parenthèses.** Change the following sentences into the tense given in brackets. You will also have to change the time phrase to the word or phrase in brackets.

a) **Pendant mes dernières vacances, j'ai logé dans un gîte.** (normally / present tense)

b) **Normalement je vais en vacances au bord de la mer pour me relaxer.** (last year / perfect tense)

c) **L'été dernier j'ai passé quinze jours dans une auberge de jeunesse à la montagne.** (next year / future tense)

[3 marks]

4 **Parlez pendant environ 45 secondes sur les thèmes suivants.** Speak for about 45 seconds about:

a) your last holiday

b) what you like doing on holiday

c) your future holiday

Give as much detail as possible.

Practice Questions

My Studies & Life at School

1 **Lisez la description des matières scolaires d'Isaac. Choisissez les mots de la case pour finir le résumé.**
Read Isaac's description of his school subjects. Choose the words from the box to fill in the summary.

J'adore l'histoire-géo parce que le prof est marrant.

Ma matière préférée c'est les mathématiques parce que je suis fort en maths!

Moi, je suis faible en EPS mais j'adore ça!

J'étudie l'espagnol et l'allemand. J'adore les langues, moi.

Je déteste l'EMT parce que c'est barbant.

Mon prof de chimie est drôle, mais la matière est inutile.

technology
mathematics
Spanish
PE
chemistry

Isaac's favourite subject is .... because he is good at it. One subject that he hates is ....
because he finds it boring. He thinks that his .... teacher is funny but he thinks the subject is not
very useful. Despite not being very good at .... , he loves it! He studies .... and German.
He loves both.

[5 marks]

2 **Lisez les opinions sur la vie scolaire. Répondez aux questions en anglais.** Read the opinions about
school life below. Answer the questions that follow in English.

**Ce que je n'aime pas, c'est le travail! Ce soir, mes devoirs consistent à écrire une dissertation en
histoire-géo! Difficile, héin! George, 12 ans**

**J'apporte mon propre repas parce que la nourriture à la cantine est dégoûtante. Mes amis
apportent eux aussi un sandwich parce qu'ils n'aiment pas la restauration à l école. Naomi, 15 ans**

**J'adore la natation donc c'est super qu'il y a une piscine près de l'école. Ma matière préférée c'est
l'EPS parce que, les jeudis on nage. Nathalie, 13 ans**

**Je n'aime pas les règles scolaires. Par exemple le chewing-gum est interdit et on n'a pas le droit
d'avoir son portable en cours. Les filles n'ont pas le droit d'êtres maquillées! Gavin, 16 ans**

**L'année prochaine je vais passer mes examens. Il y a beaucoup de pression de mes parents parce que
mes notes ne sont pas bonnes. Je ne veux pas redoubler! Loïc, 14 ans**

a) Why does Naomi bring her own lunch to school?

b) What is it about school that Gavin does not like?

c) Which person has a difficult homework task to do?

d) What does Loïc want to avoid?

e) Which person is keen on her PE lessons? Why?

[5 marks]

Education Post-16 & Career Choices and Ambitions

1 **Traduisez ces phrases en anglais.** Translate the following into English.

a) **Il est maçon.**

b) **Ma mère est professeur.**

c) **Je rêve d'avoir un boulot varié.** [6 marks]

2 **Traduisez ces phrases en français.** Translate the following into French.

a) I am a hairdresser.

b) My father is a plumber.

c) I am going to be a nurse. [6 marks]

3 **Lisez l'e-mail et décidez quelles phrases sont vraies.** Read the email and decide which of the statements below are true.

L'année prochaine je vais passer mes examens et donc je dois décider quoi faire. Moi, je n'ai pas l'intention de quitter l'école parce que je veux continuer mes études, et puis aller à la fac. Avant d'aller à la fac je vais faire une année sabbatique. Je voyagerai en Asie parce que j'adore les cultures asiatiques. J'irai avec un ami.

J'ai envie de devenir ingénieur parce que je voudrais avoir un boulot varié et enrichissant. Et bien sûr je gagnerai un bon salaire!

Guillaume

a) Guillaume is going to continue his studies after this year.

b) He does not intend to go to university.

c) He would like to travel to Asia.

d) He likes Asian culture.

e) He wants to become a teacher.

f) He aims to earn lots of money.

[4 marks]

Practice Questions

Gender, Plurals and Articles & Adjectives

1   **Mettez a–c au pluriel et mettez d–f au singulier.** Write a–c in the plural and write d–f in the singular.

a) **une pomme** (an apple) → **des** _____ (apples)

b) **un château** (a castle) → **des** _____ (castles)

c) **un cheval** (a horse) → **des** _____ (horses)

d) **des jeux** (games) → **un** _____ (a game)

e) **des journaux** (newspapers) → **un** _____ (a newspaper)

f) **des fils** (sons) → **un** _____ (a son)

[6 marks]

2   **Remplissez les blancs avec le bon article.** Fill in the gaps with the correct article.

Indefinite article	Definite article	Partitive article
un poisson (a fish)	**le poisson** (the fish)	**du poisson** (some fish)
un café (a coffee)	.... **café** (the coffee)	.... **café** (some coffee)
.... **glace** (an ice cream)	**la glace** (the ice cream)	.... **glace** (some ice cream)
un ananas (a pineapple)	**l'ananas** (the pineapple)	.... **ananas** (some pineapple)
des œufs (some eggs)	.... **œufs** (the eggs)	.... **œufs** (some eggs)

[7 marks]

3   **Copiez le texte, en choisissant la bonne forme de chaque adjectif. Puis traduisez le texte en anglais.**
Copy out the text, choosing the correct form of each adjective. Then translate the text into English.

Pour la fête d'anniversaire de mon   _meilleur / meilleure / meilleurs_   **copain, Thomas, je vais porter**
ce / cette / ces   **chemise avec un pull**   _noir / noire / noirs / noires_   **et**   _mon / ma / mes_   **baskets**
blanc / blanche / blancs / blanches.   **Comme cadeau d'anniversaire, je lui ai acheté un tee-shirt**
vert / verte / verts / vertes,   **parce que tous**   _son / sa / ses_   **tee-shirts sont trop**   _vieux / vieille / vieilles!_

[16 marks: 8 marks for each correct adjective form in French and
8 marks for translating everything correctly]

Adverbs and Expressions of Time and Place & Regular Verbs and the Present Tense

1 **Écrivez quatre listes en utilisant les adverbes dans la case et traduisez-les en anglais.**

Write four lists using the adverbs in the box and translate them into English.

Adverbs ending in –ly in English	Adverbs used to ask questions (interrogatives)	Adverbs of time and frequency	Adverbs of place or location

| seulement | combien | aujourd'hui | ici | toujours | mal | vite | partout |
| maintenant | lentement | quelquefois | pourquoi | quand | comment | en face | près |

[32 marks: 1 mark for each adverb under the correct heading and 1 for each correct translation]

2 **Recopiez les phrases en utilisant la forme correcte du verbe entre parenthèses.** Copy out the sentences, using the correct form of the verb in brackets.

a) Le matin, je (quitter) la maison à huit heures moins le quart.

b) Nous (habiter) une petite maison dans centre-ville.

c) Dans mon collège, les cours (finir) à quinze heures trente.

d) Ma sœur travaille dans un magasin; elle (vendre) des vêtements.

e) Où est-ce que tu (acheter) tes affaires scolaires?

[5 marks]

3 **Traduisez les phrases suivantes en français.** Translate the following sentences into French.

a) At my school, lessons start at nine o'clock.

b) I get up every day at seven o'clock.

c) I wait for the bus in front of the cinema.

d) I get on well with my sister, but I argue with my brother.

e) We have lived here for six years.

[10 marks: 2 marks for each sentence correctly written in French.]

Using Verbs in the Present Tense

You must be able to:

- Use common irregular verbs in the present tense
- Recognise verbs with an infinitive and verbs with prepositions
- Use the present participle.

Common Irregular Verbs

- The four most common irregular verbs in French are:
  avoir – to have, **être** – to be, **aller** – to go and **faire** – to do

Person	AVOIR	ÊTRE	ALLER	FAIRE
je (j')	ai	suis	vais	fais
tu	as	es	vas	fais
il / elle / on	a	est	va	fait
nous	avons	sommes	allons	faisons
vous	avez	êtes	allez	faites
ils / elles	ont	sont	vont	font

- They have special uses which make them even more important to know:

- **Avoir**
- used with age –
  - **J'ai quinze ans.**   I'm fifteen.
  - **avoir faim / soif**   to be hungry / thirsty
  - **avoir chaud / froid**   to be hot / cold
  - **avoir raison / tort**   to be right / wrong

  - **avoir peur**   to be frightened
  - **avoir besoin de**   to need
  - **avoir envie /**   to want / intend to
    l'intention de

- **Être**
- **être en train de:**   to be doing:
  Je suis en train   I am revising verbs.
  de réviser les verbes.

  - **être sur le point de:**   to be about to:
    Je suis sur le point   I'm about to revise.
    de réviser.

- **Aller**
- **aller bien**   to be / feel well

  - **aller mieux**   to be / feel better

- **Faire**
- used with weather expressions –
  Il fait chaud.   It's hot.
- used with the infinitive of another verb to mean 'make someone do something':
  tu me fais rire / rigoler   you make me laugh
  ça me fait sourire   that makes me smile

Modal Verbs

- Modal verbs are irregular and are always used with *another verb in the infinitive*. They are:
  devoir – to have to / must; **pouvoir** — to be able to / can; **savoir** – to know (how to do something) / can; **vouloir** – to want

Person	DEVOIR	POUVOIR	SAVOIR	VOULOIR
je	dois	peux	sais	veux
tu	dois	peux	sais	veux
il / elle / on	doit	peut	sait	veut
nous	devons	pouvons	savons	voulons
vous	devez	pouvez	savez	voulez
ils / elles	doivent	peuvent	savent	veulent

- **Je peux sortir.**   I can (am allowed to) go out.
- **Je sais nager.**   I can (know how to) swim.
- **Je veux aller au cinéma**   I want to go to the cinema…
- **…mais je dois faire mes devoirs**   …but I have to do my homework

- Other verbs can be used with an infinitive:
  adorer – to adore; **aimer** – to like to; **désirer** – to want to; **détester** – to hate; **espérer** – to hope to; **préférer** – to prefer to; **il faut** – it is necessary to; **il vaut mieux** – it is better to

- **Elle adore nager.**   She loves swimming (to swim).
- **J'espère aller à l'université.**   I hope to go to university.
- **Il vaut mieux trouver un emploi.**   It would be better to find a job.

- Some verbs need the preposition **à** or **de** before the infinitive:

apprendre à	to learn	**arrêter de**	to stop
passer du temps à	to spend time	**décider de**	to decide
s'intéresser à	to be interested in	**essayer de**	to try
réussir à	to succeed	**éviter de**	to avoid

The Present Participle

- To translate 'by doing something' or 'while doing something', use the present participle.
- In French, use the **nous** stem of the present tense and **'en –ant'**:
  danser: nous dansons   dans   › **en dansant** = by dancing / while dancing
  choisir: nous choisissons   choisiss ⟶ **en choisissant** = by choosing / while choosing

- There are three irregular present participles: **ayant** = having, **étant** = being, **sachant** = knowing.

Future Time-frame

You must be able to:

- Use **aller** with the infinitive of other verbs to express the immediate future
- Use the future tense of regular and common irregular verbs
- Use the conditional tense.

The Immediate Future

- The immediate future is translated as 'going to do something'.
- In French, use the verb **aller** (to go) and the infinitive of the other verb:

Person	Part of aller	Infinitive	English
Je	vais	manger	I'm going to eat
Tu	vas	finir	You're going to finish
Il / Elle / On	va	attendre	He / She / One is going to wait
Nous	allons	voir	We are going to see
Vous	allez	boire	You are going to drink
Ils / Elles	vont	faire	They are going to do

- **Tu vas finir tes devoirs ce soir?**   Are you going to finish your homework this evening?

- **Mes copains vont faire du ski.**   My friends are going to go skiing.

> ### Key Point
>
> Remember that **on** in French is often translated as 'we' rather than 'one':
> **On va regarder le film ensemble**.
> We're going to watch the film together.

The Future Tense

- The future tense is translated as 'will do something'.
- In French, use the *future stem* of the verb and add the correct ending for the subject of the sentence.

Regular Verbs in the Future Tense

- For regular **–er** and **–ir** verbs, the future stem is the infinitive of the verb.
- For regular **–re** verbs, take away the final **–e** from the infinitive, e.g.
  écrire = to write ⟶ **écrire**

Person	Future stem	Future tense ending	English
Je	manger	ai	I will eat
Tu	jouer	as	You will play
Il / Elle / On	finir	a	He / She / One will finish
Nous	dormir	ons	We will sleep
Vous	attendr	ez	You will wait
Ils / Elles	écrir	ont	They will write

> ### Key Point
>
> The future tense endings are like the verb 'avoir' in the present tense.

HT Irregular Verbs in the Future Tense

- Irregular verbs have to be learned separately. The *future stem* is irregular and is not the infinitive. The endings for each person are the same as for regular verbs.

Top 10 Irregular Verbs in the Future Tense

French verb	English	Future stem	Future tense	English meaning
aller	to go	ir–	j'irai	I will go
avoir	to have	aur–	tu auras	you will have
être	to be	ser–	il sera	he will be
faire	to do	fer–	nous ferons	we will do
pouvoir	to be able to	pourr–	vous pourrez	you will be able to
savoir	to know	saur–	ils sauront	they will know
vouloir	to want to	voudr–	je voudrai	I will want to
recevoir	to receive	recevr–	tu recevras	you will receive
venir	to come	viendr–	elle viendra	she will come
voir	to see	verr–	nous verrons	we will see

- **J'aurai bientôt seize ans.**   I will soon be sixteen.
- **J'espère qu'il fera beau demain.**   I hope the weather will be nice tomorrow.

HT The Conditional Tense

- The conditional tense is translated as 'would do something'.
- In French, use the *future stem* and add the correct ending for the subject of the sentence.

Person	Future stem	Conditional tense ending	English
Je	manger	–ais	I would eat
Tu	finir	–ais	You would finish
Il / Elle / On	écrir	–ait	He / She / One would write
Nous	aur	–ions	We would have
Vous	ser	–iez	You would be
Ils / Elles	ir	–alent	They would go

HT 'Si' clauses

- **Si** means 'if' and is often used with the future and conditional tenses:
- **S'il fait du soleil, nous irons à la plage.**   If it's sunny, we will go to the beach.
- **Si j'étais riche, j'aurais une voiture neuve.**   If I were rich, I would have a new car.

Key Point

Je voudrais and **j'aimerais** (I would like) are examples of the conditional tense, e.g. **Je voudrais continuer mes études** (I would like to continue my studies); **j'aimerais me marier** (I would like to get married).

Key Point

If the `si clause' is a likely event use the present tense, followed by the future tense in the main clause.
If the `si clause' is a more unlikely event use the imperfect tense, followed by the conditional tense in the main clause.

Quick Test

1. Which of these is NOT an infinitive?
   a) faire   b) allez   c) attendre   d) finir
2. Translate into English:
   On ira en ville pour mon anniversaire – j'aurai seize ans!
3. Translate into French: I would like to study languages at university.
4. Translate into French: If I were rich, I would have a big house.

Past Time-frame: Perfect Tense

You must be able to:

- Use the perfect tense with **avoir** and **être** verbs
- Use the perfect infinitive.

The Perfect Tense

- The perfect tense is used in French to talk about events that happened in the past.
- It is translated as 'have done something' or 'did something'.
- In French, use the present tense of **avoir** or **être** and the *past participle* of the main verb.
- **Avoir** and **être** are known as the *auxiliary verb.*

The Perfect Tense with 'Avoir'

- To form the past participle of:
  regular **–er** verbs: take off **–er** and add **–é**   e.g. **manger** → **mangé**
  regular **–ir** verbs: take off **–ir** and add **–i**   e.g. **finir** → **fini**
  regular **–re** verbs: take off **–re** and add **–u**   e.g. **attendre** → **attendu**

Person	AVOIR	PAST PARTICIPLE	English meanings
Je (j')	ai	mangé	I ate; I have eaten
Tu	as	joué	I (have) played
Il / Elle / On	a	fini	He / She / One (has) finished
Nous	avons	choisi	We chose; we have chosen
Vous	avez	attendu	You (have) waited
Ils / Elles	ont	perdu	They (have) lost

Irregular Verbs with 'Avoir'

- As in English, some verbs do not follow the pattern. They need to be learned separately.

avoir	j'ai eu (had)	mettre	j'ai mis (put)
boire	j'ai bu (drank)	prendre	j'ai pris (took)
connaître	j'ai connu (knew – a person)	dire	j'ai dit (said)
devoir	j'ai dû (had to)		
lire	j'ai lu (read)	écrire	j'ai écrit (wrote)
pouvoir	j'ai pu (was able to)	faire	j'ai fait (did)
savoir	j'ai su (knew – a fact)		
recevoir	j'ai reçu (received)	rire	j'ai ri (laughed)
voir	j'ai vu (saw)	ouvrir	j'ai ouvert (opened)
vouloir	j'ai voulu (wanted to)	être	j'ai été (been)

> **Key Point**
>
> To use a negative sentence in the perfect tense, make the auxiliary verb negative: e.g. **il n'a pas joué; ils n'ont pas fini.**

The Perfect Tense with 'Être'

- A small number of verbs use **être** as the auxiliary verb.
- With **être** verbs, the *past participle* agrees as if it was an adjective.

Person	ÊTRE	PAST PARTICIPLE	English meanings
Je	suis	**allé**	I went; I have gone (masculine)
Je	suis	**allée**	I went; I have gone (feminine)
Tu	es	**venu(e)**	You came; you have come
Il	est	**arrivé**	He (has) arrived
Elle	est	**arrivée**	She (has) arrived
Nous	sommes	**partis**	We (have) left (masculine or mixed group)
Nous	sommes	**parties**	We (have) left (feminine)
Vous	êtes	**monté(e)(s)(es)***	You went (have gone) up
Ils	sont	**descendus**	They went (have gone) down (masculine or mixed group)
Elles	sont	**descendues**	They went (have gone) down (feminine)

*Vous can be used for singular polite or groups, masculine or feminine

 **Perfect Infinitive**

The perfect infinitive is translated as 'to have done something'.

- In French, use the *infinitive* of **avoir** or **être** and the *past participle*:
- **Je regrette d'avoir oublié ton anniversaire.**
  I'm sorry to have forgotten your birthday.
- **Je suis désolé(e) d'être arrivé(e) en retard.**
  I'm sorry **to have arrived** late.

- It is used most commonly with **après avoir** or **après être**:
- **Après avoir mangé, nous sommes allés en ville.**
  Having eaten, we went into town.
- All **être** verb rules apply:
- **Après être arrivés en ville, nous avons fait les magasins.**
  Having arrived in town, we went shopping.

Key Point

These are the past participles of the verbs that use **être** as the auxiliary verb and one way of remembering them is MRS VAN DER TRAMP.

Monté	went up
Resté	stayed
Sorti	went out
Venu	came
Allé	went
Né	was born
Descendu	went down
Entré	went in
Rentré	went back
Tombé	fell
Retourné	returned
Arrivé	arrived
Mort	died
Parti	left

Key Point

All reflexive verbs use **être** in the perfect tense: e.g. **je me suis levé(e)** = I got up; **elle s'est réveillée** = she woke up; **nous nous sommes amusés** = we enjoyed ourselves.

Quick Test

1. Put these verbs into the perfect tense ('**je**' form):
   a) **choisir**   b) **regarder**   c) **faire**   d) **voir**
2. Put these verbs into the perfect tense ('**elle**' form):
   a) **arriver**   b) **partir**   c) **descendre**   d) **venir**
3. Make these phrases negative and translate into English:
   a) **il a écrit**   b) **nous sommes retournés**   c) **j'ai dit**

Past Time-frame: Imperfect Tense and Pluperfect Tense

You must be able to:

- Use the imperfect tense
- Understand the difference between the perfect tense and the imperfect tense
- Recognise and use the pluperfect tense.

Imperfect Tense

- The imperfect tense is used in French for descriptions and continuous actions in the past.
- It is translated as 'was doing something' or 'used to do something'.
- In French, use the **nous** stem of the present tense, remove the '**ons**' and add the imperfect endings:

Use the **nous** stem	

regarder	nous regardons
choisir	nous choisissons
attendre	nous attendons
avoir	nous avons
manger	nous mangeons
commencer	nous commençons

Person	Stem	Imperfect tense ending
je	regard	ais
tu	choisiss	ais
il / elle / on	attend	ait
nous	av	ions
vous	mang	iez
ils / elles	commenç	aient

> ### Key Point
>
> To keep the 'soft' sound in **manger**, add an **–e** before the hard vowel sound '**a**'; so '**je mangeais**'; or add **ç** to '**commencer**' – '**je commençais**'.

- **Être** (to be) is irregular – the stem is **ét–** : **j'étais, il était, ils étaient**.

Using the Imperfect Tense

1. to say 'used to do something':
   Quand j'étais plus jeune, je mangeais beaucoup de chocolat.
   When I was younger, I used to eat lots of chocolate.

2. for descriptions – for example the weather and opinions.
   Il pleuvait, mais nous étions contents.
   It was raining, but we were happy.

3. to say 'was doing something':
   Je jouais dans le parc. I was playing in the park.

Using the Perfect and Imperfect Tenses

- The perfect tense is used for a single 'event' or 'action' in the past, e.g.:
  J'ai bu de l'eau. I drank some water.

- The imperfect tense is used for continuous actions in the past, e.g.:
  Je buvais de l'eau.
  I was drinking some water. (Also means: I used to drink some water.)

- They are used together when two actions coincide:
Je jouais dans le parc quand l'accident s'est passé.
I was playing in the park when the accident happened.

- **Avant il habitait en France mais l'an dernier il a déménagé au Canada.**
Before he was living / used to live in France, but last year he moved to Canada.

HT The Pluperfect Tense

- The pluperfect tense is another past tense but it goes back further in time. It is translated as 'had done something'.
- In French, use the imperfect tense of **avoir** or **être** as the auxiliary verb and the past participle of the main verb.
- The rules and agreements of the perfect tense apply:

Person	Auxiliary	Past participle	English
Je (j')	**avais**	**mangé**	I had eaten
Tu	**étais**	**parti(e)**	You had left
Il	**avait**	**attendu**	He had waited
Elle	**était**	**tombée**	She had fallen
Nous	**avions**	**fini**	We had finished
Vous	**étiez**	**descendu(e)(s)**	You had gone down
Ils	**avaient**	**dit**	They had said
Elles	**étaient**	**venues**	They had come

- **J'avais mangé avant de partir.**
I had eaten before leaving.
- **Tu étais parti quand je suis arrivée.**
You (masculine) had left when I (feminine) arrived.

HT Reported Speech

- The pluperfect tense is used to report what someone said.
- **Céline a dit qu'elle était allée en vacances en Italie.**
Céline said that she went (had gone) on holiday to Italy.

'Je suis allée en vacances en Italie.' I went on holiday to Italy.

Céline

Quick Test

1. Put these verbs into the imperfect tense:
   a) je (regarder)   b) nous (choisir)   c) ils (attendre)   d) elle (être)
2. Which is the odd one out and why?
   a) **Je jouais dans le parc.**
   b) **L'accident s'est passé en ville.**
   c) **Il habitait en France.**
3. Translate into French: We used to drink lots of water.
4. Translate into English: **Ils avaient mangé avant d'aller au cinéma.**

Pronouns

You must be able to:

- Use personal and reflexive pronouns
- Understand what direct and indirect object pronouns are
- Use different pronouns together.

Personal and Reflexive Pronouns

- **Revision**: Pronouns replace nouns.

- Personal pronouns are used with a verb.

je	I		nous	we
tu	you informal (one person)		vous	you as a group and you formal
il	he			
elle	she		elles	they (feminine)
on	one – also used to mean we		ils	they (masculine or mixed group)

- Reflexive pronouns are used with reflexive verbs; **se disputer** is a reflexive verb.

je	me	dispute		nous	nous	disputons
tu	te	disputes		vous	vous	disputez
il / elle / on	se	dispute		ils / elles	se	disputent

- **me / te / se** become **m' / t' / s'** if the verb starts with a vowel, e.g.: **je m'appelle**

Object Pronouns

- In a sentence the *object* is the person or thing which is having the action done to it.
- The *subject* is the person or thing which is doing the action.

Object pronoun	Je **mange** la pomme – I am eating the apple
An object pronoun replaces the object in a sentence. Instead of saying *I am eating the apple* you can also say *I am eating it – it* is an object pronoun.	**Je** is the subject (*I* eat) and **la pomme** is the object (*What am I eating? the apple*)

There are two types of object pronouns: *direct* object pronouns and *indirect* object pronouns.

An *indirect* object pronoun	A *direct* object pronoun
An indirect object pronoun replaces a noun in front of which there is a *preposition*, usually **à** (to / for).	A direct object pronoun replaces a noun in front of which there is *no preposition*.

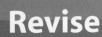

J'ai donné le cadeau à ma mère   I gave the present *to my mum*

So if we want to replace *to my mum* by a pronoun we would need to say *to her*.

J'ai donné le cadeau   I gave the present

So if we want to replace *the present* by a pronoun we would need to say *it*.
Our new sentence would be: I gave *it* (direct object pronoun) *to her* (indirect object pronoun)

Direct object pronouns		Indirect object pronouns	
me / m'	me	**me / m'**	to / for me
te / t'	you	**te / t'**	to / for you
la / l'	her / it	**lui**	to / for her
le / l'	him / it	**lui**	to / for him
nous	us	**nous**	to / for us
vous	you	**vous**	to / for you
les	them	**leur**	to / for them

Direct object pronouns:

Je ne regarde pas les actualités tous les jours.
I don't watch the news every day.

Je ne les regarde pas tous les jours.
I do not watch them every day.

Indirect object pronouns:

Elle n'a pas acheté de bonbons pour les enfants.
She didn't buy sweets for the children.

Elle ne leur a pas acheté de bonbons.
She didn't buy sweets for them.

Order of the Pronouns

- If you have two pronouns in a sentence, this is the order to follow:

me				
te	le	lui	y	en
se	la	leur		
nous	les			
vous				

- **J'ai donné les fleurs à ma mère.**   I gave the flowers to my mum.
  Je les lui ai données.   I gave *them* to *her*.

HT When your direct object pronoun is before your auxiliary in a compound tense, your past participle will agree with the direct object pronoun.
J'ai mangé les pommes. – Je les ai mangées.
I ate the apples. – I ate them.

Key Point
In French the object pronouns come in front of the verb and after the **ne** of the negative.

Key Point
With compound tenses (tense with an auxiliary) the object pronouns will come before the auxiliary.

HT ### Key Point
Use pronouns correctly in your sentence to score higher in your exam.

Key Point
In French the following verbs will be followed by **à** + person so they will need an indirect object pronoun whereas in English they have a direct object pronoun:
Téléphoner à (to phone)
demander à (to ask)
conseiller à (to advise)
dire à (to tell)

Questions

You must be able to:

- Form and recognise questions in different ways
- Use a range of question words
- Use questions in different tenses.

Asking Questions

- There are two types of questions – open and closed questions.
  Open questions will require a question word that asks for details (who / when / why…).
  Closed questions will require a 'yes or no' answer (did you… / will you…).

Asking Closed Questions

- There are three ways of asking a closed question. For example, if you want to ask if someone likes spending their holidays with their family:

  1. Change the statement into a question by raising your voice at the end of the sentence.
  Say: 'You like spending your holidays with your family?' but raise your voice at the end.
  Tu aimes passer les vacances en famille? ↑

  2. Add **Est-ce que** at the start of the sentence.
  Say: 'You like spending your holidays with your family' but add **Est-ce que** at the start.
  Est-ce que tu aimes passer les vacances en famille?
  Est-ce que? literally means 'is it that?'

  3. Change the order of the sentence by swapping the subject and the verb.
  Tu aimes passer les vacances en famille
  will become
  Aimes-tu passer les vacances en famille?

Asking Closed Questions in Different Tenses

- Identify your statement first. Think about the information you want to ask about. If you want to ask someone if they went on holiday last year, your statement will be 'you went on holiday last year'.
- Then translate that statement – **Tu es allé(e) en vacances l'année dernière**.
- Finally, choose any of the three patterns to ask your question.
  1. Raising your voice: **Tu es allé(e) en vacances l'année dernière?** ↑
  2. Adding **Est-ce que**: **Est-ce que tu es allé(e) en vacances l'année dernière?**
  3. Word order: **Es-tu allé(e) en vacances l'année dernière?**
- All three questions mean 'Did you go on holiday last year?'.

> ### Key Point
>
> It is important to remember these patterns and not to translate straight from English as you won't be able to translate, for example, the 'do' in 'do you like…?' or 'will' in 'will you study French?'

Asking Open Questions

- Another way of asking a question is to use a *question word*.
- Question words, as commonly named, can be:
  1. Interrogative pronouns
  2. Interrogative adverbs
  3. Interrogative adjectives.

Interrogative pronouns	Interrogative adverbs	Interrogative adjectives
qui who	**où** where	**quel / quelle / quels / quelles** which
que what	**quand** when	
quoi what	**pourquoi** why	**quel** will agree with the noun it goes with:
lequel / laquelle / lesquels / lesquelles which one(s) **lequel** will agree with the noun it replaces	**combien (de)** how many	**Quelle musique préfères-tu?**
	combien de temps how long	
	comment how	**Quels livres as-tu lus?**

> ### Key Point
>
> All these 'question words' can be formed with a preposition, e.g.
> **À quelle heure?**
> At what time?
> **Pour qui?**
> For whom?
> **Depuis quand?**
> Since when?

Asking Questions with Question Words

- If you want to ask at what time the train is leaving, think of your statement first and identify your question word.
- Your statement is **le train part** (the train is leaving) and your question word is **à quelle heure** (at what time).
- Add **est-ce que** after the question word.
- **À quelle heure est-ce que le train part?**
  At what time does the train leave?
- If you want to ask someone what they will do next week, think of your statement first and identify your question word.
- Your statement is **tu feras la semaine prochaine** (you will do next week) and your question word is **que** (what).
- Add **est-ce que** after the question word.
- **Qu'est-ce que tu feras la semaine prochaine?**
  What will you do next week?

> ### Quick Test
>
> 1. What is the French for: Who? For whom? When? Since when? Which one (feminine)? Which (masculine plural)?
> 2. Change this question into the other two patterns: **Tu recycles chez toi?** Do you recycle at home?
> 3. Change this question into the other two patterns: **Est-ce que tu habites ici?** Do you live here?
> 4. Ask the following question in three ways: Will you study French next year?

> ### Key Point
>
> It is important to remember that there are different ways of asking a question in French.

Prepositions and Conjunctions

You must be able to:

- Use prepositions with nouns and verbs
- Use co-ordinating conjunctions
- Use subordinating conjunctions.

Using Prepositions

- A preposition is a little word such as *to*, *from*, *for*, *between*, *beside*, *under*, *within* that comes in front of a noun or a verb.

Using Prepositions with Nouns

- Here is a list of the most common prepositions:

à	to	**malgré**	despite
contre	against	**parmi**	among
de	from / of	**pour**	for / in order to
depuis	since	**sans**	without
derrière	behind	**selon**	according to
devant	in front of	**sous**	under
en	in	**sur**	on
entre	between	**vers**	towards (direction)

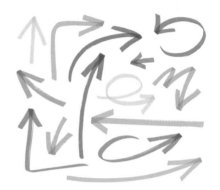

Compound Prepositions

- The following prepositions are called *compound prepositions* as they are formed of two or more words.

à côté de	next to	**au fond de**	at the back / bottom of
à travers	across / through	**au lieu de**	instead of
au bord de	at the side / edge of	**au milieu de**	in the middle of
au bout de	at the end of	**autour de**	around
au-dessous de	beneath / below	**en dehors de**	outside (of)
au-dessus de	above / over	**en face de**	opposite
près de	near	**jusqu'à**	up to

Prepositions with Disjunctive Pronouns

- When using a preposition with a personal pronoun you will need to use *disjunctive pronouns*, which are **moi / toi / lui / elle / nous / vous / eux / elles** (me / you / him / her / us / you / them)
- **J'ai acheté ce gâteau pour toi.** I bought this cake for you.
- **Selon eux, il fait trop chaud!** According to them, it is too hot!

Using Prepositions with Verbs

- When using prepositions with a verb you will need to use the *infinitive* form of the verb:
- **Il est parti sans payer.** He left without paying.

Key Point

If you use a noun with **le / la / les** after a preposition formed with '**de**' or '**à**' you will have to use **du / des / de l'** or **au / aux / à l'**.

J'étais assis à côté du mur (à côté de + le)
I was sitting next to the wall.

Je serai en vacances jusqu'au 12 juillet (jusqu'à + le)
I will be on holiday until 12 July.

Using Conjunctions

- Conjunctions will help you make your sentences longer.

Co-ordinating Conjunctions

- *Co-ordinating conjunctions* will link two sentences together.

mais	but	**donc**	so, therefore
ou	or	**or**	yet, but / now
et	and	**car**	because

- The following words can also be helpful for writing longer sentences.

à cause de	because of	**ensuite**	next
ainsi	so / therefore	**évidemment**	obviously
alors	so, therefore / then	**par contre**	on the other hand
aussi	also	**pourtant**	however
cependant	however	**puis**	then
c'est-à-dire	that is to say	**sans doute**	undoubtedly /
d'un côté /	on one hand / on		without doubt
d'un autre côté	the other hand	**y compris**	including

> **Key Point**
>
> In English you will usually use the –ing form of the verb when using a preposition ('without saying'; 'instead of going') but avoid translating this structure directly into French.

Subordinating Conjunctions

- Subordinating conjunctions will help you make a subordinate clause.
- Here is a list of the most common subordinating conjunctions.

comme	as	**puisque**	since / because
lorsque	when	**tandis que**	whereas
parce que	because	**quand**	when
pendant que	while	**si**	if

- **Lorsqu'il est arrivé, j'étais en train de manger.**
  When he arrived I was eating.
- **Maintenant j'ai les cheveux blonds tandis qu'avant j'avais les cheveux marron.** Now I have blond hair whereas before I had brown hair.

> **HT Key Point**
>
> Try to use subordinate clauses consistently throughout your written and speaking work to show great complexity.

Using Subordinating Pronouns

- Another way to make a sentence longer is to use a subordinate pronoun such as **qui, que, dont**. These pronouns relate back to something or someone you have talked about in your sentence.

- **Qui** replaces the *subject* of the verb:
- **J'ai acheté un DVD qui coûte cher.** I bought a DVD that is expensive.
- **Que** replaces the *object* of the verb:
- **J'ai acheté le DVD que je voulais depuis longtemps.**
  I have bought the DVD that I had wanted for ages.
- **Dont** means *of / about which / whom* but also replaces the object of a verb followed by the preposition **de**:
- **C'est le DVD dont je t'ai parlé. (parler de)**
  It is the DVD (about which) I have told you.

> **Key Point**
>
> *Connectives* usually connect and sequence ideas in a paragraph whereas *co-ordinating conjunctions* link two sentences together to make a sentence more complex.

> **Quick Test**
>
> Fill in the sentences with the appropriate prepositions:
> 1. J'ai acheté un beau cadeau .... **toi.**
> 2. Quel désastre! Je suis parti en vacances .... **ma valise.**
>
> Translate into French:
> 3. Instead of travelling by car, I should use my bike.

Subjunctive Mood and the Passive Voice

You must be able to:

- Understand the subjunctive mood and the passive voice
- Use the passive voice in the present, perfect, future and imperfect tenses.

The Subjunctive Mood

- The subjunctive mood expresses something that is doubtful or not factual or that is very subjective such as feelings and emotions.
- In English we use the subjunctive with phrases such as:
  If I were rich – *If I were* is in the subjunctive because *you wish* you were rich.

When to Use the Subjunctive Mood

- The subjunctive mood is triggered by certain verbs, conjunctions and phrases.

- **Verbs of uncertainty, necessity and emotion**
  Je ne pense pas que...
  I don't think that…
  Je ne crois pas que...
  I don't believe that…
  Je doute que...
  I doubt that…
  Il est important / essentiel que...
  It is important / essential that…
  Il est nécessaire que / Il faut que...
  It is necessary that…
  Je suis content(e) / heureux(se) / surpris(e) / désolé(e) que...
  I am happy / surprised / sorry that…

- **Verbs expressing a wish / a desire:**
Je veux / voudrais que...	I want / would like…
Je souhaite que...	I wish…

- **Conjunctions**
Bien que	although
Pour que	in order to
À condition que	provided that…

- **Phrases**
C'est le meilleur / pire ... que	It is the best / worst … that
Il n'y a rien que / qui	There is nothing that…
Il semble que	It seems that…

There are some irregular verbs:

être becomes **je sois / tu sois / il soit / nous soyons / vous soyez / ils soient**
avoir becomes **j'aie / tu aies / il ait / nous ayons / vous ayez / ils aient**
pouvoir becomes **je puisse / es / e / ions / iez / puissent**
faire becomes **je fasse / es / e / ions / iez / ent**
aller becomes **J'aille / es / e / allions / alliez / ent**
devoir becomes **je doive / es / e / devions / deviez / doivent**
vouloir becomes **je veuille / es / e / voulions / vouliez / veuillent**

Key Point

The subjunctive mood is formed by using the 'they' form of the present tense. Remove the –**ent** from the 'they' form and add the following endings:

–e	–es
–e	–ions
–iez	–ent

- Although he is ill.
  Bien qu'il soit malade.
- I don't think that the film is good.
  Je ne pense pas que le film soit bon.

The Passive Voice

- The passive voice is as follows:
  La classe a été nettoyée par les élèves.
  The classroom has been cleaned by the pupils.
- The active voice is:
  Les élèves ont nettoyé la classe.
  The pupils have cleaned the classroom.

Forming the Passive Voice

The passive voice is formed using **être** and the *past participle* of the verb.

Present	Perfect	Imperfect	Future
La classe est nettoyée par les élèves.	**La classe a été nettoyée par les élèves.**	**La classe était nettoyée par les élèves.**	**La classe sera nettoyée par les élèves.**
The classroom *is* cleaned by the pupils.	The classroom *has been* cleaned by the pupils.	The classroom *was / used to be* cleaned by the pupils.	The classroom *will be* cleaned by the pupils.

Key Point

The *passive voice* is used when the verb is being done to the *subject* of the sentence.

Key Point

Remember to change the ending of your past participle so that it agrees with the subject. Add **e / s /** or **es**.

Quick Test

1. Select the correct form:
   Je ne suis pas contente qu'il est / soit ici avec nous.
   Je voudrais que vous allez / alliez dehors.
2. Write the correct form of the verb in the subjunctive.
   Je ne pense pas qu'il.........................venir. (pouvoir)
   Il faut que je ....mes devoirs. (faire)

Review Questions

My Studies & Life at School

1 **Choisissez le bon adjectif pour chaque phrase. Écrivez la lettre auprès de la traduction.** Match the adjectives to the sentence in which they are mentioned. Write the letter alongside the English translation.

a) **Mon prof d'informatique est très habile.**

b) **Selon moi, l'EMT est très utile.**

c) **J'adore les mathématiques parce que c'est amusant!**

d) **J'adore la religion mais c'est un peu facile.**

e) **Mon prof de français est assez désagréable.**

f) **Madame Régis est sévère mais assez rigolote.**

g) **Le dessin? Oui c'est génial!**

h) **Je n'aime pas la couture. C'est ennuyeux.**

annoying	
great	
easy	
clever	
unpleasant	
funny	
strict	
useful	

[8 marks]

2 **Finissez les instructions en choisissant un verbe de la case.** Complete the instructions by choosing a verb from the box below.

a) _____ les livres Richard!

b) _____ attention la classe!

c) N'_____ pas vos devoirs!

d) Ne _____ pas dans les couloirs!

e) _____ les mots!

f) _____ la question entre vous!

oubliez	répétez	distribuez	faites	discutez	courez

[6 marks]

3 **Traduisez les phrases suivantes en français.** Translate the sentences into French.

a) My sister, Élise, is good at biology. **Christophe, 14 years**

b) I am very weak in mathematics. **Élise, 15 years**

c) Bradley is a bit rubbish in IT. **Kevin, 15 years**

d) My girlfriend is gifted in Spanish. **Justin, 16 years**

e) I am good at languages but I am quite weak in PE. **Patrice, 14 years**

[10 marks]

Education Post-16 & Career Choices and Ambitions

1 **Lisez, puis écrivez le nom de chaque personne décrite dans la case.** Read, then write the name of the person described in the grid below.

J'étudie pour mon BT, et je fais l'interrogation cette année. J'espère réussir avec une mention. Lisa, 16 ans

L'année prochaine je voudrais aller à la fac. Je voudrais étudier les sciences. Thomas, 17 ans

Je suis au lycée et je suis interne. Cela signifie que je rentre chez moi le week-end. Olivier, 17 ans

Je me suis spécialisé quand je suis arrivé au lycée pour pouvoir passer le bac. Par exemple j'ai laissé tombé l'informatique et les sciences et j'ai choisi les langues. Yann, 16 ans

a)	Has chosen to study science.	
b)	Is studying something other than the baccalaureate.	
c)	Decided to drop certain subjects.	
d)	Lives at school during the week.	
e)	Is being tested by continuous assessment.	
f)	Has specialised in languages.	

[6 marks]

2 **Choisissez un verbe de la case pour compléter les phrases.** Choose a verb from the box to complete the sentences.

a) **J'aurai un emploi bien payé donc je _____ riche.**

b) **J' _____ aux Caraïbes parce que j'adore le soleil.**

c) **Je _____ un tour du monde avec mes meilleurs amis.**

d) **J' _____ au travail tous les jours en hélicoptère.**

e) **J' _____ une grande voiture et une grande maison avec piscine.**

f) **Je _____ dans des bons restaurants tous les jours.**

mangerai	habiterai	irai	aurai	ferai	serai

[6 marks]

3 **Écrivez un court paragraphe au sujet de votre avenir. Essayer d'inclure toutes les choses suivantes.**
Write a short paragraph about your future. Try to include each of the following:

Je viens de + infinitive (to say what you have just done); **Je vais** + infinitive…; **J'ai l'intention de**…; The future tense

[8 marks]

Review Questions

Gender, Plurals and Articles & Adjectives

1 **Devinez le genre de ces mots et choisissez le bon article défini.** Guess the gender of these words and choose the correct definite article.

a) le / la tourisme   b) le / la violence   c) le / la condition   d) le / la bagage

e) le / la maladie   f) le / la développement   g) le / la panneau   h) le / la tartine

[8 marks]

2 **Recopiez le texte et complétez les blancs avec *du / de la / de l'* ou *des*.** Copy out the text and fill in the gaps with *du / de la / de l'* or *des*.

Pour le pique-nique demain, je vais préparer des sandwichs, alors il faut acheter _____ pain, _____ fromage et _____ pâté. Avec les sandwichs, on va manger _____ salade, donc je vais aussi acheter _____ tomates. Comme dessert, on va manger _____ fraises avec _____ crème ou peut-être _____ glace à la vanille. Les enfants vont boire _____ jus d'orange, mais pour les adultes il y aura _____ vin et _____ eau minérale.

[11 marks]

3 **Recopiez les phrases en utilisant la bonne forme de l'adjectif entre parenthèses. Puis traduisez ces phrases en anglais.** Copy out the sentences, using the correct form of the adjective in brackets. Then translate the sentences into English.

a) Ma sœur est plus (sportif) que moi, mais elle n'est pas la plus (intelligent)!

b) Le français est moins (difficile) que les maths, mais la géo est la plus (intéressant).

c) Les raisins sont aussi (cher) que les fraises, mais les fraises sont (meilleur).

d) Cette chemise (bleu) est plus (vieux) que la chemise (blanc), mais je préfère celle-ci.

e) Mes grands-parents sont plus (gentil) que mon oncle, mais ma tante est la plus (généreux).

f) Leur maison est plus (grand) que notre maison, mais notre jardin est le plus (beau).

[19 marks: 13 marks for each correct adjective and 6 marks for translating the sentences correctly]

Adverbs and Expressions of Time and Place & Regular Verbs and the Present Tense

1   **Changez ces adjectifs en adverbes. Attention, il y a un adverbe irrégulier!** Change these adjectives into adverbs. Watch out, there is one irregular adverb!

a) **doux / douce** (soft, gentle)   ⟶   (softly, gently)

b) **final / finale** (final)   ⟶   (finally)

c) **bon / bonne** (good)   ⟶   (well)

d) **régulier / régulière** (regular)   ⟶   (regularly)

e) **général / générale** (general)   ⟶   (generally)

[5 marks]

2   **Copiez et complétez les phrases, en ajoutant le bon pronom réfléchi.** Copy and complete the sentences, by adding the correct reflexive pronoun.

a) **Les jours d'école, je _____ lève à sept heures.**

b) **Mon frère _____ brosse les dents dans la salle de bains.**

c) **D'habitude, nous _____ entendons bien.**

d) **Mes parents _____ fâchent contre nous.**

e) **Tu _____ couches à quelle heure?**

[5 marks]

3   **Changez ces phrases en utilisant le pronom indiqué.** Change these sentences, using the pronoun indicated.

a) **Je quitte la maison à huit heures. ⟶ (nous)**

b) **Il aide ses parents à la maison. ⟶ (tu)**

c) **On finit les cours à trois heures et demie. ⟶ (ils)**

d) **Elle s'amuse le samedi soir. ⟶ je**

e) **Vous attendez le bus devant le café. ⟶ (on)**

[5 marks: verb endings must be correct!]

Practice Questions

Using Verbs in the Present Tense & Future Time-frame

1. **Choisissez le verbe correcte et écrivez les phrases.** Choose the correct form of the verb and write the sentences.

   a) *Veut / Veux / Voulez* -tu aller en boîte de nuit?

   b) Je *doivent / doit / dois* partir tout de suite!

   c) Nous ne *sait / savent / savons* pas où il est.

   d) *Peut / Pouvez / Pouvons* -vous m'aider, s'il vous plaît?

   e) On ne *doit / doivent / dois* pas manger en classe.

   f) Mes sœurs ainées ne *voulez / veulent / veux* jamais sortir avec moi! [6 marks]

2. **Remplissez les blancs. Utilisez la forme correcte du verbe 'aller'.** Fill in the gaps with the correct form of the verb 'aller'.

   a) Nous _____ rencontrer nos amis.

   b) Je _____ regarder les feux d'artifices.

   c) Ils _____ goûter les fruits de mer.

   d) _____ -vous souvent en ligne?

   e) _____ -tu rester au collège l'année prochaine?

   f) Mon père _____ aller à la pêche ce week-end.

   [6 marks]

3. **Soulignez les verbes au futur.** Underline the verbs in the future tense.

   Le week-end prochain sera vraiment passionnant parce que mes deux cousins viendront chez nous et que je ne les ai pas vus depuis très longtemps! Le samedi matin, nous irons à la patinoire où nous ferons du patin à glace. Après, nous retrouverons des amis en ville et nous mangerons au café, et puis le soir, on ira au concert de The Vamps!! Ce sera absolument génial, il y aura une ambiance formidable et ils chanteront leur dernier hit! J'ai trop hâte de les voir!

   [10 marks]

Past Time-frame: Perfect Tense & Imperfect Tense and Pluperfect Tense

1 **Remettez ces phrases dans le bon ordre et traduisez-les en anglais. Elles sont toutes dans le passé composé.** Unscramble these sentences in the perfect tense and translate into English:

a) chocolat / J'ai / de / mangé / trop!

b) match / nous / rugby / le / avons / de / gagné

c) cinq / elle / a / du / à / heures / fini / soir

d) nouvel / mes / choisi / un / parents / ordinateur / ont

e) Est-ce que / portable / tu / perdu / ton / as?

f) ils / devant / attendu / bus / l'église / le / ont

[6 marks]

2 **Remplissez le tableau en utilisant les verbes qui forment leur passé composé avec être.**
Fill in the grid with the verbs that take **être** in the perfect tense.

M	R	S	V	A	N	D	E	R	T	R	A	M	P

[14 marks]

3 Which other verbs take **être**? CLUE = **E X R E F L I V E** _____

Écrivez un exemple. Write one example. _____

[1 mark]

4 **Remplissez les blancs. Utilisez les verbes dans la boîte. Ils sont les verbes à l'imparfait.**
Fill in the blanks. Use the verbs in the box. They are all in the imperfect tense.

Quand j' _____ plus jeune, j' _____ un chien qui s' _____ Bruno. Il _____ vraiment
adorable et _____ le poil marron et frisé. Ses yeux _____ noirs et il _____ un collier bleu.
Tous les jours, on _____ des promenades au parc et on _____ ensemble.
Je l' _____ beaucoup.

était	étais	étaient	faisait	avait	avais	aimais	jouait	portait	appelait

[10 marks]

Pronouns & Questions

1 **Dans chaque phrase choisissez le bon pronom qui remplacera les mots soulignés.**
In each sentence choose the correct pronoun that would replace the underlined words.

a) <u>Ma mère</u> n'aime pas le chocolat.   [il ou elle?]

b) <u>Mes parents</u> ne me laissent pas sortir tard le soir.   [ils ou elles?]

c) Quelquefois je me dispute avec <u>ma meilleure amie.</u>   [il ou elle?]

d) L'année prochaine <u>mon frère</u> [il / ou / elle] ne viendra pas en vacances avec <u>mes parents et moi.</u>
[nous / ou / vous]

[5 marks]

3 **Traduisez ces phrases en français. Faites attention à vos pronoms.** Translate these sentences into French.
Pay attention to your pronouns. (The underlined words are the pronouns to focus on.)

a) I watch <u>it</u> every day after school. (<u>it</u> replaces 'television')

b) I don't like <u>them</u>. (<u>them</u> replaces 'horror films')

c) I go on holiday with <u>them</u>. (<u>them</u> replaces 'my parents').

d) I sometimes argue with <u>her</u>.

e) I don't really like <u>it</u>. (<u>it</u> replaces 'my school')

[10 marks: 5 marks for the correct pronoun and 5 marks for the correct position]

4 **Remettez les questions ci-dessous dans le bon ordre et traduisez-les en anglais.**
Unjumble the questions below and translate them into English.

a) tu / pourquoi / est-ce que / ne / pas / recycles ?

b) joues / quand / du / piano / tu / depuis ?

c) en / combien / de / as / temps / passé / Allemagne / tu ?

d) les touristes / ville / qu' / il y a / est-ce qu' / dans / pour / ta ?

e) tu / ta / avec / t' / qui / le mieux / entends / dans / famille / est-ce que ?

[10 marks: 5 marks for reordering and 5 marks for translation]

Prepositions and Conjunctions & Subjunctive Mood and the Passive Voice

1 **Comment dit-on en français…?** What is the French for…?

a) without

b) next to

c) behind

d) instead of

e) on the other hand

f) in order to

g) around

h) in front of

i) according to

j) among

[10 marks]

2 **Traduisez les phrases suivantes qui sont au subjonctif.**
Translate the following sentences which are in the subjunctive mood.

a) Je ne pense pas que le film soit bien.

b) Bien que je fasse beaucoup d'efforts je ne m'améliore pas.

c) Il semble qu'il fasse froid dehors.

d) Je suis désolée que tu sois malade.

[4 marks]

3 **Écrivez la forme correcte du verbe 'être' dans ces phrases à la voix passive. Le temps est écrit entre parenthèses.** Write the correct form of '**être**' in these sentences in the passive voice. The tense is given in brackets.

a) **Les bouteilles** _____ **recyclées par les enfants.** (future tense)

b) **L'ambulance** _____ **appelée par ma mère.** (perfect tense)

c) **La fête** _____ **organisée par mon amie.** (present tense)

d) **La radio dans notre chambre n'** _____ **pas** _____ **réparée.** (perfect tense)

[4 marks]

Review Questions

Using Verbs in the Present Tense & Future Time-frame

1 **Remplissez les blancs. Utilisez la forme correcte du verbe entre parenthèses.**
Complete the sentences. Use the correct form of the verb in brackets.

a) _____ -tu mieux aujourd'hui? (aller)

b) Nous _____ en train de manger. (être)

c) _____ - vous envie de sortir? (avoir)

d) Les dessins animés me _____ rire. (faire)

[4 marks]

2 **Reliez les bouts de phrases et traduisez en anglais.** Match the pairs and translate into English.

a) Nous nous intéressons	trouver un petit boulot.
b) Le collège décide de	de recycler tous les déchets.
c) Tous mes copains vont réussir	changer l'uniforme.
d) Mon frère espère	à la danse.
e) Ils essaient	à leurs examens!

[10 marks]

3 **Écrivez ces phrases au futur immédiat.** Write these sentences using the immediate future.

Exemple: Je fais du sport

→
le futur

Je vais faire du sport

a) Je finis à cinq heures.

b) On attend à la gare.

c) Nous voyons le film en 3D.

d) Ils ne mangent pas.

e) Elle boit de la limonade.

[5 marks]

4 **Écrivez les même phrases au futur.** Write the same sentences in the future tense.

[5 marks]

Past Time-frame: Perfect Tense & Imperfect Tense and Pluperfect Tense

1 **Soulignez les verbes qui forment leur passé composé avec être.**

Underline the verbs which take **être** in the perfect tense.

manger	aller	faire	se coucher	boire	commencer
sortir	finir	descendre	choisir	se lever	venir
perdre	monter	s'amuser			

[8 marks]

2 **Remplissez les blancs. Utilisez le participe passé du verbe entre parenthèses.**

Fill in the gaps. Use the past participle of the verb in brackets.

a) Le week-end dernier, mon copain a _____ de l'escalade. (faire)

b) Il l'a _____ vraiment passionnant. (trouver)

c) Je suis _____ à la maison et j'ai _____ mon dernier blog en ligne. (rester) (mettre)

d) As-tu _____ le dernier film de la Guerre des Etoiles? (voir)

e) Ma sœur est _____ le voir avec ses amies. (aller)

[6 marks]

3 **Écrivez les phrases de l'exercice 2 dans le plus que parfait.**

Write the sentences from exercise 2 in the pluperfect tense.

[6 marks]

4 **Passé composé ou imparfait? Écrivez le texte.** Perfect or imperfect? Rewrite the passage using the correct tense of each verb.

L'hiver dernier *nous avons passé / nous passions* des vacances à la montagne dans le sud de la France. Le temps *a été / était* superbe – il *a neigé / neigeait* tous les jours et *il y avait / il y a eu* beaucoup de choses à faire. À part le ski, *j'essayais / j'ai essayé* le snowboard et ma sœur a *fait / faisait* du patinage à glace. Après avoir fait du ski chaque jour, ma famille et moi *buvions / avons bu* toujours du chocolat chaud dans le même petit café, mais le dernier jour des vacances mes parents *choisissaient / ont choisi* un vin chaud! [8 marks]

Review Questions

Pronouns & Questions

1 **Comment dit-on en anglais...?** What is the English for...?

a) pourquoi?

b) depuis quand?

c) combien de?

d) avec qui?

e) lequel?

[5 marks]

2 **Remplissez les blancs avec les mots interrogatifs suivants.** Fill in the following sentences with the appropriate question words from the list below.

| pour qui | avec qui | pourquoi | depuis quand | laquelle |

a) Tu habites ici _____ ?

b) _____ est-ce que tu voudrais aller en Australie?

c) _____ passes-tu tes vacances normalement?

d) Voici deux paires de chaussures – _____ préfères-tu?

e) _____ as-tu acheté ces fleurs?

[5 marks]

3 **Pouvez-vous trouver un autre mot interrogatif pour chaque question de l'exercice 2?**
Can you think of another question word for each of the questions in exercise 2? [5 marks]

4 **Quelles sont les questions pour ces réponses?** What are the questions for these answers?

a) J'irai en vacances avec mes parents.

b) Je pense que je préfère le foot au rugby.

c) Quand j'étais petit je jouais au foot.

d) J'habite ici depuis cinq ans.

e) Je voudrais aller en Italie l'année prochaine.

[5 marks]

Prepositions and Conjunctions & Subjunctive Mood and the Passive Voice

1   **Lesquelles de ces phrases sont à la voix passive?** Which of these sentences are in the passive voice?

a) La fête va être organisée par ma copine.

b) Le recyclage devrait être entrepris par tout le monde.

c) Le recyclage devrait être une obligation.

d) La fête va être géniale.

e) Les vacances ont été un désastre.

[2 marks]

2   **Reliez les parties de phrases et traduisez-les en anglais.** Match the two halves of the sentences and translate into English.

a) Bien que	i) je suis nulle en maths je ne vais pas avoir une bonne note
b) Comme	ii) j'irai en vacances en Italie l'année prochaine
c) Je pense que	iii) je sois la meilleure en maths
d) Je ne pense pas que	iv) je fasse plus d'exercice
e) Il faut que	v) je fasse beaucoup d'efforts, je ne vais pas réussir

[10 marks]

3   **Complétez les phrases avec les pronoms relatifs corrects.** Complete the sentences with the correct relative pronouns – **qui / que / dont**.

a) Ma sœur Laurette, _____ est plus âgée que moi, étudie le Français à l'université.

b) C'est le film _____ je t'ai parlé.

c) Ce _____ m'intéresse c'est le patinage artistique.

d) Sur cette photo c'est la ville _____ j'ai visitée la semaine dernière.

e) C'est la fille _____ les parents sont espagnols.

[5 marks]

Mixed Exam-Style Questions

Reading

1 Read what people are saying about their towns. Write the name of the correct person for each question in English.

Homeless people and poverty

> Moi, ce que je n'aime pas c'est le nombre de sans-abris qui demandent tout le temps de l'argent devant la gare.

Florence

> Ce qui me déplaît, c'est les voyous qui se promènent la nuit dans mon quartier.

Matéo

> Malheureusement le petit magasin à côté de chez moi connaît plus de vols depuis peu.

Youssef

> Moi, je pense qu'on devrait encourager les sans-abris à retrouver un travail.

Bernard

> Pour moi c'est vrai que le chômage est inquiétant mais pas autant que le nombre de personnes qui n'ont pas de logement et dorment dans la rue.

Alissa

a) Who doesn't feel safe at night? ....

b) Who doesn't like the fact that there are too many beggars? ....

c) Who feels that crime is increasing? ....

d) Who thinks that homelessness is very worrying? ....

e) Who thinks that we should help homeless people? ....

5 marks

2 Translate this French blog into English:

> **Prenez-vous trois repas par jour? Ou mangez-vous souvent des casse-croûtes en travaillant?**
>
> **Je suis fana d'un grand petit-déjeuner avant de quitter la maison le matin. À midi, une salade et le soir un dîner plein de légumes. Cependant, pour les fêtes spéciales, on peut toujours choisir un bon dessert!**

10 marks

3 Read what these French teenagers say about where they live. Write the name of the correct person for each statement in English.

Est-ce que tu aimes l'endroit où tu habites?

J'aime ma maison, mais j'habite en ville et il y a trop de circulation.	**Benjamin, 14 ans**
Si je veux voir mes amis, je dois me déplacer en bus ou en voiture!	**Killian, 15 ans**
C'est plus propre à la campagne qu'en ville. Ici les rues sont sales.	**Lisa, 14 ans**
Par la fenêtre je vois des arbres et des collines, mais on n'a pas de voisins.	**Daniel, 14 ans**
J'adore vivre en plein centre-ville parce que c'est très animé!	**Olivier, 15 ans**
La ville est trop bruyante pour moi, et les loyers sont plus chers qu'à la campagne!	**Marlne, 19 ans**

a) Who is concerned by the high rent? ....

b) Who says that they have no neighbours? ....

c) Who likes the liveliness of the town centre? ....

d) Who cannot walk or cycle to see friends? ....

e) Who complains about the traffic? ....

f) Who is unhappy about the cleanliness of the streets? ....

6 marks

4 Read these adverts for leisure events:

A	**'Venez faire du ski cet hiver! Stages commencent le 10 décembre'**
B	**'Nouveau – stage de yoga pour débutants – mardi à 20 heures'**
C	**'Samedi matin au centre sportif – volleyball pour tous!'**
D	**'Cet été – apprenez la planche à voile!'**
E	**'Savourez le paysage rurale – faites des randonnées en groupe!'**
F	**'Essayez le skate – tous les mercredis!'**

Mixed Exam-Style Questions

Which activity would you choose if you enjoyed:

a) water sports _____

d) relaxation _____

b) being in the countryside _____

e) winter sports _____

c) playing team sports _____

☐ 5 marks

---

5 HT Read the advice from the study guide and tick the four pieces of advice that are given.

Préparez-bien pour vos examens!

Cet été vous allez passer vos examens et vous voulez réussir sans doute! Voici des avis pour ne pas échouer…et pour éviter le redoublement!

- **Venez à l'examen bien équipé. Laissez assez de temps pour votre voyage.**
- **Lisez les rubriques sur les premières pages des examens. Vous devez écrire vos détails sur la première page. La lecture des questions est très importante.**
- **On n'a pas le droit d'avoir son téléphone portable pendant l'examen. Le chewing-gum est aussi strictement interdit.**

a) You must wear uniform to the exam. ☐

b) Make sure that your details are filled in on the front page of exams. ☐

c) Mobiles are not allowed in the exam. ☐

d) Come to the exam well prepared. ☐

e) You must enter the exam hall in silence. ☐

f) Make-up is not allowed. ☐

g) Read the questions well. ☐

h) Take note of the length of time of the examinations. ☐

☐ 4 marks

6 HT Read this film review and tick the four correct sentences:

Le nouveau film de James Bond vient de sortir au cinéma. C'est le vingt-quatrième aventure de l'agent secret et comme toujours, c'est un film d'espionnage plein d'effets spéciaux. Il y a plein d'action qui a lieu dans les montagnes, soit en Europe soit aux États-Unis. Il s'agit des espionnes britanniques qui doivent éliminer les adversaires puissants. L'actrice française Léa Seydoux joue un rôle principal comme la nouvelle 'Bond Girl'.

a) The new James Bond film will soon be released. ☐

b) It is the twenty-fourth film in the Bond series. ☐

c) The special effects are disappointing. ☐

d) Lots of the action takes place in the mountains. ☐

e) The action only takes place in Europe. ☐

f) French spies have to defeat their enemies. ☐

g) The role of the 'Bond girl' is played by a French actress. ☐

h) Léa Seydoux has a main role in the film. ☐

☐ 4 marks

Mixed Exam-Style Questions

7 Read what these French teenagers say about marriage. Write the name of the correct person for each statement in English.

Kassem

Voudrais-tu te marier un jour?

Pourquoi pas? Mes parents sont mariés depuis vingt ans et ils sont contents.
Kassem, 15 ans

Manon

Oui, parce que le mariage, c'est une preuve d'amour.
Manon, 14 ans

Charlotte

Non, parce que le mariage se termine souvent par un divorce. Charlotte, 16 ans

Samuel

Si on veut avoir des enfants, c'est mieux d'être marié. Samuel, 14 ans

Naima

Le mariage, c'est une idée qui est complètement démodée. Naima, 15 ans

Yanis

Mes parents sont divorcés depuis trois ans et j'ai maintenant un beau-père.
Yanis, 15 ans

Romane

J'aime bien habiter seule, alors je crois que je vais rester célibataire.
Romane, 14 ans

Lucas

C'est plus simple d'habiter ensemble: si ça ne marche pas, on peut se séparer.
Lucas, 16 ans

a) Who is planning to stay single? _____

b) Whose parents have split up? _____

c) Who thinks living together is preferable to getting married? _____

d) Who thinks it's better for children if their parents are married? _____

e) Who thinks getting married is old-fashioned? _____

f) Whose parents have been together for a long time? _____

6 marks

8 Read the sentences below about what some pupils think about the environment and match the names to the statements.

Moi et l'environnement

Thierry:	Il est important d'essayer de marcher ou d'utiliser les transports en commun.
Mathilde:	À l'école tout le monde essaie de protéger la planète en triant ce qu'on utilise tous les jours en classe ou à la cantine.
Alain:	Je pense qu'on devrait prendre des douches au lieu de prendre des bains.
Farida:	L'énergie solaire, par exemple, est notre avenir.

a) We need to avoid using cars _____

b) We need to use more renewable energy _____

c) We need to save water _____

d) We need to recycle _____

4 marks

9 A friend who does not speak French has sent you the following extract from a magazine article about family relationships. Your friend has asked you to translate it for her into English.

> Mon demi-frère est assez grand, et il porte des lunettes. Je m'entends bien avec lui, parce qu'il est très gentil. Hier, nous sommes allés au cinéma ensemble et c'était amusant. La semaine prochaine, ma sœur aînée va partir en vacances avec son petit ami. Je me dispute souvent avec elle, car elle est trop égoïste.

9 marks

10 Julie talks about the environment. Read the passage and choose the correct sentences; there are four correct sentences. Circle them.

Moi, tous les jours j'essaie de recycler le papier, le plastique et les cannettes chez moi et à l'école; je les mets dans les poubelles appropriées. Je sais qu'il n'est pas facile de protéger l'environnement mais moi j'ai décidé de marcher au lieu de prendre le bus mais malheureusement mes amis ne suivent pas mon exemple. Aussi j'aimerais réduire ma consommation d'électricité mais de nos jours tout est électrique alors ce n'est pas facile! Il faudrait peut-être que j'arrête d'utiliser mon portable aussi souvent et je pense que je devrais éteindre mes appareils électriques quand je ne les utilise pas. Vraiment, je pense que je pourrais en faire plus pour sauver la planète.

a) Julie recycles cans at home.

b) Julie doesn't recycle anything at school.

c) Julie has decided to walk because her friends do it too.

d) Julie uses a lot of electricity.

e) Julie thinks it is easy to reduce our electricity consumption.

f) Julie thinks she uses her phone too much.

g) Julie is good at switching everything off when she is not using them.

h) Julie thinks that she doesn't do enough to help protect the environment.

4 marks

TOTAL

57 marks

Writing

1 C'est le week-end et vous écrivez à votre ami(e) français(e).

Décrivez:

- où vous êtes
- vos intérêts
- vos passetemps sportifs
- vos activités ce week-end.

Écrivez environ 40 mots en français.

8 marks

2 Vous écrivez un article sur l'amitié pour un magazine français.

Décrivez:

- votre meilleur(e) ami(e)
- pourquoi vous vous entendez bien
- ce que vous avez fait récemment avec vos ami(e)s
- vos projets pour le week-end prochain

Écrivez environ 90 mots en français. Répondez à chaque aspect de la question.

16 marks

3 Vous décrivez les fêtes pour votre blog.

Décrivez:

- votre fête préférée
- les aspects positifs et négatifs des fêtes
- une célébration récente
- comment vous voulez fêter votre prochain anniversaire

Écrivez environ 90 mots en français. Répondez à chaque aspect de la question.

16 marks

4 Vous décrivez vos études et vos projets pour votre blog.

Décrivez:

- vos matières préférées
- vos opinions de votre école
- vos projets pour l'année prochaine
- votre choix de carrière.

Écrivez environ 90 mots en français. Répondez à chaque aspect de la question.

16 marks

Mixed Exam-Style Questions

5 Translate the following sentences into French.

    a) I recycle at school.

    b) We must use public transport.

    c) People should consume less electricity.

    d) In order to save the environment we must not use too many carrier bags.

    e) Yesterday I recycled my cans at home.

10 marks

6 Translate the following sentences into French.

    a) My mother is quite small and pretty.

    b) My best friend has blue eyes and brown hair.

    c) I do my homework on my computer.

    d) I download music because it's fast.

    e) Yesterday, I spent a lot of time online.

10 marks

7 Translate the following sentences into French:

    a) The station is next to the police station.

    b) I like the town centre.

    c) You can buy some nice clothes.

    d) There is a market.

    e) I lost my wallet in the shopping centre.

10 marks

TOTAL

86 marks

Speaking

1 Role-play activity: Prepare your part in the role-play below:

Your teacher will play the part of the hotel receptionist and will speak first.

You should address the receptionist as '**vous**'.

When you see this – ! – you will have to respond to something you have not prepared – try to work out what this might be in advance.

When you see this – ? – you will have to ask a question

Vous venez d'arriver à votre hôtel en Belgique. Vous parlez avec le / la réceptionniste.

- **réservation (deux détails)**
- **nom + comment ça s'écrit**
- **Voiture – description (deux détails)**
- **!**
- **? heure – petit-déjeuner**

15 marks

2 Role-play activity: Prepare your part in the role-play below:

Your teacher will play the part of the waiter / waitress and will speak first.

You should address the waiter / waitress as '**vous**'.

When you see this – ! – you will have to respond to something you have not prepared – try to work out what this might be in advance.

When you see this – ? – you will have to ask a question.

Vous parlez avec le serveur / la serveuse dans un restaurant en France.

- **Réservation – combien de personnes**
- **Table – où**
- **entrée et plat principal – (deux choses)**
- **!**
- **? légumes**

15 marks

Mixed Exam-Style Questions

3 Role-play activity. Prepare your part in the role-play below:

Your teacher will play the part of your French friend and will speak first.

You should address your friend as '**tu**'.

When you see this – ! – you will have to respond to something you have not prepared – try to work out what this might be in advance.

When you see this – ? – you will have to ask a question

Tu parles d'où tu habites avec ton ami(e) français(e).

- **Ta maison – description (deux détails)**
- **Ta ville / ton village (deux détails)**
- **!**
- **Ta chambre (ton opinion et une raison)**
- **? ville ou campagne**

15 marks

4 Photo card: Look at the photo. Prepare <u>spoken</u> answers to the following questions:

- **Qu'est-ce qu'on voit sur la photo?**
- **Que penses-tu du recyclage?**
- **Qu'est-ce que tu as fait hier pour protéger l'environnement?**

Think of two further questions you might be asked on the topic of 'The Environment' and prepare spoken answers.

(6 marks for answering these extra questions correctly – 3 marks per question)   15 marks

5 Photo card: Look at the photo. Prepare <u>spoken</u> answers to the following questions:

- **Qu'est-ce qu'il y a sur la photo?**
- **Quelles sortes de films aimes-tu?**
- **Parle-moi d'une visite récente au cinéma.**

Think of two further questions you might be asked on the topic of 'Cinema and TV' and prepare spoken answers.

(6 marks for answering these extra questions correctly – 3 marks per question) 15 marks

6 Photo card: Look at the photo. Prepare <u>spoken</u> answers to the following questions:

- **Qu'est-ce qu'il y a sur la photo?**
- **Tu fais du sport? Pourquoi, ou pourquoi pas?**
- **Qu'est-ce que tu as fait récemment pour rester en bonne santé?**

Think of two further questions you might be asked on the topic of 'Healthy Living' and prepare spoken answers.

(6 marks for answering these extra questions correctly – 3 marks per question) 15 marks

Mixed Exam-Style Questions

7 Photo card: Look at the photo. Prepare <u>spoken</u> answers to the following questions:

- • **Qu'est-ce qu'il y a sur la photo?**
- • **Quels sont les avantages de la technologie mobile?**
- • **Qu'est-ce que tu as fait hier sur ton portable ou ton ordinateur?**

Think of two further questions you might be asked on the topic of 'Technology in everyday life' and prepare spoken answers.

(6 marks for answering these extra questions correctly – 3 marks per question)   15 marks

8 General conversation

Prepare <u>spoken</u> answers to the following questions you might be asked on the topic of 'Me, my family and friends'.

a) **Décris un membre de ta famille.**

b) **Avec qui t'entends-tu bien dans ta famille? Pourquoi?**

c) **Qu'est-ce que tu as fait avec ta famille, le week-end dernier?**

d) **Ton meilleur copain / Ta meilleure copine est comment?**

e) **Qu'est-ce que tu as en commun avec ton / ta meilleur(e) ami(e)?**

f) **Qu'est-ce que tu vas faire avec tes ami(e)s, le week-end prochain?**   30 marks

9   General conversation

Prepare <u>spoken</u> answers to the following questions you might be asked on the topic of 'School and future career'.

a) Décris ton collège.

b) Quelle est ta matière préférée? Pourquoi?

c) Comment est ta journée scolaire?

d) Que penses-tu du règlement scolaire?

e) Tu as l'intention de faire quoi l'année prochaine?

f) Qu'est-ce que tu veux faire dans la vie?

30 marks

10   General conversation

Prepare <u>spoken</u> answers to the following questions you might be asked on the topic of 'Travel and tourism'.

a) Quel genre de vacances préfères-tu généralement?

b) Que penses-tu des vacances entre amis?

c) Parle-moi de tes dernières vacances. Qu'est-ce que tu as fait?

d) Parle-moi de ton logement. Qu'est-ce que tu en as pensé?

e) Quels sont tes projets pour tes prochaines vacances?

25 marks

TOTAL

190 marks

Pronunciation Guide

La Prononciation Française

Knowing key sounds will help you improve your speaking and listening skills. Here is a summary of key French sounds.

Letters	Sounds like...	Examples
final consonants t/d/b/p/x/s/r/c	silent except **un fils**	**c'est / ans / blanc / les yeux / grand beaucoup / trop**
h	silent	**l'hôtel / l'histoire / heureux**
in / im / un / ain	nasal sound	**un / du pain / un copain important / intelligent / un lapin**
en / em / an / am	nasal sound	**ans / un enfant / dans**
on / om	nasal sound	**bon / une maison / un avion**
qu	k	**quatre / quand / qui**
a	ah	**la table / confortable / âge**
y / i	ee	**un site / une bicyclette**
o / eau / au	oh	**le bateau / le chapeau / les chevaux**
ou	oo	**tout / sous / beaucoup**
oi	wa	**coiffer / le coiffeur / moi**
eu	euh	**les yeux / les cheveux / bleus**
ai	ay	**maison / faire**
é / er	eh	**chanter / préféré**

Answers

1.

Les saisons	Les mois	Les jours de la semaine
le **printemps** [1]	**janvier** [1]	lundi
l'été	février	**mardi** [1]
l'automne	mars	**mercredi** [1]
l'**hiver** [1]	**avril** [1]	jeudi
	mai	**vendredi** [1]
	juin	samedi
	juillet [1]	**dimanche** [1]
	août [1]	
	septembre	
	octobre	
	novembre	
	décembre	

2. le premier avril – April Fool's Day **[1]**
le quatorze février – la Saint-Valentin **[1]**
le vingt-cinq décembre – le Jour de Noël **[1]**
le trente-et-un octobre – Halloween **[1]**
le premier janvier – le Jour de l'An **[1]**
le cinq novembre – Bonfire Night **[1]**

3. Answers will vary. Example answers:
   a) Je m'appelle Adam. **[1]**
   b) J'ai seize ans. **[1]**
   c) Mon anniversaire, c'est le quinze octobre. **[1]**
   d) J'habite à Bristol. **[1]**
   e) Oui, j'ai un frère et deux sœurs. **[1]**
   f) Oui, j'ai un chien et deux cochons d'Inde. **[1]**

4. **a)** 10 **[1]**   2 **[1]**   12 **[1]**
   b) 4 **[1]**   40 **[1]**   14 **[1]**
   c) 15 **[1]**   55 **[1]**   5 **[1]**
   d) 30 **[1]**   13 **[1]**   3 **[1]**
   e) 60 **[1]**   70 **[1]**   16 **[1]**
   f) 24 **[1]**   80 **[1]**   90 **[1]**

5. **a)** trente-deux **[1]**
   b) cinquante-trois **[1]**
   c) quarante-six **[1]**
   d) soixante-cinq **[1]**
   e) soixante-quatorze **[1]**
   f) quatre-vingt-deux **[1]**
   g) quatre-vingt-treize **[1]**

6. **a)** 8:00 – Il est huit heures. **[1]**
   b) 8:10 – Il est huit heures dix. **[1]**
   c) 8:15 – Il est huit heures et quart. **[1]**
   d) 8:25 – Il est huit heures vingt-cinq. **[1]**
   e) 8:30 – Il est huit heures et demie. **[1]**
   f) 8:45 – Il est neuf heures moins le quart. **[1]**
   g) 8:50 – Il est neuf heures moins dix. **[1]**

7. **a)** Il est sept heures et demie. **[1]**
   b) Il est deux heures et quart. **[1]**
   c) Il est cinq heures vingt. **[1]**
   d) Il est dix heures moins le quart. **[1]**
   e) Il est dix heures. **[1]**

Page 7 Quick Test
1. I get on very well with my uncle. He is quite old and thin, but he is always happy and nice.
2. Je ne m'entends pas très bien avec ma sœur cadette. Elle est mince et jolie, mais (elle est) très paresseuse et méchante. On se dispute tout le temps.
3. Answers will vary. Example answer: Ma sœur est assez grande et mince. Je m'entends bien avec elle parce qu'elle est toujours aimable et généreuse.

Page 9 Quick Test
1. Ma meilleure amie / copine a les yeux verts et les cheveux longs, blonds et bouclés / frisés. Elle est assez sportive.
2. Il n'est jamais de mauvaise humeur.
3. Nous aimons la même musique et les mêmes sports. – We like the same music and the same sports.
4. Answers will vary. Example answer: Ma meilleure copine est assez petite et un peu grosse. Elle a les cheveux courts et blonds et les yeux gris. Elle est très gentille et elle est toujours de bonne humeur. On aime les mêmes films et on va souvent au cinéma ensemble.

Page 11 Quick Test
1. marié(e)   divorcé(e)   séparé(e)   naître   mourir   avoir des enfants
2. **a)** I don't think I would like to get married. I would prefer to stay / remain single.
   b) My grandparents have been married for thirty years.
3. Answers will vary. Example answer: Je crois que je voudrais me marier un jour, parce que c'est plus sécurisant que simplement habiter ensemble.

Page 13 Quick Test
1. (Any four of) l'ordinateur (portable), la tablette, le clavier, la souris, la touche, l'écran, l'imprimante, la clé USB.
2. **a)** Il ne faut pas / jamais partager son mot de passe.
   b) Il faut installer un logiciel anti-virus.
3. Answers will vary. Example answer: J'utilise les réseaux sociaux pour rester en contact avec mes copains et partager des photos.

Page 15 Quick Test
1. je prends, because it is irregular / not a regular –er verb.
2. quickly   easily   regularly

3. À mon avis, la technologie portable est utile et amusante, mais elle / ça coûte trop cher (or: c'est trop cher.)

Page 17 Quick Test
1. Remember NOT to pronounce the final letters on the words 'mes' 'parents' and 'préfèrent': so, 'mes' sounds like 'may' in English, 'parents' is pronounced 'par' (not 'pair') + 'on' (no 'ts' sound) and 'préfèrent' is pronounced exactly the same as 'préfère'.
2. 'Je préfère' means 'I prefer' whereas 'mon chanteur préféré' means 'my favourite singer'. 'Je préfère' is a verb whereas 'préféré' is an adjective. They sound different, because you need to pronounce the 'é' ('eh' sound) at the end of 'préféré'.
3. The type of music that I like best is hip-hop.
The song makes me smile.
4. J'ai toujours écouté le reggae / de la musique reggae.

Page 19 Quick Test
1. What's it about?
2. It's about a man who has to / must save the planet.
3. **a)** Je préfère regarder la télé à la maison / chez moi.
   b) Il ne faut jamais payer les billets.

Page 21 Quick Test
1. une tranche de jambon; un kilo de framboises; une boîte de prunes
2. often, sometimes, usually
3. He eats nothing OR he never eats anything, she no longer eats meat; they eat neither fruit nor vegetables
4. Je n'ai jamais goûté de dinde.

Page 23 Quick Test
1. Any two from: le saumon (salmon), le thon (tuna), la truite (trout)
Any three from: l'agneau (lamb), le bœuf (beef), le veau (veal), le poulet (chicken), le canard (duck), la dinde (turkey)
2. As a main course, I'd like the lamb. What (sort of) vegetables do you have?
3. Nous avons déjeuné dans un restaurant français.
C'était parfait.

Page 25 Quick Test
1. Je joue au volley.
2. 'I ski / I am skiing' (present tense) and 'I used to ski / was skiing' (imperfect tense)
3. I used to play basketball.
4. J'allais à la patinoire.
5. I would like to try water sports.

Answers

Page 27 Quick Test

1.
   - la fête des mères — Mother's Day
   - la fête des rois — Epiphany (6 January)
   - la fête du travail — May Day
   - la fête nationale — Bastille Day
2.
   - Bon Anniversaire! — Happy Birthday!
   - Bonne Chance! — Good Luck!
   - Félicitations! — Congratulations!
   - Meilleurs Vœux — Best Wishes
3. We spent the evening eating and dancing.
4. Beaucoup de gens pensent qu'il faut conserver les fêtes traditionelles.

Pages 28–31 Practice Questions

Page 28

1. a) Ma tante est assez jeune et très jolie, mais un peu grosse. **[3]**
   b) Mon beau-père a une barbe noire. Il est trop vieux et assez laid. **[3]**
   c) Mes frères sont petits et très minces. Ils sont assez beaux. **[3]**
   d) Ma sœur est très belle. Elle est assez grande et un peu maigre. **[3]**

2. a) Je m'entends bien avec mon neveu, car il est toujours sage et très gentil. **[1]** (I get on well with my nephew, because he is always well-behaved and very nice.) **[3]**
   b) Je me dispute quelquefois avec ma mère, parce qu'elle est souvent trop sévère. **[1]** (I sometimes argue with my mother, because she is often too strict.) **[3]**
   c) Je ne m'entends pas très bien avec ma sœur aînée, car elle est agaçante et égoïste. **[1]** (I don't get on very well with my older sister, because she is annoying and selfish.) **[3]**
   d) Mon beau-père se fâche contre moi, parce qu'il est rarement heureux et trop têtu. **[1]** (My step-father gets angry with me, because he is rarely happy and too stubborn.) **[3]**

> When translating into English, take care not to miss out small words like qualifiers, or you will lose marks.

3. Samedi dernier, je suis allé au *mariage* **[1]** de mon frère. Sa femme est très *gentille*. **[1]** Ma sœur est mariée aussi *depuis* **[1]** deux ans. Mais mes parents sont *divorcés*. **[1]** Je ne sais pas encore si je *voudrais* **[1]** me marier, ou si je préférerais rester *célibataire*. **[1]** En ce moment, je n'ai pas de petite *amie* **[1]**. Mais un jour, je voudrais avoir des *enfants*. **[1]**

Page 29

1. l'ordinateur **[1]** (computer) **[1]**, la souris **[1]** (mouse) **[1]**, le page web **[1]** (web page) **[1]**, l'écran **[1]** (screen) **[1]**, la tablette **[1]** (tablet) **[1]**, le clavier **[1]** (keyboard) **[1]**, l'imprimante **[1]** (printer) **[1]**, la clé USB **[1]** (memory stick) **[1]**, la touche **[1]** (key) **[1]**, le réseau social **[1]** (social network) **[1]**.

2. a) J'envoie des SMS à tous mes amis. **[1]**
   b) Je télécharge de la musique et des applis. **[1]**
   c) Je prends beaucoup de photos sur mon portable. **[1]**
   d) Je vais sur mes sites web préférés. **[1]**
   e) Je fais des recherches pour mes devoirs. **[1]**

> Remember that word order in French is not always the same as in English.

3. a) C'est rapide et très pratique. A **[1]**
   b) On peut rester en contact avec les autres. A **[1]**
   c) Le cyberharcèlement est affreux. I **[1]**
   d) Parfois, il n'y a pas de réseau. I **[1]**
   e) Il faut recharger régulièrement son portable. I **[1]**
   f) On peut contacter quelqu'un en cas d'urgence. A **[1]**

Page 30

1. a) le jazz **[1]**   b) le reggae **[1]**
   c) le vieux rock **[1]**   d) la musique classique **[1]**   e) le hip-hop **[1]**
2. a) préfèrent **[1]**; préfère **[1]**
   b) préfère **[1]**; préfèrent **[1]**
   c) préfère **[1]**
3.

ça me plaît	I like it	**[1]**
ça m'énerve	it gets on my nerves	**[1]**
ça me détend	it relaxes me	**[1]**
ça me fait sourire	it makes me smile	**[1]**
ça me rend triste	it makes me sad	**[1]**
ça me fait rire	it makes me laugh	**[1]**
ça me fait pleurer	it makes me cry	**[1]**
ça me fait peur	it frightens me	**[1]**

4. a) les actualités **[1]**   b) un dessin animé **[1]**   c) un feuilleton **[1]**
   d) un film de guerre **[1]**   e) la télé réalité **[1]**   f) une émission **[1]**
   g) les effets spéciaux **[1]**   h) la publicité **[1]**   i) la séance **[1]**
   j) un billet **[1]**

5. Je m'intéresse à la musique pop. **[1]** Je préfère écouter la musique en direct. **[1]** J'ai toujours écouté la musique forte. **[1]** Je suis allé au festival de musique. **[1]**

Page 31

1. a) Je voudrais un kilo de carottes, s'il vous plaît. **[1]**   b) Nous dînons chez ma grand-mère deux fois par semaine. **[1]**   c) Je ne mange pas de chocolat parce que c'est trop sucré. **[1]**   d) Mes parents ne mangent jamais de poisson. **[1]**

2. a) I would like a kilo of carrots, please. **[1]**   b) We have dinner at my grandmother's house twice a week. **[1]**   c) I don't eat chocolate because it's too sweet (sugary). **[1]**   d) My parents never eat fish. **[1]**

3. a) Comme entrée (hors d'œuvre) je voudrais le potage, s'il vous plaît. **[1]**   b) Qu'est-ce que vous avez comme légumes? **[1]**   c) Je n'ai pas de couteau. **[1]**   d) C'était délicieux, merci. **[1]**

4. a) Ma sœur aime faire **des** promenades. **[1]**   b) Mon frère fait **de l'**équitation tous les samedis. **[1]**   c) Je jouais **au** volley. **[1]**   d) Mes copains vont souvent **à la** pêche. **[1]**   e) Avez-vous fait **de la** planche à voile? **[1]**

5. a) le cadeau **[1]**   b) le jour férié **[1]**   c) le feu d'artifice **[1]**   d) le défilé **[1]**   e) la mosquée **[1]**   f) une fête traditionnelle **[1]**   g) fêter (or célébrer) **[1]**   h) épouser **[1]**   i) garder **[1]**   j) donner **[1]**

Pages 32–53 Revise Questions

Page 33 Quick Test

1. I live in a small terraced house. There are seven rooms. On the ground floor there is the living room, dining room and kitchen. Upstairs there are three bedrooms and the bathroom.
2. J'habite dans une maison jumelée. À l'étage, il y a quatre chambres. Ma chambre est propre et il y a une armoire à côté de la porte. J'ai quelques posters au mur. Je nettoie ma chambre chaque semaine. La chambre de mon frère, en revanche, est sale.
3. Personal response.

Page 35 Quick Test

1. Answers will vary. Example answer: Dans ma ville il y a une zone piétonne avec des magasins et restaurants. Les transports en commun sont assez fréquents.

Answers

Mais il n'y a pas de cinéma, et on a besoin d'un grand centre commercial.
2. Personal response.
3. In town there are some shops and a department store where you can buy some nice clothes.
Can I try this jacket on?
My mother paid with her credit card.

Page 37 Quick Test
1. Il y a beaucoup de magasins en ville. Les maisons à la campagne sont plus grandes que les maisons en ville.
2. I love living in town because I can go to school on foot. My cousin lives in the country and he must take the bus.
3. Personal response.

Page 39 Quick Test
1. I do voluntary work. I distribute drinking water and hot meals to the homeless people in the streets.
2. Je livre des médicaments aux personnes âgées. À l'avenir je voudrais être infirmier / infirmière. Je voudrais travailler avec les personnes handicapées.
3. Personal response.

Page 41 Quick Test
1. Answers will vary. Example answer:
Je suis en bonne santé parce que je mange beaucoup de légumes et je bois suffisamment d'eau.
Je vais faire un régime et je vais éviter les produits gras.
2. Answers will vary. Example answer:
Il faut dormir au moins huit heures par nuit.
Il faut faire de l'exercice.
Il faut éviter les produits sucrés.
Il faut manger sainement.
Il faut manger moins de bonbons.
3. Je mange assez sainement mais je ne fais pas assez de sport. Je vais jouer au tennis et éviter les produits gras, car il faut rester en bonne santé.

Page 43 Quick Test
1. I think that there is too much pollution.
2. The most worrying problem is that there is too much packaging.
3. À mon avis les gens utilisent trop d'électricité.
4. Je pense que je gaspille trop et que je ne recycle pas assez.

Page 45 Quick Test
1. Je pense qu'on devrait recycler plus. (I think that we should recycle more.)
2. On pourrait créer plus de pistes cyclables. (We could create more cycle paths.)

3. Il faudrait protéger l'environnement en gaspillant moins. (It would be necessary to protect the environment by wasting less.)
4. en recyclant / en améliorant / en n'utilisant pas / en ne gaspillant pas
5. pour sauver / pour améliorer / pour encourager / pour ne plus polluer

Page 47 Quick Test
1. There are a lot of homeless people.
2. The most important problem is unemployment.
3. Now there are too many yobs.
4. We often hear about war on the news.
5. We should worry about the number of people who are poor.

Page 49 Quick Test
1. en / à; aux
2. avons logé; passerai

Page 51 Quick Test
1. J'ai voyagé en train.
2. Nous y avons passé deux semaines / quinze jours.
3. En vacances j'aime me promener.
4. En vacances ce que j'aime le plus c'est aller dans les parcs d'attraction.
5. Il y a trois ans j'ai passé deux semaines sur une île.

Page 53 Quick Test
1. Good evening, I have a reservation for a family bedroom for six nights.
2. I have lost my key.
3. Have you got a town plan, please?
4. Bonjour, je voudrais réserver une chambre double pour deux nuits, s'il vous plaît.
5. J'ai laissé ma valise à l'aéroport.

Pages 54–57 Review Questions

Page 54
1. Ma *meilleure* [1] copine s'appelle Yasmine. Elle a les yeux *marron* [1] et les *cheveux* [1] bruns, longs et frisés. Elle *porte* [1] des lunettes. Elle est un peu *moins* [1] grande que moi. On se connaît *depuis* [1] six ans. Elle me fait *rire* [1] et elle n'est *jamais* [1] de mauvaise humeur.
2. a) On **a** beaucoup de choses en commun. [1]
   b) Nous **aimons** la même équipe de foot. [1]
   c) **Nous** avons le même sens de l'humour. [1]
   d) On **aime** les mêmes émissions de télé. [1]
   e) **On** va au cinéma ensemble. [1]
   f) On **écoute** de la musique ensemble. [1]

> Make sure you know which present tense verb endings to use with 'on' and 'nous'. If you got any of the answers to exercise 2 wrong, look back at the second Key Point box on page 9.

3. a) Il vaut mieux habiter ensemble. [1] (It's better to live together.) [1]
   b) Le mariage se termine souvent par un divorce. [1] (Marriage often ends in divorce.) [1]
   c) J'aimerais avoir des enfants. [1] (I'd like to have children.) [1]
   d) Je préférerais rester célibataire. [1] (I'd prefer to stay single.) [1]
   e) Le mariage est complètement démodé. [1] (Marriage is completely outdated.) [1]
   f) Je voudrais me marier un jour. [1] (I'd like to get married one day.) [1]

Page 55
1. a) J'utilise mon portable pour *rester* en contact avec mes amis. [1]
   b) J'utilise mon imprimante pour *imprimer* des documents. [1]
   c) Je vais sur des sites web pour *faire* des recherches. [1]
   d) Je vais sur des sites de musique pour *télécharger* des chansons. [1]
   e) Pour se protéger en ligne, il faut *installer* un logiciel anti-virus. [1]
   f) Il ne faut jamais *communiquer* avec des inconnus. [1]

2.

Adjectifs positifs	Adjectifs négatifs
utile [1]	barbant [1]
amusant [1]	trop cher [1]
rapide [1]	ennuyeux [1]
génial [1]	affreux [1]
pratique [1]	
rigolo [1]	

> Make sure you can recognise and use a wide range of adjectives: they crop up in many different situations.

3. Answers will vary. Example answers:
   a) Je passe beaucoup de temps en ligne, parce que c'est amusant. [1] (I spend a lot of time online, because it's fun.) [1]
   b) Je ne joue pas à des jeux en ligne, parce que je trouve ça barbant. [1] (I don't play online games, because I find it boring.) [1]

Answers

c) Je prends beaucoup de photos sur mon portable, car c'est pratique. **[1]** (I take a lot of photos on my mobile, because it's practical.) **[1]**

d) Je déteste le cyberharcèlement: je trouve ça affreux. **[1]** (I hate cyber-bulling: I find it terrible.) **[1]**

e) Je fais tous mes achats en ligne, parce que c'est rapide. **[1]** (I do all my shopping online, because it's fast.) **[1]**

f) J'aimerais acheter le dernier modèle de portable, mais c'est trop cher. **[1]** (I'd like to buy the latest mobile phone model, but it's too expensive.) **[1]**

Page 56

1. a) Nous ador**ons [1]** b) Elle écout**e [1]** c) Ils télécharg**ent [1]** d) Nous chant**ons [1]** e) Elles s'intéress**ent [1]**

2. a) Je suis fana de jazz. **[1]** b) J'ai téléchargé le nouvel album de Guizmo. **[1]** c) J'ai toujours aimé le vieux rock. **[1]** d) J'ai vu mes chanteurs préférés. **[1]** e) Je suis allé au dernier concert de Mustang. **[1]**

3.

Télé	Cinéma
C **[1]**	A **[1]**
E **[1]**	B **[1]**
F **[1]**	D **[1]**
H **[1]**	G **[1]**

4. **A** (The) special effects are better on the big screen. **[1] B** (The) seats are becoming more and more expensive. **[1] C** Comfort is the most important thing for me and you can relax where you want to. **[1] D** I prefer the atmosphere because the surround sound is more powerful. **[1] E** You don't have to watch all the adverts. **[1] F** You can press pause and re-start when you want. **[1] G** Everyone likes buying popcorn and sweets at the kiosk! **[1] H** You don't have to keep quiet. **[1]**

Page 57

1.

hors d'œuvres	poissons	viandes	légumes	desserts
crudités **[1]**	truite aux amandes **[1]**	côtelette d'agneau **[1]**	chou-fleur **[1]**	crêpes flambées **[1]**
assiette de charcuterie **[1]**	saumon fumé **[1]**	filet de veau **[1]**	champignons **[1]**	tarte aux cerises **[1]**

2. a) Il y a deux ans, **je jouais** au basket au club des jeunes. **[1]** b) En ce moment **je fais** souvent des promenades à la campagne. **[1]** c) Maintenant **je joue** au volley tous les samedis. **[1]** d) Quand j'étais plus jeune, **je faisais** de la natation trois fois par semaine. **[1]**

3. a) Je voudrais essayer les sports nautiques. **[1]** b) Je me passionne pour l'escalade. **[1]** c) J'ai horreur des sports d'équipe. **[1]** d) J'ai envie essayer la planche à voile **[1]**

4. a) Les touristes regardent les défilés et les feux d'artifice. ((The) tourists watch the processions and the firework displays.) **[1]**
b) Beaucoup de gens mangent les plats traditionnels. (Lots of people eat traditional dishes (meals).) **[1]**
c) Tout le monde aime donner et recevoir les cadeaux. (Everyone loves giving and receiving presents.) **[1]**
d) On passe la journée à chanter les chansons traditionnelles. (We spend the day singing traditional songs.) **[1]**
e) En fin de soirée on danse dans les rues. (At the end of the evening, we dance in the streets.) **[1]**

Pages 58–61 Practice Questions

Page 58

1. J'habite dans une maison **individuelle**. **[1]** Il y a neuf pièces. Au **rez-de-chaussée [1]** il y a la cuisine et **la [1]** salle à manger. Le salon est **près [1]** de l'entrée. À l'étage il y a trois **chambres [1]** et une salle de bains. Ma chambre est à côté de la **chambre [1]** de ma sœur.

2. Own answer **[8]**

3. a) On peut acheter du pain ici. **[1]**
b) Je peux essayer cette chemise? **[1]**
c) On a besoin d'un cinéma. **[1]**
d) Il y a trop de circulation dans cette ville. **[1]**
e) Les transports en commun sont très fréquents. **[1]**
f) J'ai perdu mon portefeuille. **[1]**

Page 59

1. a) Henri **[1]**
b) Nadia **[1]**
c) Luc **[1]**
d) Delphine **[1]**
e) Rachel **[1]**

2. a) Il faut éviter les produits gras. **[1]**
b) Je suis en très bonne santé. **[1]**
c) Il faut se détendre pour éviter le stress. **[1]**
d) Ma mère a arrêté de fumer. **[1]**
e) Je vais essayer de suivre un régime. **[1]**

3. a) Je vais manger sainement. **[1]**
b) Je vais éviter les matières grasses. **[1]**
c) Je vais m'entraîner trois fois par semaine. **[1]**
d) Louis va aller au centre sportif. **[1]**

Page 60

1. a) gaspiller **[1]**
b) on devrait **[1]**
c) le réchauffement climatique **[1]**
d) une poubelle **[1]**
e) on pourrait **[1]**
f) l'inondation **[1]**
g) je devrais **[1]**
h) nous devons **[1]**
i) l'effet de serre **[1]**
j) endommager **[1]**

2. [1] trop **[1]** [2] assez **[1]** [3] trop **[1]** [4] assez **[1]** [5] beaucoup **[1]**

3. a) on devrait protéger l'environnement en recyclant plus **[1]** We should protect the environment by recycling more. **[1]**
b) à mon avis on pourrait gaspiller moins **[1]** In my opinion one / we should waste less. **[1]**
c) je devrais respecter la planète en ne polluant pas autant **[1]** I should respect the planet by not polluting so much. **[1]**
d) il ne faut pas gaspiller autant **[1]** We must not waste so much. **[1]**
e) on doit sauver la Terre en ne gaspillant pas nos ressources **[1]** We have to save the Earth by not wasting our resources. **[1]**

4. a) to frighten **[1]**
b) to steal **[1]**
c) unemployment **[1]**
d) war **[1]**
e) poverty **[1]**
f) a homeless person **[1]**
g) a yob **[1]**
h) poor **[1]**
i) grateful **[1]**
j) a worry **[1]**

Page 61

1. a) **en** [1]   Next year I will spend my holidays in Italy. **[1]**

   b) **à / en** [1]   I would like to go on holiday to Beijing in China. **[1]**

   c) **en** [1]   Normally we go on holiday by car because my dad likes driving. **[1]**

   d) **aux** [1]   Three years ago I spent my holidays in the USA. **[1]**

2. a) nous passons   **[1]**
   b) j'allais   **[1]**
   c) j'ai passé   **[1]**
   d) je passerai   **[1]**
   e) je passais   **[1]**

3. a) Ma salle de bains est sale.   **[1]**
   b) J'ai réservé une chambre double pas une simple.   **[1]**
   c) À quelle heure est le petit-déjeuner?   **[1]**
   d) Je crois que j'ai perdu / oublié mon passeport.   **[1]**
   e) Il me manque une serviette. / Je n'ai pas de serviette.   **[1]**

Pages 62–79 Revise Questions

Page 63 Quick Test

1. Answers will vary. Example answer:
Je suis très fort(e) en français.
Je suis assez fort(e) en maths.
Je ne suis pas très fort(e) en EPS.
Je suis faible en histoire-géo.
Je suis nul(le) en dessin.

2. History/Geography
Chemistry
PE
German
Technology
Art
Answers will vary. Example answer: Je suis très fort(e) en histoire-géo. J'aime bien cette matière parce que le prof est très intéressant.

3. At the moment I am studying for my exams. I love languages, especially Spanish because the teacher is funny and interesting. I am good at PE because I am pretty sporty, but I'm very weak in mathematics.

Page 65 Quick Test

1. Personal response.
2. Répétez le vocabulaire
Distribuez les livres
N'oubliez pas vos cahiers.
3. Je vais au collège.
Il y a 800 élèves, 38 professeurs et 29 salles de classe.

Commence à huit heures quarante cinq, finit à quinze heures quinze et les cours durent une heure.

Page 67 Quick Test

1. Les téléphones portables ne sont pas permis / autorisés.
On n'a pas le droit de parler en classe.

2. écrire (writing – to write)
redoubler (repetition of year – to repeat the year)
répondre (response – to respond)
voyager (travel – to travel)
lire (reading – to read)

3. la note – mark
réussir un examen – to pass an exam
apprendre – to learn
le cours – lesson
passer un examen – to sit an exam
interdit(e) – forbidden

Page 69 Quick Test

1. a) J'ai l'intention de continuer mes études.
   b) Je n'ai aucune idée de ce que je veux faire.
   c) L'année prochaine je vais être en terminale.

2. Answers will vary. Example answer: Après les examens j'ai l'intention de voyager en Asie. J'ai envie de voir la Chine.

3. Next year I plan to continue my studies. I want to study physics and chemistry because I would like go to university. I want to make lots of money in the future.

Page 71 Quick Test

1. Personal response.
2. Je vais être policier.
Ma mère est professeur.
Je rêve d'avoir une grande voiture.
3. J'habiterai dans une grande maison.
L'année prochaine je voyagerai.
Je gagnerai trente milles livres.

Page 73 Quick Test

1. a) une usine   b) un bureau
   c) un lycée   d) une sortie
2. a) des pommes   b) des ananas
   c) des chevaux   d) des châteaux
3. a) la patinoire   b) le lycée
   c) l'enfant   d) les livres
4. a) du pain   b) de la confiture
   c) de l'eau   d) des bonbons

Page 75 Quick Test

1. a) un tee-shirt noir   b) une jolie maison
   c) des enfants sportifs

2. a) un vieux film   b) une fille sympa
   c) un beau chat
3. a) Il est plus grand que moi. Il est le plus grand de la classe.
   b) Ma maison est moins moderne que sa maison.
   c) Je vais porter ce tee-shirt et ces baskets.

Page 77 Quick Test

1. vite / lentement   bien / mal   mieux / plus mal   loin / près   tôt / tard
2. I have looked for my mobile everywhere – here, there, upstairs and downstairs.
3. Answers will vary. Example answers:
   a) Je me douche tous les jours.
   b) Je vais en ville souvent.
   c) Je lis un livre de temps en temps.

Page 79 Quick Test

1. a) je travaille (I work / I am working)
   b) nous attendons (we wait / we are waiting)
   c) elle choisit (she chooses / she is choosing)
   d) ils achètent (they buy / they are buying)
2. a) je me lève (I get up)
   b) il se douche (he has a shower)
   c) vous vous amusez (you have fun)
   d) elles se disputent (they argue)
3. a) Je travaille ici depuis trois ans.
   b) i) Finis ton petit-déjeuner!
     ii) Achetez du pain.

Pages 80–83 Review Questions

Page 80

1. a) J'**habite** une maison jumelée à la campagne. **[1]**
   b) Je **nettoie** ma chambre tous les week-ends. **[1]**
   c) Dans ma chambre j'**ai** une grande armoire et une commode. **[1]**
   d) Je voudrais **déménager** à la campagne. **[1]**
   e) Les transports en commun **sont** très fréquents. **[1]**
   f) La bibliothèque **se trouve** près de la gare. **[1]**
   g) On **peut** faire des promenades sur les collines. **[1]**
   h) Ma mère **travaille** en centre-ville. **[1]**
2. a **[1]**, d **[1]**, f **[1]**, h **[1]**
3. J'habite une maison jumelée en centre-ville près **de la [1]** gare routière. Il y a neuf pièces en tout, y compris trois chambres.

Answers

Au rez-de-chaussée il y a le salon à côté **de la [1]** cuisine. Nous avons des toilettes qui se trouvent en face **de l' [1]** entrée, et près **de l' [1]** escalier. À l'étage il y a trois chambres. Ma chambre est en face **de la [1]** chambre de mes parents et à côté **du [1]** bureau.

Page 81

1. **a)** Je suis allé au **cabinet médical [1]** parce que j'étais malade.
    b) Je vais beaucoup **mieux [1]**, merci beaucoup.
    c) Le tabac peut **tuer [1]**.
    d) Je **vais [1]** faire plus de sport.
    e) J'ai réussi à **combattre [1]** l'obésité.
    f) Il faut suivre **les conseils [1]**.
2. **a)** relaxing [1]
    b) mineral water [1]
    c) three times per week [1]
    d) go on a diet [1]
    e) Eric's mother [1]

Page 82

1. **a)** une poubelle **[1]** **b)** le gaspillage **[1]**
    c) l'inondation **[1]** **d)** le trou dans la couche d'ozone **[1]** **e)** la déforestation **[1]**
    f) on pourrait **[1]** **g)** je pourrais **[1]**
    h) il ne faut pas **[1]** **i)** on peut **[1]**
    j) nous devons **[1]**
2. **a)** en recyclant [1]
    b) en consommant [1]
    c) en ne polluant pas [1]
    d) en évitant [1]
    e) en gaspillant [1]
3. **a)** iv) **[1]** We must recycle more [1]
    b) i) **[1]** We must not waste energy [1]
    c) v) **[1]** We shouldn't pollute our environment so much [1]
    d) ii) **[1]** We mustn't consume too much electricity [1]
    e) iii)**[1]** We could reduce our consumption [1]
4. **a)** [Je pense qu / À mon avis] il y a [trop de / beaucoup de] personnes qui sont sans-abri. **[1]**
    In my opinion there are too many / a lot of people who are homeless. **[1]**
    b) [Je pense qu / À mon avis] il y a [trop de / beaucoup de] jeunes qui sont au chômage. **[1]**
    In my opinion there are too many / a lot of people who are unemployed. **[1]**
    c) [Je pense qu / À mon avis] il y a [trop d' / beaucoup d'] ados qui sont harcelés. **[1]**

In my opinion there are too many / a lot of teenagers who are harassed. **[1]**
    d) [Je pense qu / À mon avis] il y a [trop de / beaucoup de] voyous qui volent. **[1]**
    In my opinion there are too many / a lot of yobs who steal. **[1]**
    e) [Je pense qu / À mon avis] il y a [trop de / beaucoup de] bandes qui sont effrayantes. **[1]**
    In my opinion there are too many / a lot of gangs who are scary. **[1]**

Page 83

1. **a)** la Suisse **[1]** **b)** un gîte **[1]**
    c) une clé **[1]**   **d)** le Pays de Galles **[1]**
    e) le premier étage **[1]**
    f) un ascenseur **[1]**
    g) un vol **[1]** **h)** le rez-de-chaussée **[1]**
    i) une île **[1]** **j)** à l'étranger **[1]**
2. **a)** Quand nous y étions nous sommes tombés en panne dans le désert. **[1]**
    When we were there we broke down in the desert. **[1]**
    b) J'aime bien y passer mes vacances avec ma famille. **[1]**
    I like spending my holidays there with my family. **[1]**
    c) J'aimerais y aller un jour pour rendre visite à ma tante. **[1]**
    I would like to go there one day to visit my aunt. **[1]**
3. **a)** normalement   je loge **[1]**
    b) l'année dernière   je suis allé(e) **[1]**
    c) l'année prochaine   je passerai **[1]**
4. Own answer.

Page 84

1. Isaac's favourite subject is **mathematics [1]** because he is good at it. One subject that he hates is **technology [1]** because he finds it boring. He thinks that his **chemistry [1]** teacher is funny but he thinks the subject is not very useful. Despite not being very good at **PE [1]**, he loves it! He studies **Spanish [1]** and German. He loves both.
2. **a)** Because the food in the canteen is not good. **[1]**
    b) The school rules. **[1]**
    c) George. **[1]**
    d) Having to repeat the year. **[1]**
    e) Nathalie, because she swims on a Thursday. **[1]**

Page 85

1. **a)** He is a builder. **[2]**
    b) My mother is a teacher. **[2]**
    c) I dream of having a varied job. **[2]**
2. **a)** Je suis coiffeur / coiffeuse. **[2]**
    b) Mon père est plombier. **[2]**
    c) Je vais être infirmier / infirmière. **[2]**
3. a **[1]**, c **[1]**, d **[1]**, f **[1]**

Page 86

1. **a)** une pomme (an apple) → des **pommes** (apples) **[1]**
    b) un château (a castle) → des **châteaux** (castles) **[1]**
    c) un cheval (a horse) → des **chevaux** (horses) **[1]**
    d) des jeux (games) → un **jeu** (a game) **[1]**
    e) des journaux (newspapers) → un **journal** (a newspaper) **[1]**
    f) des fils (sons) → un **fils** (a son) **[1]**

2.

	Indefinite article	Definite article	Partitive article
	un poisson (a fish)	le poisson (the fish)	du poisson (some fish)
	un café (a coffee)	**le [1]** café (the coffee)	**du [1]** café (some coffee)
	une [1] glace (an ice cream)	la glace (the ice cream)	**de la [1]** glace (some ice cream)
	un ananas (a pineapple)	l'ananas (the pineapple)	**de l' [1]** ananas (some pineapple)
	des œufs (some eggs)	**les [1]** œufs (the eggs)	**des [1]** œufs (some eggs)

3. Pour la fête d'anniversaire de mon **meilleur [1]** copain, Thomas, je vais porter **cette [1]** chemise avec un pull **noir [1]** et **mes [1]** baskets **blanches [1]**. Comme cadeau d'anniversaire, je lui ai acheté un tee-shirt **vert [1]**, parce que tous **ses [1]** tee-shirts sont trop **vieux**! **[1]**
    For my best friend Thomas' birthday party, I am going to wear this shirt, with a black jumper and my white trainers. As a birthday present, I have bought him a green tee-shirt, because all his tee-shirts are too old! **[8]**

Answers

Page 87

1.

Adverbs ending in –ly in English	Adverbs used to ask questions (interrogatives)	Adverbs of time and frequency	Adverbs of place or location
seulement **[1]** (only) **[1]** mal **[1]** (badly) **[1]** vite **[1]** (quickly) **[1]** lentement **[1]** (slowly) **[1]**	combien **[1]** (how much / many) **[1]** pourquoi **[1]** (why) **[1]** quand **[1]** (when) **[1]** comment **[1]** (how) **[1]**	aujourd'hui **[1]** (today) **[1]** toujours **[1]** (always) **[1]** maintenant **[1]** (now) **[1]** quelquefois **[1]** (sometimes) **[1]**	ici **[1]** (here) **[1]** partout **[1]** (everywhere) **[1]** en face **[1]** (opposite) **[1]** près **[1]** (near) **[1]**

2. a) Le matin, je *quitte* la maison à huit heures moins le quart. **[1]**
b) Nous *habitons* une petite maison dans centre-ville. **[1]**
c) Dans mon collège, les cours *finissent* à quinze heures trente. **[1]**
d) Ma sœur travaille dans un magasin; elle *vend* des vêtements. **[1]**
e) Où est-ce que tu *achètes* tes affaires scolaires? **[1]**

3. a) Dans mon collège, les cours commencent à neuf heures. **[2]**
b) Je me lève tous les jours à sept heures. **[2]**
c) J'attends le bus devant le cinéma. **[2]**
d) Je m'entends bien avec ma sœur, mais je me dispute avec mon frère. **[2]**
e) On habite / Nous habitons ici depuis six ans. **[2]**

Pages 88–103 Revise Questions

Page 89 Quick Test
1. a) nous avons **b)** nous faisons **c)** nous pouvons **d)** nous voulons
2. Choose from: devoir – to have to; savoir – to know how to; adorer – to adore; aimer – to like to; désirer – to want to; détester – to hate; espérer – to hope to; préférer – to prefer to; il faut – it is necessary to; il vaut mieux – it is better to
3. a) essayer de **b)** arrêter de **c)** réussir à
4. a) je sais danser **b)** je peux sortir **c)** je veux aller

Page 91 Quick Test
1. b – allez is the 'vous' form of the verb 'aller', to go (used for the imperative)
2. We will go into town for my birthday – I will be 16!
3. Je voudrais (j'aimerais) étudier les langues à l'université.
4. Si j'étais riche, j'aurais une grande maison.

Page 93 Quick Test
1. a) j'ai choisi **b)** j'ai regardé **c)** j'ai fait **d)** j'ai vu
2. a) elle est arrivée **b)** elle est partie **c)** elle est descendue **d)** elle est venue
3. a) il n'a pas écrit – he hasn't written / he didn't write **b)** nous ne sommes pas retournés – we haven't returned / we didn't return **c)** je n'ai pas dit – I haven't said / I didn't say

Page 95 Quick Test
1. a) je regardais **b)** nous choisissions **c)** ils attendaient **d)** elle était
2. b – because it is a single action in the past (the accident happened once) and the perfect tense is used; the other two sentences describe a situation in the past and the imperfect tense is used.
3. Nous buvions beaucoup d'eau.
4. They had eaten before going to the cinema.

Page 97 Quick Test
1. Elle est partie avec lui. Je ne l'ai pas vu.
2. Elle l'a aimé. Je vous le donnerai.

Page 99 Quick Test
1. qui / pour qui / quand / depuis quand / laquelle / quels
2. Est-ce tu recycles chez toi? Recycles-tu chez toi?
3. Tu habites ici? Habites-tu ici?
4. Tu étudieras le français l'année prochaine? Etudieras-tu le français l'année prochaine? Est-ce que tu étudieras le français l'année prochaine?

Page 101 Quick Test
1. pour
2. sans
3. Au lieu de voyager en voiture je devrais utiliser mon vélo.

Page 103 Quick Test
1. soit / alliez
2. puisse / fasse

Pages 104–107 Review Questions

Page 104
1.

annoying	h	**[1]**
great	g	**[1]**
easy	d	**[1]**
clever	a	**[1]**
unpleasant	e	**[1]**
funny	c	**[1]**
strict	f	**[1]**
useful	b	**[1]**

2. a) Distribuez [1] les livres Richard!
b) Faites [1] attention la classe!
c) N'oubliez [1] pas vos devoirs!
d) Ne **courez [1]** pas dans les couloirs!
e) Répétez [1] les mots!
f) Discutez [1] la question entre vous!

3. a) Ma sœur, Élise, est forte en biologie. **Christophe, 14 ans** **[2]**
b) Je suis très faible en mathématiques. **Élise, 15 ans** **[2]**
c) Bradley est assez nul en informatique. **Kevin, 15 ans** **[2]**
d) Ma petite amie est douée en espagnol. **Justin, 16 ans** **[2]**
e) Je suis fort en langues mais je suis assez faible en EPS. **Patrice, 14 ans** **[2]**

Page 105
1. a) Thomas **[1]**
b) Lisa **[1]**
c) Yann **[1]**
d) Olivier **[1]**
e) Lisa **[1]**
f) Yann **[1]**
2. a) J'aurai un emploi bien payé donc je **serai [1]** riche.
b) J'**habiterai [1]** aux Caraïbes parce que j'adore le soleil.
c) Je **ferai [1]** un tour du monde avec mes meilleurs amis.
d) J'**irai [1]** au travail tous les jours en hélicoptère.

Answers

e) J'**aurai** [1] une grande voiture et une grande maison avec piscine.

f) Je **mangerai** [1] dans des bons restaurants tous les jours.

3. Own answer. [8]

Page 106

1. a) le tourisme [1]   b) la violence [1]
   c) la condition [1]   d) le bagage [1]
   e) la maladie [1]
   f) le développement [1]
   g) le panneau [1]   h) la tartine [1]

2. Pour le pique-nique demain, je vais préparer des sandwichs, alors il faut acheter **du** [1] pain, **du** [1] fromage et **du** [1] pâté. Avec les sandwichs, on va manger **de la** [1] salade, donc je vais aussi acheter **des** [1] tomates. Comme dessert, on va manger **des** [1] fraises avec **de la** [1] crème ou peut-être **de la** [1] glace à la vanille. Les enfants vont boire **du** [1] jus d'orange, mais pour les adultes il y aura **du** [1] vin et **de l'** [1] eau minérale.

> Remember, you often have to use the word for 'some' in French, when we miss it out in English. For example: We need to buy (some) bread, (some) cheese and (some) pâté. This could trip you up when translating from English to French.

3. a) Ma sœur est plus **sportive** [1] que moi, mais elle n'est pas la plus **intelligente** [1]!
   (My sister is sportier than me, but she is not the most intelligent!) [1]

   b) Le français est moins **difficile** [1] que les maths, mais la géo est la plus **intéressante**. [1]
   (French is less difficult than / not as difficult as maths, but geography is the most interesting.) [1]

   c) Les raisins sont aussi **chers** [1] que les fraises, mais les fraises sont **meilleures** [1].
   (The grapes are as expensive as the strawberries, but the strawberries are better.) [1]

   d) Cette chemise **bleue** [1] est plus **vieille** [1] que la chemise **blanche** [1], mais je préfère celle-ci.

(This blue shirt is older than the white shirt, but I prefer this one.) [1]

   e) Mes grands-parents sont plus **gentils** [1] que mon oncle, mais ma tante est la plus **généreuse**. [1]
   (My grandparents are kinder than my uncle, but my aunt is the most generous.) [1]

   f) Leur maison est plus **grande** [1] que notre maison, mais notre jardin est le plus **beau**. [1]
   (Their house is bigger than our house, but our garden is the most beautiful.) [1]

> Always look closely at the gender of a noun to make sure you use the correct adjective agreement. Take care with irregular adjectives such as **beau / belle** and **vieux / vieille.**

Page 107

1. a) **doucement** (softly, gently) [1]
   b) **finalement** (finally) [1]
   c) **bien** (well) [1]
   d) **régulièrement** (regularly) [1]
   e) **généralement** (generally) [1]

> Using adverbs can enhance your speaking or writing and will impress an examiner. When writing adverbs, make sure you know which ones need accents, which type of accent and on which letters.

2. a) Les jours d'école, je **me** lève à sept heures. [1]
   b) Mon frère **se** brosse les dents dans la salle de bains. [1]
   c) D'habitude, nous **nous** entendons bien. [1]
   d) Mes parents **se** fâchent contre nous. [1]
   e) Tu **te** couches à quelle heure? [1]

3. a) **Nous quittons** la maison à huit heures. [1]
   b) **Tu aides** tes parents à la maison. [1]
   c) **Ils finissent** les cours à trois heures et demie. [1]
   d) **Je m'amuse** le samedi soir. [1]
   e) **On attend** le bus devant le café. [1]

> Using correct verb endings to go with each pronoun (I, he, we, they, etc.) is key to success in your speaking and writing exam papers.

> Remember, not all verbs are reflexive! You will need to use a mix of reflexive and non-reflexive verbs in most topic areas.

Pages 108–111 **Practice Questions**

Page 108

1. a) **Veux**-tu aller en boîte de nuit? [1]
   b) Je **dois** partir tout de suite! [1]
   c) Nous ne **savons** pas où il est. [1]
   d) **Pouvez**-vous m'aider, s'il vous plaît? [1]   e) On ne **doit** pas manger en classe. [1]   f) Mes sœurs ainées ne **veulent** jamais sortir avec moi! [1]

2. a) Nous **allons** rencontrer nos amis. [1]   b) Je **vais** regarder les feux d'artifices. [1]   c) Ils **vont** goûter les fruits de mer. [1]   d) **Allez**-vous souvent en ligne? [1]   e) **Vas**-tu rester au collège l'année prochaine? [1]   f) Mon père **va** aller à la pêche ce week-end. [1]

3. Le week-end prochain <u>sera</u> [1] vraiment passionnant, parce que mes deux cousins <u>viendront</u> [1] chez nous et je ne les ai pas vus depuis très longtemps! Le samedi matin, <u>nous irons</u> [1] à la patinoire où nous <u>ferons</u> [1] du patin à glace. Après, nous <u>retrouverons</u> [1] des amis en ville et <u>nous mangerons</u> [1] au café et puis le soir, <u>on ira</u> [1] au concert de The Vamps!! Ce <u>sera</u> [1] absolument génial, <u>il y aura</u> [1] une ambiance formidable et <u>ils chanteront</u> [1] leur dernier hit! J'ai trop hâte de les voir!

Page 109

1. a) J'ai mangé trop de chocolat! [1]
   b) Nous avons gagné le match de rugby. [1]   c) Elle a fini à cinq heures du soir. [1]   d) Mes parents ont choisi un nouvel ordinateur. [1]   e) Est-ce que tu as perdu ton portable? [1]   f) Ils ont attendu le bus devant l'église. [1]

2.

M	R	S	V	A	N	D	E	R	T	R	A	M	P
Monter [1]	Rester [1]	Sortir [1]	Venir [1]	Aller [1]	Naître [1]	Descendre [1]	Entrer [1]	Rentrer [1]	Tomber [1]	Retourner [1]	Arriver [1]	Mourir [1]	Partir [1]

3. REFLEXIVE verbs – e.g. se lever, se coucher, s'amuser **[1]**

4. Quand j'<u>étais</u> **[1]** plus jeune, j'<u>avais</u> **[1]** un chien qui <u>s'appelait</u> **[1]** Bruno. Il <u>était</u> **[1]** vraiment adorable et <u>avait</u> **[1]** le poil marron et frisé. Ses yeux <u>étaient</u> **[1]** noirs et il <u>portait</u> **[1]** un collier bleu. Tous les jours, on <u>faisait</u> **[1]** des promenades au parc et on <u>jouait</u> **[1]** ensemble. Je l'<u>aimais</u> **[1]** beaucoup.

Page 110

1. a) elle **[1]**
   b) ils **[1]**
   c) elle **[1]**
   d) il **[1]**, nous **[1]**

3. a) Je la regarde tous les jours après l'école. **[2]**
   b) Je ne les aime pas. **[2]**
   c) Je vais en vacances avec eux. **[2]**
   d) Je me dispute quelquefois avec elle. **[2]**
   e) Je ne l'aime pas vraiment. **[2]**

4. a) Pourquoi est-ce que tu ne recycles pas? **[1]**
      Why don't you recycle? **[1]**
   b) Tu joues du piano depuis quand? **[1]**
      How long have you played the piano for? **[1]**
   c) Tu as passé combien de temps en Allemagne? **[1]**
      How long did you spend in Germany? **[1]**
   d) Qu'est-ce qu'il y a dans ta ville pour les touristes? **[1]**
      What is there for tourists in your town? **[1]**
   e) Avec qui est-ce que tu t'entends le mieux dans ta famille? **[1]**
      Who do you get on the best with in your family? **[1]**

Page 111

1. a) sans **[1]**
   b) près de **[1]**
   c) derrière **[1]**
   d) au lieu de **[1]**
   e) d'un autre côté **[1]**
   f) pour **[1]**
   g) autour de **[1]**
   h) devant **[1]**
   i) selon **[1]**
   j) parmi **[1]**
2. a) I don't think that the film is good. **[1]**
   b) Although I make a lot of effort I am not improving. **[1]**
   c) It seems to be cold outside. **[1]**
   d) I am sorry that you are ill. **[1]**
3. a) seront **[1]**
   b) était **[1]**
   c) est **[1]**
   d) a été **[1]**

Page 112

1. a) **Vas**-tu mieux aujourd'hui? **[1]**
   b) Nous **sommes** en train de manger. **[1]**   c) **Avez**-vous envie de sortir? **[1]**   d) Les dessins animés me **font** rire. **[1]**
2. a) Nous nous intéressons à la danse. **[1]** (We are interested in (i.e. love) dance.) **[1]**   b) Le collège décide de changer l'uniforme. **[1]** (The school is deciding to change the uniform.) **[1]**   c) Tous mes copains vont réussir à leurs examens! **[1]** (All my friends are going to pass their exams!) **[1]**   d) Mon frère espère trouver un petit boulot. **[1]** (My brother is hoping to find a part-time job.) **[1]**
   e) Ils essaient de recycler tous les déchets. **[1]** (They try to recycle all (their) waste.) **[1]**
3. a) Je vais finir à cinq heures. **[1]**
   b) On va attendre à la gare. **[1]**
   c) Nous allons voir le film en 3D. **[1]**
   d) Ils ne vont pas manger. **[1]**
   e) Elle va boire de la limonade. **[1]**
4. a) Je finirai à cinq heures. **[1]**
   b) On attrendra à la gare. **[1]**
   c) Nous verrons le film en 3D. **[1]**
   d) Ils ne mangeront pas. **[1]**
   e) Elle boira de la limonade. **[1]**

Page 113

1. manger   <u>aller</u> **[1]**   faire   <u>se coucher</u> **[1]**   boire   commencer   <u>sortir</u> **[1]**   finir   <u>descendre</u> **[1]**   choisir <u>se lever</u> **[1]**   <u>venir</u> **[1]**   perdre   <u>monter</u> **[1]**   <u>s'amuser</u> **[1]**
2. a) Le week-end dernier, mon copain a **fait** de l'escalade. **[1]**   b) Il l'a **trouvé** vraiment passionnant. **[1]**   c) Je suis **resté(e)** à la maison et j'ai **mis** mon dernier blog en ligne. **[2]**   d) As-tu **vu** le dernier film de la Guerre des Etoiles? **[1]**   e) Ma sœur est **allée** le voir avec ses amies. **[1]**
3. All answers as exercise 2 but change verbs to:
   a) – avait fait **[1]**
   b) – l'avait trouvé **[1]**
   c) – j'étais resté(e) **[1]** + j'avais mis **[1]**
   d) – avais-tu **[1]**
   e) – était allée **[1]**
4. L'hiver dernier ***nous avons passé*** **[1]** des vacances à la montagne dans le sud de la France. Le temps ***était*** **[1]** superbe – il ***neigeait*** **[1]** tous les jours – et ***il y avait*** **[1]** beaucoup de choses à faire. À part le ski, ***j'ai essayé*** **[1]** le snowboard et ma sœur ***a fait*** **[1]** du patinage à glace. Après avoir fait du ski chaque jour, ma famille et moi

buvions **[1]** toujours du chocolat chaud dans le même petit café, mais le dernier jour des vacances mes parents ***ont choisi*** **[1]** un vin chaud!

Page 114

1. a) why? **[1]**
   b) since when? **[1]**
   c) how much / many? **[1]**
   d) who with? **[1]**
   e) which one? **[1]**
2. a) depuis quand **[1]**
   b) pourquoi **[1]**
   c) avec qui **[1]**
   d) laquelle **[1]**
   e) pour qui **[1]**
3. a) avec qui **[1]**   b) quand **[1]**
   c) où **[1]**   d) n/a **[1]**   e) quand / où / pourquoi **[1]**
4. a) Avec qui iras-tu en vacances? **[1]**
   b) Tu préfères le foot ou le rugby? **[1]**
   c) Qu'est-ce que tu faisais quand tu étais petit? **[1]**
   d) Tu habites ici depuis combien de temps? **[1]**
   e) Où voudrais-tu aller l'année prochaine? **[1]**

Page 115

1. a **[1]**, b **[1]**
2. a) v) **[1]** Even though I make a lot of effort, I am not going to succeed. **[1]**
   b) i) **[1]** As I am no good at maths I am not going to get a good mark. **[1]**
   c) ii) **[1]** I think that I will go on holiday to Italy next year. **[1]**
   d) iii) **[1]** I don't think that I am the best at maths. **[1]**
   e) iv) **[1]** I must do more exercise. **[1]**
3. a) qui **[1]**
   b) dont **[1]**
   c) qui **[1]**
   d) que **[1]**
   e) dont **[1]**

Reading

1. a) Matéo **[1]**
   b) Florence **[1]**
   c) Youssef **[1]**
   d) Alissa **[1]**
   e) Bernard **[1]**
2. Do you have (eat) three meals a day? Or do you often eat snacks while working? I'm a fan of a big breakfast before leaving the house in the morning. At lunchtime (noon) I have a salad and in the evening a dinner with lots of vegetables. However, for / on special occasions, you can always choose a good dessert! **[10]**

Answers

3. **a)** Marine [1]
    b) Daniel [1]
    c) Olivier [1]
    d) Killian [1]
    e) Benjamin [1]
    f) Lisa [1]
4. **a)** D [1]; **b)** E [1]; **c)** C [1]; **d)** B [1];
    e) A [1]
5. b [1], c [1], d [1], g [1]
6. b [1], d [1], g [1], h [1]
7. **a)** Romane [1]
    b) Yanis [1]
    c) Lucas [1]
    d) Samuel [1]
    e) Naima [1]
    f) Kassem [1]
8. **a)** Thierry [1]
    b) Farida [1]
    c) Alain [1]
    d) Mathilde [1]
9. My half-brother / step-brother is
    quite tall, and he wears glasses. I
    get on well with him, because he is
    very kind. Yesterday, we went to the
    cinema together and it was fun. Next
    week, my older sister is going to go
    on holiday with her boyfriend. I often
    argue with her, as / because she is
    too selfish. [9]

> When you translate into English,
> stick as closely as possible to the
> original, but make the English
> sound natural.

10. a [1], d [1], f [1], h [1]

Writing

1. Answers will vary. Example answer:

    Salut! Je suis chez moi (à la maison),
    dans ma chambre. J'aime la musique
    et les jeux vidéo. Comme sport, je
    joue au tennis et je fais du vélo. Le
    samedi, je vais en ville avec mes amis
    et j'achète des vêtements. [8]

2. Answers will vary. Example answer:

    Ma meilleure copine s'appelle Sarah.
    Elle a les yeux gris et les cheveux
    blonds, assez longs et frisés. Elle
    est un peu plus petite que moi.
    Elle est assez timide, mais très
    aimable. On se connaît depuis cinq
    ans et on s'entend toujours bien
    ensemble, parce qu'elle n'est jamais
    de mauvaise humeur. Nous aimons
    la même musique et samedi dernier,
    nous sommes allées à un concert de
    notre chanteur préféré. Nous avons
    chanté et dansé. C'était génial! Le
    week-end prochain, on va regarder
    une vidéo du concert à la télé. [16]

> When describing someone, using
> correct adjective endings is key.
> Make sure you know how to make
> regular and irregular adjectives
> agree correctly.

3. Answers will vary. Example answer:

    Ma fête préférée est Noël, parce que
    j'aime l'ambiance. Tout le monde est
    content et on s'amuse bien.
    J'adore donner et recevoir les cadeaux,
    mais de l'autre côté je mange trop de
    chocolat et de bonbons qui n'est pas si
    bon pour la santé!
    L'été dernier j'avais l'occasion d'aller
    au mariage de ma cousine. Après
    les noces à l'église, nous avons
    fait la fête dans un grand château.
    C'était excellent.
    Pour mon prochain anniversaire, je
    voudrais visiter un parc d'attractions avec
    mes amis. Nous pourrions passer toute la
    journée sur les attractions et à regarder
    les spectacles. Ce serait magnifique! [16]

4. Answers will vary. Example answer.

    À l'école j'aime bien les sciences
    parce que le professeur est super sympa
    et je trouve ça très intéressant. Ma
    matière préférée pourtant, c'est
    les maths. C'est pour cette raison que je
    voudrais devenir ingénieur.
    Les professeurs de mon collège sont
    calmes et assez gentils. Le collège
    est très grand et les salles sont très
    modernes et la salle omnisport est
    énorme, ce qui est formidable parce
    que j'adore jouer au basket.
    Je vais passer mes examens cette
    année et puis je vais aller au lycée.
    J'ai l'intention de passer un bac
    scientifique. Après j'irai à la fac pour
    continuer mes études. [16]

> Ensure that you cover all the
> elements of the question and that
> you give some thought to what
> grammatical features are being
> sought. For example, it is clear
> that in this question you need to
> talk about the future, so think of
> a number of ways you can do this
> without repeating yourself.

5. **a)** Je recycle à l'école. (*present tense
    ending* needed) [2]
    b) Il faut utiliser les transports en
    commun. (*il faut* needed) [2]
    c) On devrait consommer moins
    d'électricité. (*on devrait + moins de*
    needed) [2]

    d) Pour sauver l'environnement on
    ne doit pas / nous ne devons pas
    utiliser trop de sacs en plastique.
    (*on ne doit pas / nous ne devons
    pas / trop de* needed) [2]
    e) Hier j'ai recyclé mes cannettes chez
    moi. (*perfect tense* needed) [2]

> 5 marks for communication
> 5 marks for application of grammar

6. **a)** Ma mère est assez petite et jolie. [2]
    b) Mon meilleur ami/copain / Ma
    meilleure amie/copine a les yeux
    bleus et les cheveux bruns. [2]
    c) Je fais mes devoirs sur
    mon ordinateur. [2]
    d) Je télécharge de la musique, parce
    que c'est rapide. [2]
    e) Hier, j'ai passé beaucoup de temps
    en ligne. [2]

7. **a)** La gare se trouve / est près du
    commissariat. [2]
    b) J'aime le centre-ville. [2]
    c) On peut acheter des bons
    vêtements. [2]
    d) Il y a un marché. [2]
    e) J'ai perdu mon portefeuille dans
    le centre commercial. [2]

Speaking

1. Answers will vary. Example answers:
    *   (Bonjour je peux aider?)
        Oui, j'ai une réservation pour
        deux nuits pour 3 personnes, s'il
        vous plait. [3]
    *   (Quel est votre nom?)
        Je m'appelle [SMITH]...et ça s'écrit
        S.M.I.T.H [3]
    *   (J'ai vu que vous avez une voiture.)
        Oui, c'est une (Renault / Peugeot / ...)
        et elle est (rouge / verte / ...) [3]
    *   ! 'Vous payez comment?'
        Par carte / en liquide/ chèque [3]
    *   ? le petit-déjeuner est à quelle
        heure s'il vous plait? [3]
2. Answers will vary. Example answers:
    *   (Bonjour, madame / monsieur) –
        j'ai réservé une table pour
        quatre personnes. [3]
    *   (Nous voudrions) une table (au coin)
        près de la fenêtre, s'il vous plaît. [3]
    *   (Je vais prendre) les escargots (pour
        commencer) et le poulet (comme
        plat principal). [3]
    *   ! 'qu'est-ce que vous voulez boire?'
        Je voudrais une limonade, s'il vous
        plaît. [3]
    *   ? Qu'est-ce que vous avez comme
        légumes? [3]
3. *   Talk about the levels (e.g. le rez-de-
        chaussée) and the rooms. Can you

include some prepositions too? (Le bureau est <u>en face de la</u> chambre de ma sœur). **[3]**

- You could mention shops, amenities, transport, etc. You might add if something is needed (on a besoin de…) and whether where you live is quiet, busy or lively. **[3]**
- ! Possible areas to think about include traffic in town (la circulation) and whether you like where you live. **[3]**
- You might say what is in your room, using prepositions to be clearer. **[3]**
- ? Ask the teacher whether he / she prefers living, or would prefer to live, in the town or country. This could be something like 'Vous préfères habiter…?' **[3]**

4. Answers will vary. Example answers:

Sur la photo on voit une fille et son père, je crois. La petite fille porte une chemise rose et elle a les cheveux blonds et raides. Le père porte une chemise bleue et il a les cheveux courts et bruns. **[3]**
La petite fille fait du recyclage – elle met les boîtes dans la poubelle et son père met une bouteille en plastique dans la poubelle. **[3]**
Moi, je pense qu'il est très important de recycler pour protéger la planète. À mon avis tout le monde devrait recycler à la maison. Malheureusement il y a trop de gaspillage. **[3]**
Hier j'ai marché au collège au lieu de prendre la voiture et j'ai éteint les lumières quand j'ai quitté une pièce. Aussi j'ai encouragé mes amis à recycler leurs cannettes à l'école au lieu de les jeter par terre! **[3]**

Examples of other questions you might be asked:

- Qu'est-ce qu'on devrait faire pour encourager les gens à recycler plus?
- Est-il facile de protéger l'environnement? Pourquoi? Pourquoi pas?

To score the highest marks for this task you need to answer all questions clearly and develop them by giving details, justification and express your opinion.

5. Answers will vary. Example answers:

Sur la photo il y a un couple qui est dans une salle de cinéma. La femme et l'homme portent des lunettes car ils regardent un film en 3D. C'est peut-être une comédie, parce que tout le monde sur la photo rigole. Ils semblent très heureux. Je pense qu'ils sortent ensemble et qu'ils s'amusent bien. Je crois que l'homme a acheté le pop-corn que la femme est en train de manger. **[3]**
Personnellement, j'aime tous genres de films, sauf les films d'horreur. Je ne les regarde jamais parce qu'ils me font peur. J'aime bien les films d'amour (même si l'histoire me fait pleurer de temps en temps!) mais je préfère les comédies parce qu'elles sont amusantes et je peux les regarder avec tous mes amis. **[3]**
La dernière fois que je suis allé(e) au cinéma, c'était pour fêter l'anniversaire de mon frère. Après être arrivés, nous avons décidé de voir un film d'aventure, parce que mon frère aime les effets spéciaux et l'action. Mon père a acheté les billets et mon frère et moi ont choisi des bonbons au kiosque. Nous nous sommes très bien amusés, le film était superbe et je le conseillerais à tous. **[3]**

Examples of other questions you might be asked:

- Préfères-tu regarder les films au cinéma ou à la télé? Pourquoi?
- Voudrais-tu devenir acteur / actrice? Pourquoi (pas)?

6. Answers will vary. Example answer:

Sur la photo, il y a des jeunes femmes. Elles jouent au foot pour une équipe. Je crois qu'elles jouent un match parce que je vois une fille d'une autre équipe. Deux filles portent chacune un maillot rouge et deux autres filles, de l'autre équipe, portent chacune un maillot jaune. **[3]**

To impress an examiner, you could use a variety of words to place objects within the picture. '**Au premier plan**' (in the foreground), '**à l'arrière-plan**' (in the background), '**à la droit de**' (to the right of), '**à la gauche de**' (to the left of).

Je fais de la natation depuis l'âge de onze ans. Je vais à la piscine trois fois par semaine pour m'entrainer. J'adore nager parce que j'adore la compétition et par ailleurs, je suis membre d'un club. Ma sœur n'aime pas ça parce qu'elle dit que c'est trop fatigant! **[3]**

Notice in this example that a variety of vocabulary has been used to talk about the same activity. *La natation, nager, à la piscine*; even *s'entraîner* is a nod to the same activity, but repetition has been avoided.

Le week-end dernier j'ai fait du vélo avec mes cousins. Dimanche matin je suis allé(e) à la piscine pour faire de la natation. Depuis l'été j'évite les produits gras. Par exemple hier j'ai mangé du poisson avec des légumes et j'ai bu de l'eau minérale. J'ai bien dormi cette nuit! Huit heures et demie de sommeil! **[3]**

As well as saying what you personally do be aware that the question is asking what can be done, so some impersonal suggestions have been added at the end using 'on doit' plus the infinitive.

Examples of other questions you might be asked:
- Que font tes amis pour être en bonne santé? (F)

En général mes amis vivent sainement. Le week-end on va au McDo, mais autrement on mange à la cantine ou on apporte un casse-croûte. Mon meilleur copain s'appelle Ollie et il joue au hockey avec moi. On s'entraine deux fois par semaine et on joue un match le dimanche. Je vais au gymnase de temps en temps avec mes amis Rachel et Jack pour faire de la musculation. **[3]**

You can answer this question without using other tenses if you so wish. The key point is that you vary the structures and language that you do use. For example, here the '**on**' form of the verb has been used as well as '**il**', and you may like to use the plural form too (they – **ils / elles**). There is a good variety of language including information about how often things are done. There is little repetition.

- Qu'est-ce que tu vas faire à l'avenir pour rester en bonne santé? (H)

Answers

Je suis assez sportif et je mange assez bien en ce moment mais je peux faire plus d'efforts pour vivre sainement. L'année prochaine je vais jouer au rugby pour une équipe locale parce que mes amis y jouent. En plus j'éviterai les produits sucrés parce que les gâteaux et les biscuits, c'est ma faiblesse. Enfin je dois boire plus d'eau minérale que de sodas. **[3]**

Variety is key here. Begin with what you currently do and go into both types of future tense to indicate changes that are going to be made. You do not have to be totally truthful – it is more important to show off your language skills. This is also a good opportunity to use modal verbs such as 'I must' – **je dois** + infinitive.

7. Answers will vary. Example answers:

Sur la photo, il y a un jeune homme et une jeune femme. Ils ne se regardent pas – ils regardent leurs portables. Je crois qu'ils lisent des SMS, ou qu'ils regardent quelque chose d'intéressant sur l'internet. **[3]**

To impress an examiner, you could use **être en train de** + an infinitive (to be in the process of / in the act of…). e.g.: **Ils sont en train de regarder leurs portables**.

Les avantages de la technologie mobile sont qu'on peut rester en contact avec les autres et qu'on peut contacter quelqu'un en cas d'urgence. Cependant, il y a des inconvénients. Par exemple, il faut recharger souvent son portable et il coûte trop cher d'acheter le dernier modèle. **[3]**

Although the question only asks about the advantages, always try to present the other side of the argument, too.

Hier, j'ai envoyé des SMS à mes copains et j'ai fait des recherches en ligne, pour mes devoirs d'anglais. Ce soir, je vais télécharger la dernière chanson de mon groupe préféré, parce que c'est rapide et ce n'est pas cher. **[3]**

Again, always try to go beyond the question and show what you can do. The example above shows how to answer using the perfect tense, then uses the near future tense, to refer to future plans.

Examples of other questions you might be asked:

• Penses-tu que certaines personnes passent trop de temps sur leur portable?
• Est-il interdit d'utiliser son portable dans ton collège? Que penses-tu de cette règle?

8. Answers will vary. Example answers:
   a) Ma sœur est assez grande et mince. Elle a les cheveux courts, bruns et raides et les yeux bleus. Elle est très gentille, mais parfois elle est un peu impatiente. **[5]**
   b) Je m'entends très bien avec mon père, parce qu'il est toujours aimable et très généreux. Il n'est jamais fâché contre moi. **[5]**
   c) Je suis allé(e) au cinéma avec mes parents. Nous avons vu un film de science-fiction qui était assez intéressant. Ensuite, nous sommes allés au restaurant où nous avons mangé de la pizza. C'était délicieux! **[5]**
   d) Mon meilleur copain est petit et un peu gros. Il a les cheveux roux et les yeux verts. Il est plus intelligent que moi, mais je suis le plus sportif. **[5]**
   e) On a beaucoup de choses en commun. Il me fait beaucoup rire, car nous avons le même sens de l'humour. On ne se dispute jamais. **[5]**
   f) Le week-end prochain, je vais retrouver mes amis en ville. On va faire les magasins et après, on va jouer au bowling. Le soir, on va rentrer chez moi, où on va manger des hamburgers et on va écouter de la musique dans ma chambre. **[5]**

The general conversation questions will try to find out whether you can use past, present and future tenses correctly. Make sure you know all your tenses really well. Also, try to show that you can use other parts of the verb, (not just '**je**'), such as '**on**' and '**nous**'.
Make sure you include opinions!

9. Answers will vary. Example answers:
   a) Mon collège s'appelle Carlton Academy et il est assez grand car il y a 900 élèves. La directrice s'appelle Madame Johnson. Il y a un grand terrain de sport, une piscine et 50 salles de classe. Dans chaque salle de classe il y a un tableau et quelques ordinateurs. **[5]**
   b) Ma matière préférée est l'informatique parce que j'adore les ordinateurs et que le professeur, Monsieur Jordan, est très drôle. Je suis fort en langues aussi, surtout en français. Je pense que les langues sont très utiles. Je n'aime pas la physique parce que le prof est trop sévère et qu'il y a trop de devoirs. **[5]**
   c) À mon avis, la journée n'est pas trop longue en comparaison avec la journée scolaire française! Le car de ramassage arrive vers huit heures vingt et les cours commencent à neuf heures. Il y a cinq cours de soixante minutes par jour ainsi qu'une récré à onze heures et la pause déjeuner à une heures et quart. Moi, je mange à la cantine parce que la restauration n'est pas trop mauvaise. On finit à trois heures et demie et je rentre à la maison à seize heures. **[5]**
   d) À mon avis, il y a trop de règles! On n'a pas le droit d'avoir son téléphone portable allumé en cours et le chewing-gum est interdit. On doit porter un uniforme mais ça, j'aime bien parce qu'on n'a pas besoin de choisir ses vêtements chaque matin. **[5]**
   e) Je suis en train de préparer mes examens et puis, l'année prochaine je vais aller au lycée pour faire des 'A-levels'. J'espère réussir mes examens parce que je veux étudier les langues et l'informatique et qu'il faut avoir des bonnes notes. Il y a beaucoup de pression pour les élèves parce qu'on ne veut pas échouer à ses examens. **[5]**
   f) J'ai envie d'aller à la fac parce que je veux avoir un boulot où je pourrai gagner beaucoup d'argent! Après avoir fini mes examens, je prendrai une année sabbatique et je voyagerai parce que je ne suis jamais allé(e) en Australie et que je voudrais y aller avant de trouver un emploi. **[5]**

10. Answers will vary. Example answers:

a) Généralement je préfère plutôt les vacances actives comme les vacances à la montagne pour faire du ski en hiver ou en été on peut faire des randonnées. Je pense que les vacances actives sont plus revitalisantes que les vacances au bord de la plage. **[5]**

b) Personnellement je ne suis jamais allé(e) en vacances avec mes amis, seulement avec mes parents. Je pense que partir en vacances avec ses amis doit être très amusant puisqu'il n'y a pas de règles. Cependant j'aime passer mes vacances avec ma famille car on s'entend bien et aussi mes parents paient tout pour moi en vacances! **[5]**

c) Mes dernières vacances c'était il y a deux ans je suis allé(e) en Normandie avec ma famille. La Normandie se trouve dans l'ouest de la France et c'est près de la mer. En Normandie j'ai pu faire beaucoup d'activités comme de l'escalade et de la randonnée. J'ai trouvé la région formidable et j'aimerais y retourner un jour. **[5]**

d) En Normandie, nous avons fait du camping et c'était vraiment génial. Le camping se trouvait très près de la mer et près de petits magasins où j'allais acheter du pain tous les matins. Le camping était très bien équipé, avec une piscine et une salle pour les jeunes. Le seul problème, c'est qu'il y avait trop de monde. **[5]**

e) Je ne sais pas vraiment. Ma mère dit qu'elle voudrait aller dans un pays chaud mais mon père n'est pas d'accord puisqu'il ne supporte pas trop le soleil. Moi, j'aimerais retourner en Normandie mais mon père n'aime pas aller deux fois au même endroit. Je pense que nous resterons peut-être en Angleterre pour rendre visite à notre famille mais aussi pour profiter de notre pays! **[5]**

Index

Collins

French with Audio

AQA GCSE Revision

French
with Audio

AQA GCSE Revision

French

with Audio

AQA GCSE

Workbook

Clive Bell, Karine Harrington,
Robert Pike and Vanessa Salter

Contents

Contents

Visit our website at **www.collins.co.uk/collinsgcserevision** to download the audio material for the Listening Paper on pages 180–191 of this workbook.

Me, My Family and Friends

My Family, My Friends & Marriage and Partnerships

1 **Choisissez la bonne réponse à chaque question dans la case. Il y a quatre mots de trop.** Choose the correct answer to each question from the box. There are four words too many.

a) Qui est le père de votre mère? ....

b) Qui est la sœur de votre père? ....

c) Qui est le fils de votre frère? ....

d) Qui est le mari de votre sœur? ....

e) Qui est la fille de votre oncle? ....

f) Qui est la deuxième femme de votre père? ....

mon oncle	mon grand-père	ma grand-mère	ma tante	mon neveu
ma nièce	mon beau-frère	ma cousine	mon beau-père	ma belle-mère

[6 marks]

2 **Complétez les phrases pour décrire la personnalité de chaque personne. Utilisez la bonne forme des adjectifs dans la case.** Complete the sentences to describe the personality of each person. Use the correct form of the adjectives from the box.

Il est toujours .... et ....

Elle est toujours .... et ....

Il n'est jamais .... ou ....

Elle n'est jamais .... ou ....

agaçant(e)	aimable	de bonne humeur	de mauvaise humeur
égoïste	généreux / généreuse	gentil / gentille	heureux / heureuse
méchant(e)	patient(e)	pénible	sage	sympa	têtu(e)	triste

[8 marks for logical use of adjectives and correct agreement]

3 **Recopiez et complétez ces phrases sur votre famille et vous.** Copy and complete these sentences about your family and you.

a) Je m'entends bien avec _____ parce qu'il / elle est _____ .

b) Je ne m'entends pas très bien avec _____ , puisqu'il / elle _____ .

c) Je me dispute souvent avec _____ , car _____ .

[6 marks. Words for 'my' must be correct and adjectives must agree.]

4 **Faites des lignes pour relier les deux parties de chaque phrase.** Draw lines to connect the two halves of each sentence.

Ma meilleure copine est mince et …

Elle a les yeux noisette et les cheveux …

On se connaît depuis …

Elle est toujours honnête et elle n'est jamais …

On a beaucoup de choses en commun. On aime …

En plus, on a le même sens de l'humour, donc elle …

On se retrouve en ville tous les week-ends et on …

la même musique et les mêmes films.

me fait toujours rire.

un peu plus grande que moi.

jalouse ou fâchée contre moi.

noirs, courts et raides.

fait les magasins ensemble.

sept ans et on s'entend très bien ensemble.

[7 marks]

5 **Écrivez une description de votre meilleur(e) ami(e). Attention à l'accord des adjectifs!** Write a description of your best friend. Take care with adjective agreement!

[10 marks]

6 **Complétez les phrases, puis écrivez pour chaque phrase: P (pour le mariage) ou C (contre le mariage).** Complete the sentences, then write for each sentence: P (for marriage) or C (against marriage).

a) Je préférerais _____ célibataire.

b) Je voudrais me _____ un jour.

c) Le mariage se _____ souvent par un divorce.

d) À mon avis, le mariage, c'est _____ démodé.

e) C'est mieux pour les _____ si on est mariés.

f) Il vaut mieux habiter _____ au lieu de se marier.

[12 marks: 6 marks for completing the sentences correctly and 6 for labelling them correctly P or C.]

Me, My Family and Friends

Social Media & Mobile Technology

1 **Complétez les phrases, en utilisant les bons verbes de la case. Il y a trois verbes de trop.** Complete the sentences, using the correct verbs from the box. There are three verbs too many.

a) Je _____ beaucoup de temps en ligne. (I spend a lot of time online.)

b) Je _____ sur mes sites web préférés. (I go on to my favourite websites.)

c) J'_____ et je _____ des messages. (I send and I receive messages.)

d) Je _____ des recherches pour mes devoirs. (I do research for my homework.)

e) Je _____ des photos en ligne. (I upload photos.)

f) Je _____ sur le clavier, je _____ sur la souris et

j'_____ des documents sur l'imprimante. (I type on the keyboard, I click the mouse and I print documents on the printer.)

clique	envoie	fais	imprime	mets	passe
reçois	surfe	tape	tchatte	télécharge	vais

[9 marks]

2 **Écrivez cinq phrases sur ce que vous faites en ligne, en utilisant les mots ci-dessous.** Write five sentences about what you do online, using the words below.

Exemple:

Chaque jour, je vais sur mes sites web préférés.

Chaque jour,	
Souvent,	
Quelquefois,	
Une fois par semaine,	
De temps en temps,	

[5 marks]

3 **Mettez les mots dans le bon ordre, pour créer un poster sur la sécurité en ligne.** Put the words into the correct order, to create a poster about online safety.

a) jamais ne détails faut Il partager personnels ses

b) installer Il un anti-virus faut logiciel

c) ne pas inconnus faut des communiquer avec Il

d) révéler faut ne passe jamais son mot de Il

e) régulièrement faut passe changer Il son de mot

Protégez-vous en ligne!
✓ _____
• _____
• _____
✗ _____
• _____
• _____
• _____

[5 marks]

4 **Lisez les opinions sur la technologie portable et répondez aux questions.** Read the opinions about mobile technology and answer the questions.

> Avec mon portable, je peux toujours contacter quelqu'un en cas d'urgence. **Nolan**
>
> Parfois, quand on a besoin d'appeler quelqu'un, il n'y a pas de réseau. **Yasmine**
>
> La technologie change trop vite et ça coûte cher d'acheter la dernière version. **Alizée**
>
> J'utilise mon portable pour organiser des sorties et des rendez-vous avec mes amis. **Hugo**
>
> C'est pratique, parce qu'on peut faire des achats en ligne. **William**
>
> Certaines personnes passent trop de temps sur leur portable – et elles parlent trop fort! **Lola**
>
> J'ai téléchargé mes chansons préférées sur mon portable, donc je peux les écouter quand je veux. **Karim**
>
> Il faut recharger trop souvent son portable. Ma batterie est toujours à plat! **Mélissa**

a) Who likes listening to music on a phone? _____

b) Who thinks it's expensive to upgrade to the latest model? _____

c) Who finds a mobile phone useful in an emergency? _____

d) Who complains about a phone running out of power? _____

e) Who thinks some people spend too much time on their phone? _____

f) Who uses their phone to arrange social events? _____

g) Who complains that there is sometimes no network coverage? _____

h) Who finds a phone useful for internet shopping? _____

[8 marks]

5 **Traduisez ces phrases en français.** Translate these sentences into French.

a) Every day, I send text messages to my friends.

_____

b) I use my phone to download and listen to music.

_____

c) Yesterday, I bought the latest model, but it was expensive.

_____

d) Tomorrow, I am going to do some research for my homework.

_____

[8 marks]

Free-time Activities

Music & Cinema and TV

1 **Reliez les questions et les réponses.** Match the questions and answers:

Écoutes-tu souvent la musique?	Ma chanteuse anglaise préférée c'est Adele. Elle a une voix superbe et elle écrit des chansons fabuleuses.
Quel genre de musique préfères-tu?	Oui, l'été dernier j'avais la chance de voir mon groupe favori en tournée. C'était magnifique!
Est-ce que tu as un chanteur ou une chanteuse préféré(e)?	Parce que j'adore les mélodies et en plus, même si les paroles sont tristes, ses chansons me détendent.
Pourquoi aimes-tu ses chansons?	Je m'intéresse à tous styles de musique, mais le genre que j'aime le plus, c'est la musique pop.
Es-tu déjà allé(e) à un concert ou un festival de musique?	Oui, je télécharge la musique et je l'écoute sur mon lecteur MP3 ou mon portable tous les jours.

[5 marks]

2 **Écrivez cinq phrases. Utilisez un groupe de mots de chaque colonne.** Make five sentences using a phrase from each column.

Exemple: Je préfère le hip-hop parce que le rythme me plaît.

Je préfère J'adore J'aime mieux	la musique pop l'électro le hip-hop la musique classique	parce que	la mélodie le rythme	me fait sourire me plaît me détend
			les paroles les chansons	me rendent heureux me font rire
Je (ne) m'intéresse (pas) au Je (ne) suis (pas) fana du	reggae jazz vieux rock	à cause	du rythme vif de la mélodie vive des paroles profondes des chansons monotones	

....

....

....

....

[5 marks]

3 **Remplissez les blancs. Utilisez les mots donnés.** Fill in the blanks with the words from the box:

La musique _____ un rôle important dans la vie de ma famille. Mes parents se
sont _____ à un festival de musique _____ mon père jouait
dans un groupe. Nous avons _____ écouté de la musique chez nous et on n'a
_____ choisi un genre préféré. Mes sœurs _____ dans une chorale
mais mon frère aîné aime _____ jouer du violon dans un orchestre. Mon père joue
toujours de la guitare, _____ ma mère dit que ses chansons sont démodées.

chantent	joue	même si	où	rencontrés	mieux	jamais	toujours

[8 marks]

4 **Complétez les phrases.** Choose types of films and TV programmes for your own likes and dislikes. (Choose from the list provided or write your own.) Then choose from each column to give reasons for your opinions to complete the sentences below.

films d'horreur
dessins animés
feuilletons
comédies
documentaires
jeux télévisés

parce qu'ils	sont	amusant(e)s barbant(e)s tristes éducatifs/éducatives
car ils		
même s'ils		
parce qu'ils	me font	rire
car ils		pleurer
même s'ils		peur

a) Personnellement, je préfère les _____

b) Quelquefois j'aime regarder les _____

c) Je ne regarde jamais les _____

d) Le genre de films que j'aime le plus, c'est _____

e) Mes émissions préférées à la télé sont _____

[10 marks]

5 **Trouvez les phrases.** Unscramble the sentences and write them correctly:

a) Le pendant en film a lieu Allemagne la guerre

b) s'agit fille veut sa famille Il qui retrouver d'une

c) éliminent s'agit des les qui soldats Il adversaires

[3 marks]

Free-time Activities

Food and Eating Out, Sport & Customs and Festivals

1 **Lisez la carte et trouvez les mots en français.**
Read the menu and find the French for:

a) plate of cold meats **b)** tuna marinated in
spices **c)** duck pâté **d)** peppered beef steak
e) fried vegetables **f)** lamb chop **g)** garlic-
sautéed green beans **h)** fillet of veal **i)** roasted
figs **j)** coconut

[10 marks]

2 **Répondez aux questions suivantes en anglais.**
Answer the following questions:

a) What is included in the menu price of
€39.00?

....

b) What is NOT included in the price?

....

c) When is this menu NOT available?

....

d) What is the maximum group size?

....

[4 marks]

3 **Écrivez une conversation 'Au Restaurant'.**
Utilisez la carte. Prepare a conversation in a
restaurant using the menu.

[4 marks]

Entrée + Plat + Dessert: 39,00€

(Menu hors boissons, valable pour un
maximum de dix personnes, valable tous les
jours – sauf jours de fêtes)

les entrées

Assiette de charcuterie

Thon mariné aux épices

**Foie gras de canard, chutney oignon rouge-
gingembre**

Carpaccio d'ananas et fruits exotiques

les plats

Entrecôte de bœuf poivré, poêlée de légumes
Côtelette d'agneau, haricots verts sautés à l'ail
Filet de veau, gratin de pomme de terre

Fricassée de champignons, riz maison

les desserts

Plateau de fromages
Figues rôties, crème glacée à la vanille
Panna cotta à la noix de coco
Crêpes flambées

---

4 **Traduisez les phrases en anglais.** Translate the sentences into English:

a) Quand j'étais plus jeune, j'avais envie de faire de l'équitation.

....

b) Auparavant ma sœur aimait faire des randonnées à la montagne.

....

c) De nos jours elle est amateur des sports d'hiver.

....

d) Avant je faisais du VTT tous les samedis, mais maintenant je n'ai plus de temps libre.

....

e) Nous voudrions essayer les sports extrêmes, même s'ils sont un peu dangereux!

....

[5 marks]

5 **Traduisez en français.** Translate into French:

a) I play volleyball at the sports centre.

    ....

b) I used to go to the swimming pool three times a week.

    ....

c) When I was younger I wanted to go skate-boarding.

    ....

d) Before, I used to go fishing every weekend, but now I prefer team sports.

    ....

e) We would like to try water sports.

    ....

[5 marks]

6 **Écrivez quatre phrases. Donnez vos opinions sur les fêtes. Utilisez les bouts de phrases donnés.**

Write four sentences giving your opinions on festivals and celebrations. Use the phrases in the box.

Exemple: Selon moi, pour faire la fête, il est important d'être en famille et avec des amis.

Pour célébrer Noel / Ramadan Le jour de la fête nationale Pour fêter un mariage Pendant les fêtes traditionnelles Pendant les jours fériés	je pense qu'il faut je crois qu'il est important d(e) je pense qu'on (ne) doit (pas) l'essentiel est d(e) selon moi, il (ne) faut (pas) à mon avis, on doit il n'est pas important de	aller à l'église / à la mosquée chanter des chansons traditionnelles donner des cadeaux féliciter les nouveaux mariés danser dans les rues recevoir des cadeaux manger des repas traditionnels

    ....

    ....

    ....

    ....

[4 marks]

Environment and Social Issues

At Home, Where I Live & Town or Country?

1 **Trouvez la bonne réponse à chaque question.** Match the questions and answers.

1. Tu habites en ville ou à la campagne?	a) J'adore vivre en ville mais je voudrais déménager à la campagne.
2. Qu'est-ce qu'il y a dans ta ville?	b) À l'étage, il y a quatre pièces: la salle de bains, la chambre de mes parents, la chambre de ma sœur et la mienne.
3. Où voudrais-tu habiter?	c) Il y a un centre commercial et une grande bibliothèque.
4. Comment est la vie à la campagne?	d) Il n'y a pas assez de distractions pour les jeunes. On a besoin d'un cinéma.
5. Il y a combien de chambres dans ta maison?	e) Moi, j'habite à la campagne.
6. De quoi est-ce que ta ville a besoin?	f) C'est trop calme et on doit se déplacer en voiture pour voir ses amis.

[6 marks]

2 **Complétez les phrases, en utilisant les bons mots de la case. Il y a trois mots de trop.** Complete the sentences, using the correct words from the box. There are three words too many.

a) J'habite dans une _____ mitoyenne.

b) Il y _____ pièces.

c) Le salon est à _____ de l'entrée.

d) Dans ma chambre j'ai une _____ armoire.

e) Je _____ ma chambre tous les week-ends.

f) Il y a des posters au _____ .

petit	grande
étagère	maison
huit	nettoie
déménage	côté
mur	

[6 marks]

3 **Écrivez cinq phrases sur ce que vous avez fait en centre-ville, en utilisant les verbes ci-dessous.** Write five sentences about what you did in town, using the verbs below.

Exemple: J'ai perdu mon portefeuille.

dépenser	manger	perdre	acheter	essayer

_____

_____

_____

_____

[10 marks: 5 marks for conjugated verbs and 5 marks for full correct sentences]

4 **Lisez les opinions sur la vie en ville et répondez aux questions.** Read the opinions about life in town and answer the questions.

> Là où j'habite il y a trop de circulation.
>
> **Georges**

> Je voudrais déménager en ville parce que c'est plus animé qu'à la campagne.
>
> **Karine**

> La ville est très bruyante et les rues sont sales. Non merci!
>
> **Mélissa**

> Il y a un grand choix d'activités.
>
> **Karim**

> On a besoin d'un centre commercial mais dans l'ensemble, ce n'est.
>
> **Simon**

> J'aimerais y habiter parce que les transports en commun sont plus fréquents.
>
> **Benoît**

a) Who points out something that their town needs? _____

b) Who is happy with the range of things to do? _____

c) Who comments on the traffic in town? _____

d) Who would like to move somewhere more lively? _____

e) Who would like to live where there is more regular public transport? _____

f) Who thinks the streets are dirty in town? _____

[6 marks]

5 **Traduisez ces phrases en français.** Translate these sentences into French.

a) My bedroom is always clean.

_____

b) Upstairs there are four bedrooms.

_____

c) The bathroom is found opposite the office.

_____

d) There is no market or shopping centre but the parking is free.

_____

e) There is more traffic in town than in the countryside.

_____

[10 marks: 2 per question. Award 1 for communication, 1 for precision.]

Environment and Social Issues

Charity and Voluntary Work & Healthy and Unhealthy Living

1 **Écrivez cinq phrases en utilisant un choix de chaque colonne.** Make five sentences using a choice from each column:

Exemple: Je voudrais travailler comme infirmière.

Je voudrais	aider	à des personnes âgées
J'aimerais	livrer	des repas
	rendre visite	des médicaments
	travailler	comme infirmier(ière)
	faire	des collectes d'argent
		les SDF

[5 marks]

2 **Traduisez en anglais chacune des phrases que vous avez écrites.** Translate each sentence that you wrote into English.

Exemple: Je voudrais travailler comme infirmière. – I would like to work as a nurse.

[10 marks: 2 per question. Award 1 for communication, 1 for precision.]

3 **Mettez les mots dans le bon ordre.** Put the words into the correct order.

a) faut   manger   sainement   Il _____ .

b) forme   mange   parce que   Je   la   garde   je   bien _____ .

c) vais   de   faire   un   essayer   Je   régime _____ .

[3 marks]

4 **Faites les paires pour écrire des phrases.** Match up the sentence parts to make full sentences.

1. Je dors	a) bonne santé.
2. Je m'entraîne deux	b) bien.
3. Je mange les	c) aliments sains.
4. Il faut se détendre	d) fois par semaine.
5. Le tabac	e) peut tuer.
6. Il faut	f) éviter les produits malsains.
7. Je suis en	g) pour éviter le stress.

[7 marks]

5 **Lisez les opinions et remarques sur la charité et le travail bénévole et répondez aux questions.** Read the opinions and comments about charity and voluntary work and answer the questions.

Tous les week-ends, je distribue de l'eau potable aux SDF. **Sandrine**

Après avoir fini le lycée je vais voyager en Afrique pour y apporter mon aide. **Loïc**

Je surveille des enfants qui jouent au basket dans un club. Comme ça je fais quelque chose d'utile. **Valérie**

On a livré des médicaments ce week-end. C'était fatigant, mais c'est important. **Paul**

a) What did Paul do this weekend? _____

b) What does Loïc intend to do after finishing his A-levels? _____

c) What does Sandrine give out to homeless people? _____

[3 marks]

6 **Traduisez les phrases en français.** Translate the sentences into French.

a) I stay in good shape because I sleep well. _____

b) I don't eat unhealthy products. _____

c) It is necessary to eat well. _____

d) She always eats a balanced diet. _____

e) My mother has stopped smoking. _____

[10 marks: 2 per question. Award 1 for communication, 1 for precision]

Environment and Social Issues

The Environment & Poverty and Insecurity

1 **Traduisez les phrases en anglais.** Translate the following sentences into English.

a) On ne doit pas gaspiller nos ressources naturelles.

.... [3 marks]

b) Il est important de protéger notre environnement en recyclant davantage.

.... [5 marks]

c) Je pense qu'on devrait encourager tout le monde à trier ses déchets.

.... [6 marks]

2 **Traduisez les phrases en français.** Translate the following sentences into French.

a) I think that it is important to protect our natural resources. [4 marks]

....

b) We should protect our environment by sorting out our rubbish. [5 marks]

....

c) There are more and more people who waste energy. [6 marks]

....

3 **Lisez les résultats d'une enquête sur ce qui inquiète le plus les gens dans leur ville.** Read the results of an online survey about what people are most worried about in their towns.

Quel est le problème le plus inquiétant dans votre ville?	
Le chômage	15%
Les voyous	20%
Les bandes	5%
Les sans-abris	25%
La pauvreté	10%
Le recyclage	5%

What percentage of people are the most worried about …?

a) problems with the environment ☐

b) people who don't have enough money ☐

c) people who do not have a home ☐

d) people with no jobs ☐

e) people who hang about in groups ☐

[5 marks]

4 **Remettez les mots dans le bon ordre et traduisez les phrases en anglais.** Unjumble the sentences and translate them into English.

a) de plus en plus de / personnes / il y a / sont/ dans ma ville / qui / au chômage

....

....

b) augmente / le nombre de / sans-abris / dans mon village / rapidement

....

....

c) de plus en plus de / dans ma ville / malheureusement / voit/ depuis / pauvreté / on / peu

....

....

d) tout le monde / des bandes / dans mon quartier /un souci / l'augmentation / est / pour

....

....

[8 marks: 4 marks for correct order, 4 marks for correct translation]

5 **Remplissez les blancs avec les mots de l'encadré ci-dessous. Seulement huit seront utilisés.** Fill in the gaps with the correct words from the box below. Only eight words will be needed.

1. après	2. combattre	3. maintenant
4. avant	5. passive	6. était
7. davantage	8. recyclage	9. travail
10. est	11. active	12. chômage
13. sans-abris	14. moins	15. encourager

[a] ....] dans ma ville il y a de plus en plus de personnes qui sont au
[b] ....] et qui sont sans domicile. [c] ....] le
problème le plus inquiétant [d] ....] les bandes de voyous qui volaient
dans les petits magasins. La police dans ma ville a été très [e] ....] et a mis
fin à ce problème. Malheureusement le chômage et les [f] ....] inquiètent
[g] ....] de nos jours et j'espère que le gouvernement va faire quelque
chose pour [h] ....] ces problèmes.

[8 marks]

Travel and Tourism

Travel and Tourism 1, 2 and 3

1 Mes vacances

Lisez les phrases suivantes et décidez qui dit quoi. Read the following sentences and decide who says what.

Zoe **Normalement pendant mes vacances je loge dans un hôtel quatre étoiles.**

Isidor **Il y a deux ans je suis allé en vacances avec mes amis en Suisse et nous sommes restés dans une auberge de jeunesse.**

Martine **J'aimerais bien loger dans un chalet à la montagne un jour – ça doit être très relaxant!**

Karim **D'habitude on reste chez ma tante qui habite au bord de la mer.**

Write their names in the spaces.

Who…	
1…spends their holiday with a relative?	
2…is talking about a past holiday?	
3…has visited Switzerland?	
4…has been on holiday without their parents?	
5…goes to the seaside?	

[5 marks]

2 Des problèmes en vacances

Ces cinq personnes ont eu des problèmes en vacances. Lisez leurs propos et décidez de ce dont elles parlent. These five people had problems during their holidays. Read what they are saying and decide what they are talking about.

Sylvie **On a attendu trois heures à l'aéroport! C'était vraiment pénible!**

Martin **Ils ont cassé la fenêtre et ils ont volé nos passeports!**

Farida **Mes vacances ont mal commencé car j'ai dû acheter de nouveaux vêtements parce que nos valises ne sont pas arrivées!**

Hugo **La nourriture était vraiment dégoûtante et les chambres très sales. On n'y retournera pas!**

Laure **J'ai été malade du début à la fin. J'avais mal au cœur car la mer était très agitée!**

Write their names in the spaces.

1. lost suitcases	
2. a bad hotel	
3. a disastrous cruise	
4. a delay	
5. a robbery	

[5 marks]

3 L'Hôtel de la Mer

Lisez cette brochure sur L'Hôtel de la Mer. Read the following leaflet about L'Hôtel de la Mer.

L'Hôtel de la Mer

Situé à cinq cents mètres de la mer.

Cinquante chambres disponibles sur trois étages, avec douche et vue sur la mer.

Piscine chauffée en plein air, ouverte de 9 heures à 20 heures tous les jours (fermeture à 18 heures les jours fériés).

Notre restaurant à thèmes avec terrasse est au deuxième étage (entrée au rez-de-chaussée et accès par ascenseur)

Les animaux sont interdits dans notre hôtel.

Ces phrases sont-elles vraies ou fausses? Are these statements true or false?

a) All rooms have a sea view.

b) There is an indoor swimming pool.

c) The swimming pool closes at 8pm every day all year round.

d) Pets are not allowed.

e) The restaurant is on the ground floor.

[5 marks]

4 **Traduisez en anglais.** Translate into English:

a) L'année prochaine, je voudrais loger dans une villa.

....

b) Normalement je vais en vacances à la montagne avec ma famille pendant deux semaines.

....

c) L'été dernier j'ai passé un mois dans une auberge de jeunesse à la campagne.

....

d) Il y a deux ans nous avons passé nos vacances dans un camping 3 étoiles au bord de la mer.

....

e) D'habitude j'aime me lever très tard car j'aime bien faire la grasse matinée en vacances.

....

[5 marks]

Studies and Employment

My Studies and Life at School

1 **Lisez l'e-mail et écrivez les matières dans l'ordre qu'ils sont mentionnés. Attention, il y a trois matières de trop.** Read the email and write the subjects in the order that they are mentioned. Be careful, there are three subjects too many.

> Le lundi, je commence par deux heures de français. Puis c'est la récré pendant vingt minutes. À onze heures on va au gymnase pour l'EPS, et j'adore ça parce que je suis sportive. Après le déjeuner, on a un cours de dessin suivi par la chimie. Et enfin on a une heure d'allemand. Ça fait beaucoup, hein?

PE	Mathematics	RE	Art	German	French	Chemistry	IT

[5 marks]

2 **Lisez les opinions au sujet des matières scolaires. Répondez aux questions ci-dessous.** Read the opinions about school subjects. Answer the questions below.

> Je trouve l'instruction civique facile. J'aime bien ça.

Franck

> Ma matière préférée c'est le dessin parce que c'est concret et que le prof est marrant.

Wendy

> Je suis assez faible en maths, ce qui est embêtant car j'adore ça.

Bronwyn

> Je n'aime pas les langues vivantes sauf l'anglais. Je suis plus forte en chimie et biologie.

Amélie

> Mon copain, Richard, est très fort en histoire-géo, mais moi, je suis assez nul.

Yann

> Mon professeur dit que je suis très forte en anglais, mais je pense que je suis plutôt faible.

Enid

a) Whose friend is better at history and geography than he? .... [1]

b) Who is stronger in science than in languages? .... [1]

c) Why does Franck like citizenship? .... [1]

d) Why does Enid disagree with her English teacher? .... [2]

e) Why is Bronwyn frustrated by maths? .... [2]

f) Why does Wendy like art? .... [2]

[9 marks]

3 **Complétez l'e-mail en choisissant un mot pour chaque trou. Attention, il y a trois mots de trop.**
Complete the email by choosing a word for each gap. There are three words too many.

Salut, Joseph!

Merci pour ton e-mail. Oui je vais au collège, et je suis en _____. J'aime bien l'école et ma matière préférée c'est l'histoire-géo. Je n' _____ pas l'EPS parce que je ne suis pas sportif.

On _____ à huit heures quinze, et on a cinq _____ par jour. Il y a une récré de vingt minutes et une _____ déjeuner d'une heure et demie. Je vais à l'école en _____ scolaire et je mange à la cantine.

Il y a un règlement, bien sûr. Le chewing-gum et le _____ ne sont pas autorisés et on n'a pas le droit d'avoir son téléphone portable en cours. Pourtant on ne _____ pas d'uniforme scolaire comme en Angleterre!

Bon, je te dis au revoir parce que je dois finir mes devoirs!

À bientôt

Kévin

interdit	commence	porte	car	école	pause	maquillage	seconde	voiture
aime	cours							

[8 marks]

4 **Traduisez ces phrases en anglais.** Translate the sentences into English.

a) Cet été je vais passer mes examens.

_____

b) Si on ne comprend pas il faut demander à un professeur.

_____

c) J'apporte mon propre repas à l'école.

_____

d) Fabrice doit redoubler car il n'a pas réussi ses examens.

_____

e) Il y a trop de pression sur les élèves.

_____

[10 marks: 2 per question. Award 1 for communication, 1 for precision.]

Studies and Employment

Education Post-16 & Career Choices and Ambitions

1 **Relier entre elles les deux parties de chaque phrase.** Match up the sentence parts.

1. J'ai laissé	a) aller à la fac l'année prochaine.
2. J'ai envie	b) tomber la technologie.
3. Cette année	c) vais continuer mes études.
4. Je viens de	d) passer mes examens.
5. L'année prochaine je	e) je suis en première.
6. Je voudrais	f) de voyager en Asie.

[6 marks]

2 **Lisez les projets des jeunes. Répondez aux questions.** Read the teenagers' plans. Answer the questions.

Moi, je n'ai aucune intention de continuer mes études.
Justine

Après une année sabbatique j'ai l'intention de faire un apprentissage.
David

Je mets de l'argent de côté pour faire un tour du monde.
Simone

J'aimerais étudier les langues parce que je veux être journaliste. Aller à la fac? Je ne sais pas encore.
Rachel

Je ne sais pas quoi faire mais j'ai envie de gagner beaucoup d'argent!
Farah

Je voudrais étudier les sciences à la fac.
Lisa

a) Who is going to do an apprenticeship? _____

b) Who is saving money? _____

c) Who does not know what to do? _____

d) Who wants to study languages? _____

e) Who plans to end their studies at the end of the year? _____

f) Who has decided to go to university? _____

[6 marks]

3 **Traduisez ces phrases en français.** Translate these sentences into French.

a) I would like to go to university next year. _____

b) I dropped art last year. _____

c) I intend to travel when I leave school. _____

d) I am going to go to university. _____

e) I have no idea what to do. _____

[10 marks: 2 per question. Award 1 for communication, 1 for precision.]

4 **Lisez l'e-mail et répondez aux questions.** Read the email and answer the questions.

Je rêve d'avoir un boulot intéressant et varié, mais je ne sais pas encore ce que je veux faire. Mon père est plombier et il adore travailler à son compte. Il dit que c'est un emploi enrichissant, et il gagne suffisamment d'argent. Ma mère est la patronne d'une petite entreprise qui fabrique des gâteaux et des pâtisseries.

Moi, j'ai envie de voyager pour mon métier, et je veux gagner beaucoup d'argent. Je rêve d'avoir une grande maison donnant sur la plage et, si possible, j'habiterai aux États-Unis. J'aurai une famille, un avion et je serai vedette de musique ou de cinéma.

Inès

a) Name two features of Inès' dream job. _____ [2]

b) What does her father do? _____ [1]

c) Why does he like his job? _____ [2]

d) What role does her mother play in the company for which she works? _____ [1]

e) Where would Inès like her house to be? _____ [2]

[8 marks]

5 **Écrivez un court paragraphe sur vos projets en utilisant les phrases dans la case.** Write a short paragraph about your future plans by using the phrases in the box.

J'ai l'intention de…	Je voudrais…	Je vais…	Je serai…	J'aurai…
Je ferai…	Je gagnerai…	J'habiterai…		

_____

_____

_____

_____

[10 marks. Award 5 for communication, 5 for precision.]

Grammar 1

Gender, Plurals and Articles & Adjectives

Gender, Plurals and Articles

1 Complétez le tableau en français. Complete the grid in French.

Singular	Plural
un enfant (a child)	des _____ (children)
une _____ (a flower)	**des fleurs** (flowers)
un _____ (an animal)	**des animaux** (animals)
un chapeau (a hat)	des _____ (hats)
un _____ (a game)	**des jeux** (games)
un Français (a French person)	des _____ (French people)

[6 marks]

2 Complétez ces phrases, en utilisant la bonne forme de l'article (*un / une / des; le / la / l' / les*), selon l'exemple. Complete these sentences, using the correct form of the article (*un / une / des; le / la / l' / les*), following the example.

Exemple: **Dans ma ville, il y a <u>un</u> cinéma. <u>Le</u> cinéma est dans le centre-ville.**

a) Dans ma ville, il y a _____ piscine. _____ piscine est dans le centre sportif.

b) Dans mon village, il y a _____ café. _____ café est tout près de ma maison.

c) Dans la rue où j'habite, il y a _____ magasins. _____ magasins sont utiles.

d) Dans notre village, il y a _____ église. _____ église est très vieille et historique.

e) Dans ma ville, il y a _____ centre commercial. _____ centre commercial est énorme.

f) Dans le quartier où j'habite, il y a _____ restaurants, mais _____ restaurants sont trop chers.

[12 marks]

3 Complétez les phrases avec *du / de la / de l'* ou *des*. Complete the sentences with *du / de la / de l'* or *des*.

a) Tu veux _____ glace? Elle est vraiment délicieuse.

b) Tu veux _____ fromage? Il a très bon goût.

c) Tu veux _____ carottes? Elles sont bonnes pour la santé.

d) Tu veux _____ eau? Il faut boire beaucoup d'eau.

e) Tu veux _____ gâteau? Il est au chocolat!

f) Tu veux _____ raisins? Ils ne coûtent pas trop chers.

[6 marks]

Adjectives, Comparatives and Superlatives

4 **Complétez le texte avec les bons adjectifs possessifs de la case.** Complete the text with the correct possessive adjectives from the box.

J'habite avec _____ père, _____ mère et mes deux frères. Notre maison est assez moderne, mais _____ jardin est très petit. Je partage ma chambre avec mon frère cadet: mon lit est dans le coin et _____ lit est devant la fenêtre. Mon frère aîné a la meilleure chambre: _____ chambre est plus grande que la mienne. Nous avons aussi deux chiens. _____ chiens s'appellent Boule et Bill. _____ parents travaillent pour la même entreprise. _____ bureau n'est pas loin de notre maison. Et toi? Il y a combien de personnes dans _____ famille? Où travaillent _____ parents?

mon	leur	nos	sa	son	notre	mes	ma	ta	tes

[10 marks]

5 **Ajoutez la bonne forme de l'adjectif à chaque phrase. Il va avant ou après le substantif?** Add the correct form of each adjective to each sentence. Does it go before or after the noun?

a) C'est un film. (bon / bonne / bons / bonnes)

_____

b) C'est une fille. (joli / jolie / jolis / jolies)

_____

c) C'est une voiture (noir / noire / noirs / noires)

_____

d) Ce sont des garçons (intelligent / intelligente / intelligents / intelligentes)

_____

e) Ce sont les baskets (meilleur / meilleure / meilleurs / meilleures)

_____

[10 marks: 1 mark for each correct form of the adjective and 1 mark for positioning it correctly.]

6 **Traduisez les phrases suivantes en français.** Translate the following sentences into French.

a) Your house is more beautiful than my house.

_____

b) My dog is less intelligent than your dog.

_____

c) She is the tallest girl in the school.

_____

[6 marks]

Grammar 1

Adverbs and the Present Tense

Adverbs and the Present Tense of Regular Verbs

1 Complétez chaque phrase en utilisant l'un des adverbes de l'encadré ci-dessous (il y a trois adverbes de trop). Make logical sentences by adding an adverb from the box (there are three adverbs too many).

a) Je n'ai pas beaucoup d'argent. J'ai _____ trois euros!

b) _____ je ne peux pas venir à ta fête, parce que je suis malade.

c) Tu marches trop _____ ! Le film commence dans cinq minutes!

d) Oh, merci! Des chocolats! C'est _____ très gentil.

e) Tu connais mon frère? Ah, oui, je le connais très _____ .

f) Hier, j'étais malade, mais aujourd'hui, je vais beaucoup _____ .

| bien | lentement | mal | malheureusement | mieux | rarement | seulement | vite | vraiment |

[6 marks]

2 Regardez les verbes du premier tableau, puis complétez le deuxième tableau. Look at the verbs in the first grid, then complete the second grid.

Regular –**er** verb	Regular –**ir** verb	Regular –**re** verb
jouer (to play)	**finir** (to finish)	**vendre** (to sell)
je joue (I play)	**je finis** (I finish)	**je vends** (I sell)
tu joues (you play)	**tu finis** (you finish)	**tu vends** (you sell)
il / elle / on joue (he / she / one plays)	**il / elle / on finit** (he / she / one finishes)	**il / elle / on vend** (he / she / one sells)
nous jouons (we play)	**nous finissons** (we finish)	**nous vendons** (we sell)
vous jouez (you play)	**vous finissez** (you finish)	**vous vendez** (you sell)
ils / elles jouent (they play)	**ils / elles finissent** (they finish)	**ils / elles vendent** (they sell)

Regular –**er** verb	Regular –**ir** verb	Regular –**re** verb
donn**er** (to give)	chois**ir** (to choose)	attend**re** (to wait)
je _____ (I give)	**je** _____ (I choose)	**j'** _____ (I wait)
tu _____ (you give)	**tu** _____ (you choose)	**tu** _____ (you wait)
il / elle / on _____ (he / she / one gives)	**il / elle / on** _____ (he / she / one chooses)	**il / elle / on** _____ (he / she / one waits)
nous _____ (we give)	**nous** _____ (we choose)	**nous** _____ (we wait)
vous _____ (you give)	**vous** _____ (you choose)	**vous** _____ (you wait)
ils / elles _____ (they give)	**ils / elles** _____ (they choose)	**ils / elles** _____ (they wait)

[18 marks. Each verb ending must be correct.]

The Present Tense, Reflexive Verbs, Depuis, Imperatives

3 **Traduisez les verbes en français, puis complétez les phrases, en utilisant vos propres idées.** Translate the verbs into French, then complete the sentences, using your own ideas.

Exemple:

She eats / is eating (**manger**) ⟶ **Elle mange une glace.**

a) He wears / is wearing (**porter**) ....

b) We help (**aider**) ....

c) They (**elles**) work (**travailler**) ....

d) You (**tu**) lose (**perdre**) ....

e) I reply (**répondre**) ....

f) You (**vous**) choose (**choisir**) ....

[12 marks: 1 for each correct verb form and 1 for a correct sentence]

4 **Complétez les phrases, en choisissant les bons mots de la case. Puis traduisez-les.** Complete the sentences, using the words in the box. Then translate them.

a) Je .... lève de bonne heure. ....

b) .... s'entend bien avec sa sœur. ....

c) Mes parents .... fâchent contre moi. ....

d) .... nous amusons bien au parc. ....

e) .... te couches à quelle heure? ....

f) Vous .... ennuyez le dimanche? ....

il	me	nous	se	tu	vous

[12 marks: 1 for each correct pronoun and 1 for each correct translation]

5 **Traduisez ces phrases en français, selon l'exemple.** Translate these sentences into French, following the example.

Exemple:

I have been playing the guitar for three years. ⟶ **Je joue de la guitare depuis trois ans.**

a) I have been living here for five years. ....

b) I have been doing judo for two years. ....

c) I have been studying French for six years. ....

[3 marks]

6 **Changez ces questions en commandes, selon l'exemple.** Change these questions into commands, following the example.

Exemple:

Tu manges tes carottes? ⟶ **Mange tes carottes!**

a) Tu écoutes le professeur? ....

b) Vous allez aux magasins? ....

[2 marks]

Grammar 2

Using Verbs in the Present Tense & Future Time-frame

Irregular Verbs in the Present Tense; Using the Present Participle

1 **Écrivez les phrases au pluriel.** Put these sentences into the plural (**je** ⟶ **nous, tu** ⟶ **vous,**
il / elle ⟶ **ils / elles**):

a) Je n'ai pas envie de rentrer. _____

b) Il est en train de tchatter en ligne. _____

c) Tu veux sortir samedi soir? _____

d) Elle ne peut pas venir. _____

e) Tu me fais rigoler! _____

f) Je vais passer des vacances à la plage. _____

[6 marks]

2 **Complétez le tableau en utilisant les verbes dans la case.** Put the verbs in the box into the correct
column in the table.

+ infinitive only	+ à + infinitive	+ de + infinitive

adorer	apprendre	aimer	arrêter	commencer	décider
espérer	essayer	éviter	s'intéresser	préférer	réussir

[12 marks]

Future Time-frame

3 **Traduisez les phrases en français.** Translate the sentences into French.

a) I am going to spend the weekend in Paris.

_____

b) We are going to visit the Eiffel Tower.

_____

c) We are going to eat in a famous French restaurant.

_____

d) The girls are going to play volleyball.

_____

e) Are you (singular) going to go out tonight (this evening)?

_____

[5 marks]

4 **Remplissez les blancs en utilisant un verbe au futur proche ou au futur.** Fill in the blanks using a future time-frame (either the immediate future or the future tense).

L'année prochaine je _____ (rester) au collège. Si j'ai de bonnes notes, j(e) _____ (étudier) les sciences. Ce _____ (être) plus amusant de choisir ce qu'on apprend! Après les examens, je _____ (partir) en vacances avec mes copains. Nous _____ (aller) à la campagne et nous _____ (faire) du camping sauvage. S'il fait beau, on _____ (vouloir) essayer l'escalade et l'équitation. En fait, on _____ (pouvoir) faire tout ce qu'on veut! Quelle aventure! [8 marks]

5 **Traduisez le paragraphe suivant en anglais.** Translate the following paragraph into English:

Si j'étais ministre de l'environnement, je changerais beaucoup de choses! Tout le monde devrait recycler les déchets. Les adultes ne gaspilleraient pas d'énergie. Les enfants économiseraient l'eau. Le gouvernement voudrait vraiment protéger les animaux en danger. Ce serait un monde idéal.

_____

_____

_____

_____

_____

_____

_____

[7 marks]

6 **Récrivez les phrases en utilisant l'imparfait et le conditionnel.** Rewrite the 'si clause' sentences using the imperfect and conditional tenses.

Exemple: S'il fait beau, on ira à la plage.   If the weather is nice, we will go to the beach.

S'il faisait beau, on irait à la plage.   If the weather was nice, we would go to the beach.

a) S'il pleut, nous ferons des achats en ville. _____

b) S'il vient chez nous, on visitera Paris. _____

c) Si je réussis à mon bac, je chercherai un emploi. _____

_____

d) Si nous avons plus d'argent, nous achèterons une voiture de sport. _____

e) Si je gagne à la loterie, j'aiderai les sans-abris. _____

[5 marks]

Grammar 2

Past Time-frame: Perfect Tense & Imperfect Tense and Pluperfect Tense

Perfect Tense with Avoir and Être; the Perfect Infinitive

1 **Trouvez l'erreur dans chaque phrase et écrivez la phrase correcte.** Find the error in each sentence and rewrite it correctly.

a) **Nous avons venus trop tard.** _____

b) **Je n'ai rien bois.** _____

c) **Vous n'ont pas vu le film.** _____

d) **Elles sont ne pas parties en vacances.** _____

e) **Ils ont mangés des escargots.** _____

[5 marks]

2 **Lisez l'histoire bizarre.** Read the bizarre story.

Les aventures de Luc Lebrave

Le petit <u>Luc est né</u> dans une petite maison dans une grande forêt. Un jour, à l'âge de six ans, <u>il est parti</u> de chez lui et <u>il est allé</u> dans la forêt tout seul. Après une heure de route, <u>il est venu</u> à une grande montagne. <u>Il est monté</u>, monté, monté. Enfin, tout fatigué, <u>il est arrivé</u> au sommet de la montagne et qu'est-ce qu'il a trouvé? – quelle surprise ! – un café! <u>Il est entré</u> dans le café, <u>il y est resté</u> peu de temps (il n'avait pas d'argent pour acheter quelque chose) et puis <u>il est sorti</u> du café. <u>Il est descendu</u> – descendu, descendu, mais soudain – <u>il est tombé</u> – tombé, tombé, tombé jusqu'au bas de la montagne. Quel horreur! Est-ce qu'<u>il est mort</u>, le pauvre petit Luc? Mais non, <u>il est rentré</u> dans la forêt et <u>il est retourné</u> chez lui sain et sauf. (N.B. À l'âge de seize ans, <u>il est devenu</u> alpiniste célèbre!)

Écrivez une histoire semblable au sujet de 'Lucille Lebrave'. Attention à l'accord! Write a similar adventure about Lucille Lebrave – remember the agreements! [10 marks]

_____

_____

_____

_____

_____

_____

_____

3 **Reliez les deux phrases en utilisant 'après avoir' ou 'après être'.** Join the two sentences together, using the perfect infinitive ('**après avoir**' or '**après être**').

Exemple: J'ai déjeuné chez moi. Je suis allé en ville. Après avoir déjeuné chez moi, je suis allé en ville.

a) **Il a entendu les nouvelles. Il a téléphoné à son copain.** _____

_____

b) **Nous avons fait une promenade. Nous avons mangé un gâteau au café.**

c) **Nous sommes arrivés au marché de Noël. Nous avons acheté des cadeaux.**

d) **Elle s'est levée très tôt le matin. Elle est partie à l'étranger.**

[4 marks]

Past Time-frame

4 **Dessinez des lignes pour relier les phrases anglaises et françaises, qui sont à l'imparfait.** Match the English and French sentences. They are in the imperfect tense.

a) Elle ne voulait pas sortir.	It was too noisy.
b) Il y avait trop de monde.	She didn't want to go out.
c) C'était trop bruyant.	It was too hot.
d) Il faisait trop chaud.	There were too many people.

[4 marks]

5 **Faut-il utiliser le passé composé ou l'imparfait? Complétez les phrases avec les verbes entre parenthèses.** Perfect or imperfect? Complete the following sentences using the verbs in brackets.

a) **Pour fêter mon dernier anniversaire, ma famille (organiser) _____ une surprise partie.**

b) **Mes parents (louer) _____ une salle dans le centre-ville, mais je n'en (savoir) _____ rien.**

c) **Tous mes amis (venir) _____ vers sept heures et demie – ils (être) _____ très excités!**

d) **Quand je (arriver) _____ à huit heures, tout le monde (se cacher) _____ derrière un grand rideau!**

e) **C' (être) _____ une soirée inoubliable – nous (danser) _____ et (célébrer) _____ jusqu'à minuit.**

[10 marks]

6 **Complétez ce tableau.** Complete the table.

Infinitive	Perfect tense	Imperfect tense	Pluperfect tense
avoir	j'ai eu – I had	j'avais – I was having	j'avais eu – I had had
mettre			
devoir			
sortir			
se coucher			

[12 marks]

Grammar 3

Pronouns and Questions

1 **Choisissez le bon pronom.**

Choose the correct pronoun to render the English translation.

a) Je ne   <u>la / les</u>   recycle jamais.   *I never recycle them.*

b) Je voudrais   <u>le / la</u>   protéger plus efficacement.   *I would like to protect it. (it = the planet)*
   more efficiently.

c) Il faudrait   <u>les / l'</u>   aider plus.   *We should help them more.*

d) Je ne   <u>l' / la</u>   aime pas.   *I don't like it. (the song)*

e) Il ne faut pas   <u>la / les</u>   gaspiller.   *We mustn't waste it.*

[5 marks]

2 **Remplacez les mots soulignés par un pronom. Choisissez-les dans la liste ci-dessous.**
Replace the underlined elements with a pronoun. Choose from the list below.

elle   il   les   elles   nous   ils

a) Je pense que <u>ma sœur</u> est très sympa. ....

b) Malheureusement <u>ma ville</u> est très polluée. ....

c) <u>Ma mère et moi</u> aimons passer des heures au bord de la piscine. ....

d) <u>Mon père et mon frère</u> préfèrent aller se promener. ....

e) <u>Mes sœurs</u> sont au chômage. ....

[5 marks]

3 **Traduisez en français.** Translate into French:

a) I do not like them. ....

b) I agree with her. ....

c) I don't agree with them. ....

d) I stayed at mine yesterday (use **chez**). ....

e) I do not waste them. ....

[5 marks]

4 **Quelle est la traduction française pour…?** What is the French for…?

a) who ....   e) with whom ....

b) where ....   f) how ....

c) how long ....   g) why ....

d) when ....   h) for whom ....

[8 marks]

5 **Remettez les mots dans l'ordre pour former des questions.** Unjumble the questions.

a) tu   est-ce que   recycles?

....

b) est-ce que   avec qui   en vacances   tu   normalement   vas?

....

c) est-ce que   tu   pourquoi   gaspilles   l'électricité?

....

d) où   en vacances   voudrais   est-ce que   tu   aller?

....

[4 marks]

6 **Regardez l'image et posez des questions en utilisant les mots interrogatifs suivants.** Look at the picture below and ask five questions using the following question words:

où   comment   pourquoi   quand   avec qui

....

....

....

....

....

[5 marks]

Grammar 3

Prepositions and Conjunctions & Subjunctive Mood and the Passive Voice

Prepositions and Conjunctions

1 **Choisissez la préposition correcte.** Choose the correct preposition.

a) **Elle vient** <u>de / par</u> **Belgique.** *She comes from Belgium.*

b) **Nous sommes allés en vacances** <u>sans / parmi</u> **lui.** *We went on holiday without him.*

c) **Je recycle** <u>pour / par</u> **protéger la planète.** *I recycle to protect the planet.*

d) **J'habite** <u>en / au</u> **Angleterre.** *I live in England.*

e) **Nous vivons ici** <u>depuis / pour</u> **toujours.** *We have always lived here.*   [5 marks]

2 **Traduisez en français.** Translate into French:

a) according to my mum _____

b) without spending _____

c) in order to protect _____

d) among the problems _____

e) despite my efforts _____   [5 marks]

3 **Choisissez la conjonction de coordination correcte.** Choose the correct connectives.

a) **L'hôtel m'a beaucoup plu**   <u>pourtant / parce que</u>   **la plage était décevante.**

b) **Trop de gens sont au chômage**   <u>puis / alors</u>   **je pense qu'on devrait les aider.**

c) **La planète est en danger**   <u>car / à cause de</u>   **la pollution.**

d) **La piscine était   trop froide**   <u>donc / par contre</u>   **je n'y suis pas allé(e).**

e) **Le vol a eu deux heures de retard**   <u>parce qu' / à cause de</u>   **il neigeait beaucoup.**

[5 marks]

4 a) **D'abord traduisez les conjonctions en anglais.** First translate the following conjunctions into English.   [5 marks]

b) **Puis reliez les phrases ci-dessous en choisissant une conjonction de la case.** Then link the sentences below choosing the appropriate conjunctions from the box.

| comme | lorsque | si | puisque | tandis que |

1. _____ **je vais en vacances avec mes amis, j'aurai plus de liberté.**

2. _____ **on ne recycle pas assez, il y a trop de pollution.**

3. **Je ne me sens pas en sécurité dans ma ville** _____ **il y a de plus en plus de violence.**

4. _____ **je suis arrivée dàns mon hôtel, je me suis aperçue que j'avais perdu mon passeport.**

5. **Je fais beaucoup pour la protection de l'environnement** _____ **mes amis ne font rien.**   [5 marks]

Subjunctive Mood and the Passive Voice

5 **Identifiez les phrases qui sont au subjonctif.** Identify the sentences in the subjunctive.

a) Je doute que ma ville soit très agréable pour les touristes.

b) Je pense que mes vacances l'année dernière étaient les meilleures.

c) Je ne pense que je puisse faire davantage pour protéger l'environnement.

d) On devrait faire tout ce qu'on peut pour aider les sans-abris.

e) Selon ma mère mes amis n'ont pas une bonne influence sur moi.

[5 marks]

6 **Décidez si les verbes doivent être au subjonctif ou non. Choisissez le bon verbe.** Decide whether the verbs should be in the subjunctive or not. Choose the correct verb.

a) Bien que ma ville   <u>soit / est</u>   assez moderne, il y a beaucoup de problèmes de pauvreté.

b) Je ne doute pas que l'hôtel   <u>est / soit</u>   assez décevant.

c) Il faut que je   <u>fais / fasse</u>   plus pour protéger l'environnement.

d) Je suis contente que mon amie   <u>peut /puisse</u>   venir avec nous en vacances cet été.

e) Même s'il   <u>est/ soit</u>   parfois difficile de recycler les déchets, il faut faire de son mieux.

[5 marks]

7 **Traduisez les phrases de l'exercice 6 en anglais.** Translate the sentences in exercise 6 into English.

....

....

....

....

....

[5 marks]

8 **Lesquelles de ces phrases sont à la voix passive?** Which of these sentences are in the passive voice?

a) Malheureusement notre ville a été endommagée par les inondations récentes.

b) L'hôtel que nous avons choisi pour nos vacances se trouve au bord de la mer.

c) L'environnement est constamment attaqué par nos actions égoïstes!

d) Je suis contente que la croisière cette année soit encore organisée par la même équipe que l'année dernière.

e) Il est inquiétant que les voyous harcèlent la population.

[5 marks]

Collins

GCSE
French

Higher Tier Paper 1 Listening

Time allowed: 45 minutes

(including 5 minutes' reading time before the test)

Instructions

- Download the audio material to use with this test from **www.collins.co.uk/collinsgcserevision**
- Use black ink or black ball-point pen.

Instructions

- The marks for questions are shown in brackets.
- The maximum mark for this paper is 50.
- You must **not** use a dictionary.

Advice

For each item, you should do the following:

- Carefully listen to the recording. Read the questions again.
- Listen again to the recording. Then answer the questions.
- You may write at any point during the test.
- In **Section A**, answer the questions in **English**. In **Section B**, answer the questions in **French**.
- Answer all questions in the spaces provided.
- Write down all the information you are asked to give.
- You have 5 minutes to read through the question paper before the test begins. You may make notes during this time.

Name: ....

Section A   Questions and answers in **English**

News Reports

While on holiday in Switzerland, you hear these news reports on the local radio.

A	pollution
B	an accident
C	a robbery
D	a competition
E	unemployment
F	gangs

For each report choose the topic from the list and write the correct letter.

0 1 [ ]   **[1 mark]**

0 2 [ ]   **[1 mark]**

0 3 [ ]   **[1 mark]**

0 4 [ ]   **[1 mark]**

Practice Exam Paper 1: Listening

An Excursion

While on holiday in France you visit the tourist office and you hear this announcement.

Choose the correct answer and write the letter in the box.

0 5 **The cruise is**

A	on every day
B	is not on at the weekend
C	is not on Monday

[1 mark]

0 6 **You can benefit from the price reduction if**

A	you book online
B	you book in the next few days
C	you book at the tourist office

[1 mark]

0 7 **On board**

A	you are allowed to bring your own food
B	you can't bring your own food
C	the food is cheap

[1 mark]

Hiring a Bike: the Vélo'v Scheme

You hear a podcast sent by your French partner school in Lyon. In this extract you hear an interview with Émeline who talks about **'le Vélo'v'**, a scheme to promote bike hiring in her town to reduce pollution.

Answer both parts of the question.

0 8 · 1 Le Velo'v

A	is available all the time
B	is not available between 7pm and 7am
C	is available from 300 stations

[1 mark]

0 8 · 2 The popularity of the Velo'v is growing among

A	people living in Lyon
B	tourists
C	both tourists and people living in Lyon

[1 mark]

Answer both parts of the question.

0 9 · 1 Compared with the Velo'v, Émeline finds other means of transport

A	less enjoyable
B	not as environmentally friendly
C	not as convenient

[1 mark]

0 9 · 2 Émeline's friends

A	do not agree with her
B	agree with her
C	do not really have an opinion on it

[1 mark]

Answer both parts of the question.

1 0 · 1 Émeline says that the Velo'v

A	is not always cheap but is worth it
B	is affordable
C	is sometimes free

[1 mark]

1 0 · 2 According to Émeline, accidents happen

A	because the number of cars on the roads has increased
B	because of the lack of cycle tracks
C	because some roads are too narrow

[1 mark]

Online Shopping

Listen to this French radio phone-in programme where listeners are discussing the advantages and disadvantages of online shopping.

For each speaker, write down **one** advantage and **one** disadvantage.

Answer in **English**.

1 1 Françoise

Advantage	Disadvantage

[2 marks]

1 2 Didier

Advantage	Disadvantage

[2 marks]

Fashion

Listen to these teenagers discussing fashion.

Complete the sentences in **English**.

1 3 For the first speaker, having a fashion style is ....

This is because it gives her ....

[2 marks]

1 4 The second teenager thinks that everyone should wear ....

If everyone followed fashion, we would ....

[2 marks]

Sport

You listen to a Belgian radio programme about sport.

Answer in **English**.

1 5 · **1** Why does Pierre NOT enjoy sport at school?

....

[1 mark]

1 5 · **2** What does he say about sport in the summer holidays? Give **two** details.

....

....

[2 marks]

Practice Exam Paper 1: Listening

Paris Celebrates the 14th July!

You listen to this online advert about the French National Day in Paris.

Answer in **English**.

1 6 · **1** The festivities in Paris are designed for:

A	tourists
B	children
C	all ages

[1 mark]

1 6 · **2** At what time does the military parade start?

[1 mark]

1 6 · **3** What **two** suggestions are made for watching the firework display?

[2 marks]

Local Environment

While in France you hear a radio report about the proposed building of a large shopping centre on the edge of a small town called Neuvic.

Listen to the report and answer the questions in **English**.

Example

Why are people unhappy? *They believe that the local shops will suffer.*

According to Monsieur David, why will the small businesses in town be affected, and what might be the consequences?

| 1 | 7 | · | 1 |

[1 mark]

| 1 | 7 | · | 2 |

[1 mark]

What does the developer Madame Félix say will happen as a result of the construction?

Give **two** details.

| 1 | 8 | · | 1 |

[1 mark]

| 1 | 8 | · | 2 |

[1 mark]

How does the local student Danny suggest that a compromise could be made? Give **two** details.

| 1 | 9 | · | 1 |

[1 mark]

| 1 | 9 | · | 2 |

[1 mark]

Practice Exam Paper 1: Listening

Health

While on the internet, you hear two advertisements about health related issues.

Choose the correct answer to complete each sentence. Write the letter in the box.

Answer both parts of the question.

2 0 · 1 This advert is about…

A	smoking
B	drugs
C	drinking alcohol

[1 mark]

2 0 · 2 It makes the point that the consequences of electronic cigarettes are

A	less dangerous than tobacco
B	more dangerous than tobacco
C	less known about than tobacco

[1 mark]

2 1 · 1 This advert stresses the need to avoid

A	sugary drinks
B	tap water
C	canned drinks

[1 mark]

2 1 · 2 It promotes the drink's

A	fat content
B	place of manufacture
C	price

[1 mark]

Radio Interview

While on holiday in France, you hear an interview on French radio.

Choose the correct answer and write the letter in the box.

2 2 · 1 The young man

A	is a volunteer for a charity
B	works for a charity
C	lives in Africa

[1 mark]

2 2 · 2 In the future he wants to

A	travel throughout Asia
B	deliver medicines throughout France
C	work as a doctor

[1 mark]

Practice Exam Paper 1: Listening

Section B — Questions and answers in **French**

Les Rapports Familiaux

Écoutez cet extrait d'une émission de radio. On invite des jeunes à discuter de leurs problèmes avec leurs parents.

Choisissez deux phrases qui sont vraies et écrivez les bonnes lettres dans les cases.

2 3

A	Maxime ne voit pas souvent son père.
B	Maxime ne s'intéresse pas à ses parents.
C	La belle-mère de Maxime va avoir un bébé.
D	Le père de Maxime est souvent triste.
E	Avant le divorce, Maxime s'entendait bien avec son père.

[2 marks]

2 4

A	Maxime se dispute tout le temps avec sa mère.
B	La mère de Maxime est au chômage.
C	S'il a des problèmes, Maxime peut en parler à sa mère.
D	La mère de Maxime n'est pas toujours contente de lui.
E	Maxime ne peut pas aider à la maison, à cause de ses études.

[2 marks]

Les Réseaux Sociaux

2 5 Dans un café français, vous écoutez ces jeunes qui parlent des réseaux sociaux.

Complétez les phrases suivantes en français.

2 5 · 1 Pour Nabila et ses amis, Facebook est une invention très _____.

[1 mark]

2 5 · 2 Nabila trouve que rester en contact avec ses amis en ligne est _____.

[1 mark]

2 5 · 3 Selon Malik, il est plus important de retrouver ses amis en personne pour _____.

[1 mark]

2 5 · 4 Malik dit que sur internet, on peut facilement écrire quelque chose de _____.

[1 mark]

Conseils

2 6 Vous écoutez un podcast dans lequel on donne des conseils pour se protéger en ligne.

Pour chaque personne qui parle, choisissez le conseil correct et écrivez la lettre dans la case.

A	Il ne faut jamais partager vos détails personnels.
B	Il faut changer régulièrement son mot de passe.
C	Ne communiquez pas en ligne avec des inconnus.
D	Évitez de tchatter sur des forums.
E	Il est essentiel d'installer un logiciel anti-virus.

(i)

[1 mark]

(ii)

[1 mark]

END OF QUESTIONS

Collins

GCSE
French

Higher Tier Paper 2 Speaking

H

Candidate's material – Role-play

Candidate's material – Photo card

Time allowed: 12 minutes
(+ 12 minutes' preparation time)

Instructions

- During the preparation time, you are required to prepare **one** Role-play card and **one** Photo card.
- During the General Conversation, you are required to ask at least one question.

Information

- The test will last a maximum of 12 minutes and will consist of a Role-play card (approximately 2 minutes) and a Photo card (approximately 3 minutes), followed by a General Conversation. The General Conversation is based on two out of the three Themes (5–7 minutes).
- You must **not** use a dictionary, either in the test or during the preparation time.

Name: ....

Role-play

Prepare your <u>spoken</u> answers to this Role-play.

Instructions to candidates

Your teacher will play the part of your French friend and will speak first.

You should address your friend as 'tu'.

When you see this – ! – you will have to respond to something you have not prepared.

When you see this – ? – you will have to ask a question.

Tu parles avec ton ami(e) français(e) de l'environnement dans ta ville

- L'environnement dans ta ville – (**deux** problèmes)
- !
- Protection de l'environnement – (**deux** actions récentes)
- Changement et **une** raison
- ? Recyclage à la maison

Photo card

- Look at the photo.

- Prepare your <u>spoken</u> answers to the three questions that follow.

- **Qu'est-ce qu'il y a sur la photo?**

- **À ton avis, est-il important d'avoir de bons amis? Pourquoi?**

- **Parle-moi d'une sortie que tu as faite récemment avec tes amis.**

In the examination, your teacher will ask you **two** further questions, which you have not prepared.

Think of other questions you might be asked on the topic of 'Friendship' and prepare answers to those, too.

General Conversation

The questions on the Photo card are followed by a General Conversation. The first part of this conversation will be from your nominated Theme and the second part on a Theme chosen by the examiner. The total time of the General Conversation will be between five and seven minutes and a similar amount of time will be spent on each Theme.

Themes for this example General Conversation are:

- Local, national, international and global areas of interest

- Current and future study and employment

Remember!

It is a requirement for you to ask at least **one** question during the General Conversation; this can happen at any time during this section of the test.

Collins

GCSE
French

H

Higher Tier Paper 3 Reading

Time allowed: 1 hour

Instructions

- Use black ink or black ball-point pen.
- Answer **all** questions.
- You must answer the questions in the spaces provided.
- In **Section A**, answer the questions in **English**. In **Section B**, answer the questions in **French**.
  In **Section C**, translate the passage into **English**.

Information

- The marks for questions are shown in brackets.
- The maximum mark for this paper is 60.
- You must **not** use a dictionary.

Name: ....

Practice Exam Paper 3: Reading

Section A   Questions and answers in English

0 1 Marriage and Relationships

Read these posts by two French students, in which they talk about whether they want to get married.

Même si on dit que le mariage est une preuve d'amour, pour moi, l'idée de passer sa vie entière avec une seule personne est complètement démodée. Mieux vaut habiter ensemble: au cas où ça ne marche pas, il est plus facile de se séparer. Pourtant, il faut penser aux enfants; si on veut fonder une famille, c'est plus sécurisant d'être marié.

Olivia

0 1 · 1 Which two statements are true? Write the letters in the boxes.

A	Olivia thinks she would like to get married one day.
B	Olivia believes it's possible to spend your whole life with one person.
C	Olivia thinks living together makes it easier to end the relationship.
D	Olivia thinks getting married is a good idea if you want to have children.

[2 marks]

Selon les statistiques, un grand nombre de mariages se terminent par un divorce. Cependant, je connais beaucoup de couples qui sont toujours ensemble. Mes parents sont mariés depuis plus de vingt ans et se disputent rarement. L'important c'est d'avoir plein de choses en commun, tout en respectant nos différences. Rester célibataire, c'est garder sa liberté, mais je n'aimerais pas vivre seul.

Raphaël

0 1 · 2 Which two statements are true? Write the letters in the boxes.

A	Raphaël knows a lot of couples who have got divorced.
B	Raphaël's parents generally get on well with one another.
C	Raphaël thinks you shouldn't marry someone who is from a different background.
D	Raphaël does not want to stay single all his life.

[2 marks]

0 2 Cinema and TV

Read what these two people say in a forum about cinema and TV. Identify the people.

Write A   (Alice)
      B   (Benoît)
      A + B   (Alice + Benoît)

<table>
<tr><td colspan="4" align="center">Vas-tu souvent au cinéma?</td></tr>
<tr>
<td>Alice</td>
<td></td>
<td>Pas trop souvent. Les billets sont assez chers et la plupart du temps on peut voir les mêmes films chez soi. Mais s'il s'agit de l'anniversaire d'un ami, par exemple, il vaut la peine d'y aller.</td>
<td>Benoît  Comme famille on va au cinéma assez régulièrement, je dirais une fois par mois peut-être, surtout les jours fériés ou pour faire la fête.</td>
</tr>
</table>

0 2 · 1 Who goes to the cinema on special occasions?

[1 mark]

<table>
<tr><td colspan="4" align="center">Quel genre de film aimes-tu le plus?</td></tr>
<tr>
<td>Alice</td>
<td></td>
<td>Je n'ai pas de genre préféré; il y a beaucoup de films que j'adore … en fin de compte, les films que j'aime le plus sont toujours amusants et drôles … il faut bien s'amuser et passer la soirée en rigolant.</td>
<td>Benoît  J'aime bien l'aventure et l'action! Cependant, si le film ne me fait pas rire, ce n'est pas pour moi!</td>
</tr>
</table>

0 2 · 2 Who enjoys comedy films?

[1 mark]

Que penses-tu des émissions télé réalité?			
Alice 	Tout dépend de l'émission – par exemple, à mon avis *Nouvelle Star* offre la possibilité à de jeunes talents de réaliser leur rêve et de changer leur vie, d'autres séries ne sont pas si intéressantes.	Benoît 	Avant j'aimais les regarder, mais maintenant il y en a trop et je m'ennuie de regarder les gens qui se disputent dans une maison pendant les mois.

0 2 · 3 Who has changed their opinion about reality TV programmes?

[1 mark]

0 2 · 4 Who has a negative opinion towards reality TV?

[1 mark]

0 3 Holidays

You are doing a project about young people and holidays. Read these posts that you find on a French website.

Answer the questions in **English**.

	*Lucille* a écrit: Les vacances en famille … oui, c'est sûr on devrait tous vouloir partir avec ses parents et ses frères et sœurs, mais moi ça ne me plaît pas du tout. Les règles et les sorties qui m'ennuient … non merci. Qui ne préférerait pas la liberté avec ses amis!
	Abdul a écrit: Lucille … comment peux-tu dire ça? N'as-tu pas honte de ne pas vouloir passer tes vacances avec ta famille? On grandit tellement vite alors moi, je veux vraiment passer autant de temps que possible avec mes proches.

0 3 · 1 What does Lucille think about spending her holiday with her family?

[1 mark]

0 3 · 2 How does Abdul react to what Lucille has written?

[1 mark]

0 3 · 3 Why does Abdul think that family holidays are important?

[1 mark]

0 4 At the Hairdresser's

Read this extract from the *Petit Nicolas* stories by Sempé-Goscinny. Nicolas tells the story of going to get his hair cut.

Le coiffeur qui s'appelait Marcel, d'une voix toute tremblante, a dit:

– Bon, je suis libre, qui est le premier d'entre vous?

Moi, j'ai répondu que j'étais le premier, et non seulement que j'étais le premier, mais que j'étais le seul. M. Marcel a regardé mes trois copains et il a demandé:

– Et eux?

– Nous, on vient pour rigoler, a répondu Alceste.

– Oui, a dit Clotaire, quand Nicolas sort de chez vous, il a l'air d'un guignol*, on veut voir comment vous faites.

M. Marcel est devenu tout rouge.

– Voulez-vous partir d'ici tout de suite! Ce n'est pas la cour de récréation, ici! […]

Mais Rufus, Clotaire et Alceste ne voulaient pas partir de la boutique.

– Si vous nous faites sortir, a dit Rufus, je me plaindrai à mon papa, qui est agent de police!

– Et moi, a dit Alceste, je le dirai à mon papa à moi, qui est un ami du papa de Rufus!

L'autre coiffeur s'est approché et il a dit:

– Du calme, du calme. Vous pouvez rester, les enfants, mais vous allez être sages, n'est-ce pas?

*un guignol = puppet, clown

0 4 · 1 How does M. Marcel feel, at the beginning, about seeing Nicolas and his friends in his hairdressing shop?

A	Pleased
B	Nervous
C	Curious

Write the correct letter in the box.

[1 mark]

0 4 · 2 Give **one** reason why Nicolas' friends have come with him to the hairdresser's.

Answer in **English**.

....

....

[1 mark]

0 4 · 3 What makes the hairdresser change his mind and let Nicolas' friends stay?

Answer in **English**.

....

....

[1 mark]

0 4 · 4 What does the hairdresser say the boys must be, if he allows them to stay?

A	Quiet
B	Polite
C	Well-behaved

Write the correct letter in the box.

[1 mark]

0 5 The Environment

You read this article in a Belgian magazine. Laurence has written in to explain what her school does to help protect the environment.

Read the article and answer the questions in **English**.

<u>**Votre lycée est-il propre?**</u>

Notre lycée est beaucoup plus propre qu'il y a un an et notre directeur vient de nous dire qu'il en était très fier. Et comment? Notre lycée a dû acheter beaucoup plus de poubelles récemment pour encourager les jeunes à ne pas jeter leurs déchets par terre… Apparemment il n'y avait pas assez de poubelles partout. Il est vraiment dommage d'avoir acheté plus de poubelles – quel gaspillage! Le lycée aurait dû nous encourager à utiliser celles qu'on avait déjà! Le problème c'est la paresse! La plupart des jeunes dans mon lycée ne veulent pas marcher ni se lever pour utiliser les poubelles. C'est comme le bus… le lycée devrait encourager les élèves à ne pas utiliser les transports en commun parce que la plupart n'ont vraiment pas besoin de les prendre – ils habitent si près!

0 5 · 1 What is the head teacher proud of?

_____

[1 mark]

0 5 · 2 How does Laurence feel about the purchase of more rubbish bins?

_____

[1 mark]

0 5 · 3 What reason does she give for feeling like this?

_____

[1 mark]

0 5 · 4 According to Laurence, what are the other pupils like?

_____

[1 mark]

Practice Exam Paper 3: Reading

0 6 The Festival of Music

Your French friend has sent you a magazine. You read this article about the Festival of Music.

La Fête de la Musique célèbre la musique vivante, la diversité des pratiques musicales et tous les genres musicaux en France. Elle est ouverte à tous les musiciens, amateurs de tous niveaux ou professionnel. Les musiciens de tous les âges jouent bénévolement et les concerts sont gratuits pour tout le monde. Chaque année on choisit un thème différent pour la fête, mais la date reste toujours pareil – le 21 juin, jour du solstice d'été.

La fête de la musique est majoritairement une manifestation de plein air qui se déroule dans les rues, les jardins publics et les places dans les villes et les villages partout en France. Mais c'est aussi l'occasion d'ouvrir au public des lieux qui ne sont pas traditionnellement des lieux de concerts, comme des musées et des hôpitaux.

Depuis sa création en 1982, la fête de la musique devient l'une des plus grandes manifestations culturelles françaises. L'an dernier, plus de dix millions de Français sont descendus dans les rues pour en participer, sans compter les 4,5 millions de téléspectateurs qui ont regardé des émissions diffusées en direct. La fête a pris une ampleur considérable à l'étranger aussi et plus de 120 pays l'ont célébré partout au monde.

0 6 · 1 Who can take part in the Festival of Music?

A	only professional musicians
B	only amateur musicians
C	both professional and amateur musicians

Write the correct letter in the box.   [1 mark]

0 6 · 2 Why is the Festival of Music so popular?

A	the musicians are well paid
B	the organisers raise money for charity
C	the concerts are free

Write the correct letter in the box.   [1 mark]

0 6 · 3 Where do most of the concerts take place?

A	outdoors
B	indoors
C	in museums and hospitals

Write the correct letter in the box.   [1 mark]

0 6 · 4 How many French people participated in the event last year?

A	about 4.5 million
B	over 10 million
C	more than 120 million

Write the correct letter in the box.   [1 mark]

0 7 Mobile Phones

You have texted your French friend Noémie about the banning of mobile phones in school.

Read her reply and answer the questions in **English**.

> À mon lycée, comme dans la majorité des établissements scolaires, il est interdit d'utiliser son portable. Tous mes amis trouvent ça injuste, en disant que la technologie portable est essentielle pour se tenir au courant ou de contacter quelqu'un en cas d'urgence. Cependant, moi, je suis d'autre avis. Avec l'accès internet, il est trop facile de tricher en classe ou dans une épreuve, puisqu'on peut trouver rapidement des informations sur tout.
>
> Options   Exit

0 7 · 1 How does Noémie feel about the banning of mobile phones in her school?

_____

[1 mark]

0 7 · 2 Give a reason for her view.

_____

[1 mark]

0 8 Health and Sport

A French doctor's blog discusses the results of a recent survey on physical activity.

Read the blog and answer the questions in **English**.

> **Les jeunes français ne font pas assez de sport!**
>
> **Une étude récente révèle que moins de la moitié des adolescents (15–17 ans) atteint un niveau d'activité physique « entraînant des bénéfices pour la santé ».**
>
> **La différence entre les sexes est marquée: plus de 6 garçons sur 10 atteignent un niveau d'activité physique favorable à la santé, alors que moins d'une fille sur 4 est concernée.**
>
> **17% des adolescents ont un faible niveau d'activité physique.**
>
> **Le problème? Trop de jeunes ont une image négative de l'activité physique.**
>
> **Faire du sport, ce n'est pas forcément se prendre la tête à courir autour d'une piste ou à se rentrer dedans en pratiquant un sport traumatisant comme le rugby.**
>
> **Faire du sport, c'est aussi marcher sur une plage, aller nager dans la mer et pourquoi pas prendre quelques vagues sur une planche de surf?**

0 8 · 1 According to the survey, how many 15–17 year olds do enough physical activity?

....

[1 mark]

0 8 · 2 What is particularly noticeable in the results of the survey?

....

[1 mark]

0 8 · 3 According to the doctor, what causes the problem for too many young people?

....

[1 mark]

0 8 · 4 He suggests that more people could

A	climb mountains
B	go surfing
C	play rugby

[1 mark]

0 9 School Life

You have emailed your French friend Émilie about life in school. Read her reply and answer the questions in **English**.

Moi, je trouve que la vie dans mon école n'est pas facile!

D'abord il y a le règlement! Déjà le maquillage est interdit, et mon prof a dit que c'est parce qu'on portait trop. Mais moi, je suis ado et je veux être jolie entre mes amis! Le proviseur a décidé que les téléphones portables ne sont pas permis dans les cours. Il a dit que c'est parce qu'ils sont une distraction. Je veux l'utiliser pour trouver des sites internet ou pour ses fonctions comme calculatrice.

Puis il y a la pression parce que cette année je passe mes examens et je veux réussir. Mais je suis trop fatiguée parce que la journée scolaire est trop longue. On commence à huit heures et quart et on finit à dix-sept heures.

C'est comme ça dans ton école?

Complete the grids below in English to indicate what the problems were and why.

Example

	Reason	Complaint
Make-up banned	*Too much worn*	*Wants to look pretty*

0 9 · 1

	Reason	Complaint
Mobile phones not allowed in class		

[2 marks]

0 9 · 2

	Reason	Complaint
Pressures		

[2 marks]

Section B Questions and answers in **French**

1 0 Belle et Sébastien

Lisez cet extrait du livre *Belle et Sébastien* de Cécile Aubry. Belle est une chienne et Sébastien, un petit garçon, qui vient de la trouver dans les montagnes.

Complétez le texte suivant avec les mots de la liste ci-dessous.

Écrivez la bonne lettre dans chaque case.

Example

«Moi? Je G comme tout le monde moi…Tu promets de rentrer un peu plus ☐ que d'habitude?»

«Oui», accepta Sébastien, «je rentrerai aussitôt que ☐ commencera à tomber. Pour Angelina et aussi parce que Belle doit manger son lard. Tu sais, je crois que maintenant elle ne chasse plus, elle préfère la soupe qu'Angelina lui ☐ ! Je la pose tous les soirs au pied de l'escalier et ☐ il n'y a plus rien. Il n'y a pas longtemps de ça, tu sais, deux ou trois jours seulement. Avant elle ☐ mais elle ne touchait pas à la soupe.»

A	prépare
B	tôt
C	s'approchait
D	mange
E	le matin
F	rapide
G	déjeune
H	la nuit
I	ne venait pas

[5 marks]

Practice Exam Paper 3: Reading

1 1 Un E-mail

Lisez l'e-mail de Bradley qui parle de la santé.

From: Brad624@hotmail.fr

Subject: **Ma vie saine**

Salut!

Tu m'as demandé si je suis sportif et sain! Eh bien, je dirais que oui, mais je ne suis pas parfait bien sûr! Le problème, c'est que j'aime plus manger que faire du sport!

Je mange des aliments pas trop sucrés. Par exemple, j'évite les pâtisseries et les sodas parce que je sais qu'ils ne sont pas bons pour la ligne. Je ne mange pas assez de fruits ni des légumes, même si je préfère la nourriture végétarienne aux viandes. Le poisson, j'aime bien ça, mais je n'en mange pas assez.

Je fais du sport, mais je pourrais en faire encore plus. Je fais du jogging de temps en temps, mais je trouve ça ennuyeux. Je préfère les sports d'équipe. Je vais essayer de jouer au foot avec mes amis pendant l'été et j'ai l'intention de faire un peu de natation.

À plus!

Bradley

Répondez aux questions en français.

Exemple: **Pourquoi Bradley n'est-il pas parfait selon lui?**

> **Il préfère manger plutôt que faire du sport.**

1 1 · 1 Qu'est-ce que Bradley évite de manger et de boire?

[1 mark]

1 1 · 2 Qu'est-ce qu'il aime manger, mais qu'il ne mange pas en quantité suffisante?

[2 marks]

1 1 · 3 **Que pense Bradley du jogging?**

....

[1 mark]

1 1 · 4 **Que va-t-il faire pour être plus actif?**

....

[2 marks]

1 2 Les Boulots

Lisez ces conseils trouvés dans le magazine 'Au travail!'

Il est facile de penser que l'argent est la chose la plus importante dans la vie. Mais ce n'est pas toujours le cas. Avant de choisir sa carrière il faut bien réfléchir aux conséquences de ses choix. Généralement, on est bien payé lorsqu'on doit voyager pour son travail et passer beaucoup de temps au bureau. C'est bien quand on est jeune, mais est-ce toujours le cas quand on est marié et qu'on a de jeunes enfants?

1 2 · 1 **Que devrait-on considérer en choisissant sa future carrière?**

A	Le trajet
B	Les sacrifices
C	La durée du contrat

[2 marks]

Sylvain était comptable mais il l'a laissé pour devenir plombier.

«Je voulais travailler à mon compte. Oui je gagne un peu moins d'argent, et il y a des jours où je travaille de longues heures, mais je suis mon propre chef. Je décide de mes disponibilités et de la quantité de travail que je peux accepter.»

1 2 · 2 **Pourquoi Sylvain a-t-il changé de carrière?**

A	Plus d'indépendance
B	Plus d'argent
C	Moins d'heures

[2 marks]

Practice Exam Paper 3: Reading

1 3 Un Séjour dans les Montagnes

Lisez ce rapport sur un séjour dans les Alpes. Répondez aux questions en français.

La famille Hébras vient aux Alpes chaque été pour fuir la circulation et le bruit de sa ville de Bordeaux. Hugo, Marine et leurs enfants restent pour une quinzaine de jours dans un gîte.

Ils viennent parce que la vie ici est plus calme. Pas de rues sales, et pas de loyers chers.

«Mais ce n'est qu'une vacances» dit Hugo. «Moi, j'aime bien me reposer ici mais on a besoin d'une voiture. En ville les transports en commun sont fréquents donc on peut aller au travail en bus. En plus si un de mes enfants veut aller chez un ami, il peut y aller à pied. Ici il faut aller en voiture!»

1 3 · 1 Mentionnez deux problèmes de la vie en ville.

1 ....

[1 mark]

2 ....

[1 mark]

1 3 · 2 Mentionnez un problème de la vie dans les montagnes.

....

[1 mark]

Section C Translation into **English**

1 4   Your sister has seen this post on Facebook and asks you to translate it for her into **English**.

[9 marks]

> Nous allons de temps en temps aux grands concerts à Paris, parce qu'on peut toujours voir les groupes les plus populaires. La dernière fois que j'y suis allé, on a utilisé les transports en commun pour arriver au stade. Même si c'est pire pour l'environnement, mes amis préfèreraient prendre un taxi à l'avenir!

END OF QUESTIONS

Collins

GCSE
French
Higher Tier Paper 4 Writing

Time allowed: 1 hour 15 minutes

Instructions

- Use black ink or black ball-point pen.
- You must answer **three** questions.
- Answer all questions in **French.**
- Answer the questions in the spaces provided.

Information

- The marks for questions are shown in brackets.
- The maximum mark for this paper is 60.
- You must **not** use a dictionary during this test.
- In order to score the highest marks for Question 1 you must write something about each bullet point. You must use a variety of vocabulary and structures and include your opinions.
- In order to score the highest marks in Question 2 you must write something about both bullet points. You must use a variety of vocabulary and structures and include your opinions and reasons.

Name: _____

Question 1

Vous décrivez votre école pour votre blog.

Décrivez:

- vos matières préférées
- l'école et ses profs
- une journée scolaire récente
- vos projets pour l'année prochaine

Écrivez environ 90 mots en français. Répondez à chaque aspect de la question.

[16 marks]

Question 2

Vous écrivez un article sur les vacances pour un magazine français.

Décrivez:

- les activités que vous aimez normalement faire en vacances.
- des vacances désastreuses.

Écrivez environ 150 mots en français. Répondez aux deux aspects de la question.

[32 marks]

Question 3

Translate the following passage into **French**.

I use social media to stay in contact with my friends. It's very useful, because you can send messages, or share photos. Last weekend, I bought a tablet which is quicker than my computer and I did some research for my homework. Tomorrow, I am going to do some online shopping and I would like to download some music.

[12 marks]

END OF QUESTIONS

Answers

Me, My Family and Friends

Pages 148–149: My Family, My Friends & Marriage and Partnership

1. a) mon grand-père [1]
   b) ma tante [1]
   c) mon neveu [1]
   d) mon beau-frère [1]
   e) ma cousine [1]
   f) ma belle-mère [1]

2. Answers will vary. Example answer:
   (Description of boy) Il est toujours aimable et de bonne humeur. **[2]** Il n'est jamais égoïste ou têtu. **[2]**
   (Description of girl) Elle est toujours triste et agaçante. **[2]**
   Elle n'est jamais gentille ou heureuse. **[2]**

3. Answers will vary. Example answers:
   a) Je m'entends bien avec ma mère parce qu'elle est toujours patiente et gentille. **[2]**
   b) Je ne m'entends pas très bien avec mon cousin, puisqu'il n'est jamais sage ou aimable. **[2]**
   c) Je me dispute souvent avec ma sœur cadette, car elle est trop têtue et égoïste. **[2]**

4. Ma meilleure copine est mince et un peu plus grande que moi. **[1]**
   Elle a les yeux noisette et les cheveux noirs, courts et raides. **[1]**
   On se connaît depuis sept ans et on s'entend très bien ensemble. **[1]**
   Elle est toujours honnête et elle n'est jamais jalouse ou fâchée contre moi. **[1]**
   On a beaucoup de choses en commun. On aime la même musique et les mêmes films. **[1]**
   En plus, on a le même sens de l'humour, donc elle me fait toujours rire. **[1]**
   On se retrouve en ville tous les week-ends et on fait les magasins ensemble. **[1]**

5. Answers will vary. **[10]**

> **Tip**
> You can adapt the text in exercise 4 to describe your best friend. Make sure adjectives agree and that you use the correct definite article in '**le / la / les même(s)**…' to match the noun that follows.

6. Pour le mariage:
   b) Je voudrais me **marier** un jour. **[2]**
   e) C'est mieux pour les **enfants** si on est mariés. **[2]**
   Contre le mariage:
   a) Je préférerais **rester** célibataire. **[2]**
   c) Le mariage se **termine** souvent par un divorce. **[2]**
   d) À mon avis, le mariage, c'est **complètement** démodé. **[2]**
   f) Il vaut mieux habiter **ensemble** au lieu de se marier. **[2]**

Pages 150–151: Social Media & Mobile Technology

1. a) Je **passe** beaucoup de temps en ligne. [1]
   b) Je **vais** sur mes sites web préférés. [1]
   c) J'**envoie** et je **reçois** des messages. [2]
   d) Je **fais** des recherches pour mes devoirs. [1]
   e) Je **mets** des photos en ligne. [1]
   f) Je **tape** sur le clavier, je **clique** sur la souris et j'**imprime** des documents sur l'imprimante. [3]

2. Answers will vary. Example answer:
   Chaque jour, je vais sur mes sites web préférés. [1]
   Souvent, je reçois et j'envoie des messages. [1]
   Quelquefois, je fais des recherches pour mes devoirs. [1]
   Une fois par semaine, je mets des photos en ligne. [1]
   De temps en temps, j'imprime des documents. [1]

> **Tip**
> Saying how often you do things enhances what you say or write. Make sure you know a range of expressions of frequency.

3. a) ✗ Il ne faut jamais partager ses détails personnels. [1]
   b) ✓ Il faut installer un logiciel anti-virus. [1]
   c) ✗ Il ne faut pas communiquer avec des inconnus. [1]
   d) ✗ Il ne faut jamais révéler son mot de passe. [1]
   e) ✓ Il faut changer régulièrement son mot de passe. [1]

4. a) Karim [1]
   b) Alizée [1]
   c) Nolan [1]
   d) Mélissa [1]
   e) Lola [1]
   f) Hugo [1]
   g) Yasmine [1]
   h) William [1]

5. a) Tous les jours / Chaque jour, j'envoie des SMS à mes amis / copains. [2]
   b) J'utilise mon portable pour télécharger et écouter de la musique. [2]
   c) Hier, j'ai acheté le dernière modèle, mais c'était il m'a coûté cher. [2]
   d) Demain, je vais faire des recherches pour mes devoirs. [2]

Free-time Activities

Pages 152–153: Music & Cinema and TV

1. • Écoutes-tu souvent la musique?
     Oui, je télécharge la musique et je l'écoute sur mon lecteur MP3 ou mon portable tous les jours. [1]
   • Quel genre de musique préfères-tu?
     Je m'intéresse à tous styles de musique, mais le genre que j'aime le plus, c'est la musique pop. [1]
   • Est-ce que tu as un chanteur ou une chanteuse préféré(e)?
     Ma chanteuse anglaise préférée c'est Adele. Elle a une voix superbe et elle écrit des chansons fabuleuses. [1]
   • Pourquoi aimes-tu ses chansons?
     Parce que j'adore les mélodies et en plus, même si les paroles sont tristes, ses chansons me détendent. [1]
   • Es-tu déjà allé(e) à un concert ou un festival de musique?
     Oui, l'été dernier j'avais la chance de voir mon groupe favori en tournée. C'était magnifique! [1]

2. Examples:
J'adore la musique pop parce que les chansons me rendent heureux; J'aime mieux l'électro à cause du rythme vif; Je m'intéresse au vieux rock parce que la mélodie me plaît; Je ne suis pas fana du reggae à cause des paroles monotones. **[5]**

3. La musique <u>joue</u> **[1]** un rôle important dans la vie de ma famille. Mes parents se sont <u>rencontrés</u> **[1]** à un festival de musique <u>où</u> **[1]** mon père jouait dans un groupe. Nous avons <u>toujours</u> **[1]** écouté de la musique chez nous et on n'a <u>jamais</u> **[1]** choisi un genre préféré. Mes sœurs <u>chantent</u> **[1]** dans une chorale mais mon frère aîné aime <u>mieux</u> **[1]** jouer du violon dans un orchestre. Mon père joue toujours de la guitare, <u>même si</u> **[1]** ma mère dit que ses chansons sont démodées.

4. Examples:
a) Personnellement, je préfère les comédies parce qu'elles sont amusantes. **[2]** b) Quelquefois j'aime regarder les documentaires même s'ils sont tristes. **[2]** c) Je ne regarde jamais les films d'horreur car ils me font peur. **[2]** d) Le genre de films que j'aime le plus, c'est les dessins animés parce qu'ils me font rire. **[2]** e) Mes émissions préférées à la télé sont les jeux télévisés même s'ils ne sont pas éducatifs. **[2]**

5. a) Le film a lieu en Allemagne pendant la guerre. **[1]**
   b) Il s'agit d'une fille qui veut retrouver sa famille. **[1]**
   c) Il s'agit des soldats qui éliminent les adversaires. **[1]**

Pages 154–155: Food and Eating Out, Sport & Customs and Festivals

1. a) assiette de charcuterie **[1]**; b) thon mariné aux épices **[1]**; c) foie gras de canard **[1]**; d) entrecôte de bœuf poivré **[1]**; e) poêlée de légumes **[1]**; f) côtelette d'agneau **[1]**; g) haricots verts sautés à l'ail **[1]**; h) filet de veau **[1]**; i) figues rôties **[1]**; j) noix de coco **[1]**

2. a) a starter, a main course and a dessert are included in the €39.00 price **[1]**; b) drinks are not included **[1]**; c) this menu is not available on Bank Holidays **[1]**; d) the maximum group size is 10 (ten) people. **[1]**

3. Own answer. **[4]**

4. a) When I was younger, I wanted to go horse-riding. **[1]** b) In the past, my sister loved walking in the mountains. **[1]** c) Nowadays she is a winter sports enthusiast. **[1]** d) Before I used to go mountain-biking every Saturday, but now I no longer have any free time. **[1]** e) We would like to try extreme sports, even if they are a bit dangerous! **[1]**

5. a) Je joue au volley au centre sportif. **[1]** b) J'allais à la piscine trois fois par semaine. **[1]** c) Quand j'étais plus jeune, je voulais faire du skate. **[1]** d) Avant j'allais à la pêche tous les week-ends, mais maintenant je préfère les sports d'équipe. **[1]** e) Nous voudrions essayer les sports nautiques. **[1]**

6. Example sentences:

Pour célébrer Noël / Ramadan je crois qu'il est important d'aller à l'église / à la mosquée. **[1]**
Il n'est pas important de recevoir des cadeaux. **[1]**
Le jour de la fête nationale je pense qu'on (ne) doit (pas) danser dans les rues. **[1]**
Pour fêter un mariage, l'essentiel est de féliciter les nouveaux mariés. **[1]**

Pendant les fêtes traditionnelles à mon avis, on doit chanter des chansons traditionnelles. **[1]**
Pendant les jours fériés je pense qu'il faut manger des repas traditionnels. **[1]**
(1 mark for each sentence, up to a maximum of 4 marks.)

Environment and Social Issues

Pages 156–157: At Home, Where I Live & Town or Country?

1. 1. e) **[1]**
   2. c) **[1]**
   3. a) **[1]**
   4. f) **[1]**
   5. b) **[1]**
   6. d) **[1]**

2. a) maison **[1]**
   b) huit **[1]**
   c) côté **[1]**
   d) grande **[1]**
   e) nettoie **[1]**
   f) mur **[1]**

3. Answers will vary. Example answers:
   J'ai dépensé tout mon argent. **[2]**
   J'ai mangé une pizza. **[2]**
   J'ai perdu mon porte-monnaie. **[2]**
   J'ai acheté une robe. **[2]**
   J'ai essayé un pantalon. **[2]**

4. a) Simon **[1]**
   b) Karim **[1]**
   c) Georges **[1]**
   d) Karine **[1]**
   e) Benoît **[1]**
   f) Mélissa **[1]**

5. a) Ma chambre est toujours propre. **[2]**
   b) À l'étage il y a quatre chambres. **[2]**
   c) La salle de bains se trouve en face du bureau. **[2]**
   d) Il n'y a pas de marché ni de centre commercial, mais on peut se garer gratuitement. **[2]**
   e) Il y a plus de circulation en ville qu'à la campagne. **[2]**

Pages 158–159: Charity and Voluntary Work & Healthy and Unhealthy Living

1. Example sentences:
   Je voudrais aider les SDF. **[1]**
   J'aimerais livrer des médicaments. **[1]**
   Je voudrais faire des collectes d'argent. **[1]**
   J'aimerais visiter les personnes âgées. **[1]**
   (1 mark for each sentence, up to a maximum of 5 marks.)

2. Example responses:
   Je voudrais aider les SDF. – I would like to help the homeless. **[2]**
   J'aimerais livrer des médicaments. – I would like to deliver medicines. **[2]**
   Je voudrais faire des collectes d'argent. – I would like to collect money for charity. **[2]**
   J'aimerais rendre visite à des personnes âgées. – I would like to visit older people. **[2]**
   (2 marks for each sentence, up to a maximum of 10 marks.)

3. a) Il faut manger sainement. **[1]**
   b) Je garde la forme parce que je mange bien. **[1]**
   c) Je vais essayer de faire un régime. **[1]**

4. 1. b) [1]
2. d) [1]
3. c) [1]
4. g) [1]
5. e) [1]
6. f) [1]
7. a) [1]

5. a) He delivered medication. [1]
b) Go to Africa to help there. [1]
c) Drinking water. [1]

6. a) Je reste en forme parce que je dors bien / j'ai suffisamment de sommeil. [2]
b) Je ne mange pas de produits malsains. [2]
c) Il faut manger sainement. [2]
d) Elle mange toujours équilibré. [2]
e) Ma mère a arrêté de fumer. [2]

Pages 160–161: The Environment & Poverty and Insecurity

1. a) We mustn't [1] waste [1] our natural resources [1].
b) It is important [1] to protect [1] our environment [1] by recycling [1] more [1].
c) I think that [1] we should [1] encourage [1] everyone [1] to sort out [1] their rubbish [1].

2. a) Je pense qu' [1] il est important de [1] protéger [1] nos ressources naturelles [1].
b) On devrait [1] protéger [1] notre environnement [1] en triant [1] nos déchets [1].
c) Il y a [1] de plus en plus de [1] gens [1] qui [1] gaspillent [1] l'énergie [1].

3. a) 5% [1] b) 10% [1] c) 25% [1] d) 15% [1] e) 5% [1]

4. a) [dans ma ville] il y a de plus en plus de personnes qui sont au chômage [dans ma ville] [1]
In my town there are more and more people who are unemployed. [1]
b) [dans mon village] le nombre de sans-abris augmente rapidement [dans mon village] [1]
In my village the number of homeless people is increasing rapidly. [1]
c) malheureusement on voit de plus en plus de pauvreté dans ma ville [1]
Unfortunately we can see more and more poverty in my town. [1]
d) l'augmentation des bandes dans mon quartier est un souci pour tout le monde [1]
The increase of gangs in my neighbourhood is a worry for everyone. [1]

5. a) maintenant [1]   b) chômage [1]   c) avant [1]
d) était [1]   e) active [1]   f) sans-abris [1]
g) davantage [1]   h) combattre [1]

Travel and Tourism

Pages 162–163: Travel and Tourism 1, 2 and 3

1. 1. Karim [1]
2. Isidor [1]
3. Isidor [1]
4. Isidor [1]
5. Karim [1]

2. 1. Farida [1]
2. Hugo [1]
3. Laure [1]
4. Sylvie [1]
5. Martin [1]

3. a) true [1]
b) false [1]
c) false [1]
d) true [1]
e) false [1]

4. a) Next year I would like to stay in a villa. [1]
b) Normally I go on holiday in the mountains with my family for two weeks. [1]
c) Last summer I spent one month in a youth hostel in the countryside. [1]
d) Two years ago we spent our holiday in a 3 star campsite by the sea. [1]
e) Usually I like to get up very late because I like to have a lie-in on holiday. [1]

Studies and Employment

Pages 164–165: My Studies and Life at School

1. French [1]
PE [1]
Art [1]
Chemistry [1]
German [1]

2. a) Yann [1]
b) Amélie [1]
c) He finds it easy. [1]
d) Her teacher thinks she is very good at it [1], she thinks that she is a bit weak at it [1].
e) She loves it [1] but she is weak at it [1].
f) It's practical [1] and the teacher is funny [1].

3. seconde [1]
aime [1]
commence [1]
cours [1]
pause [1]
car [1]
maquillage [1]
porte [1]

4. a) This summer I am going to sit my exams. [2]
b) If you don't understand you must ask a teacher. [2]
c) I bring my own lunch to school. [2]
d) Fabrice must resit the year because he did not pass his exams. [2]
e) There is too much pressure for the students. [2]

Pages 166–167: Education Post-16 & Career Choices and Ambitions

1. 1. b) [1]
2. f) [1]
3. e) [1]
4. d) [1]
5. c) [1]
6. a) [1]

2. a) David [1]
b) Simone [1]
c) Farah [1]
d) Rachel [1]
e) Justine [1]
f) Lisa [1]

3. a) Je voudrais aller à la fac l'année prochaine. [2]
b) J'ai laissé tomber le dessin l'année dernière. [2]
c) J'ai l'intention de voyager quand j'aurai quitté l'école. [2]
d) Je vais aller à la fac. [2]
e) Je n'ai aucune idée de ce que je veux faire. [2]

4. a) interesting, varied, includes travel, well paid (any 2) [2]
   b) plumber [1]
   c) rewarding, he likes working for himself, he earns enough money (any 2) [2]
   d) boss [1]
   e) on the beach, United States [2]

5. Example paragraph:
L'année prochaine j'ai l'intention de continuer mes études parce que je voudrais aller à la fac pour étudier les sciences. À l'avenir je vais être ingénieur et je serai riche et célèbre. Je gagnerai deux cent mille euros par an. J'habiterai en Suisse ou j'aurai une grande maison à la campagne. Tous les jours je ferai du ski et je serai très heureux et en forme. [10]

Grammar 1

Pages 168–169: Gender, Plurals and Articles & Adjectives

1.

Singular	Plural
un enfant (a child)	des **enfants** children) [1]
une **fleur** (a flower) [1]	des fleurs (flowers)
un **animal** (an animal) [1]	des animaux (animals)
un chapeau (a hat)	des **chapeaux** (hats) [1]
un **jeu** (a game) [1]	des jeux (games)
un Français (a French person)	des **Français** (French people) [1]

2. a) Dans ma ville, il y a **une** piscine. **La** piscine est dans le centre sportif. [2]
   b) Dans mon village, il y a **un** café. **Le** café est tout près de ma maison. [2]
   c) Dans la rue où j'habite, il y a **des** magasins. **Les** magasins sont utiles. [2]
   d) Dans notre village, il y a **une** église. **L'**église est très vieille et historique. [2]
   e) Dans ma ville, il y a **un** centre commercial. **Le** centre commercial est énorme. [2]
   f) Dans le quartier où j'habite, il y a **des** restaurants, mais **les** restaurants sont trop chers. [2]

3. a) Tu veux **de la** glace? Elle est vraiment délicieuse. [1]
   b) Tu veux **du** fromage? Il a très bon goût. [1]
   c) Tu veux **des** carottes? Elles sont bonnes pour la santé.[1]
   d) Tu veux **de l'**eau? Il faut boire beaucoup d'eau. [1]
   e) Tu veux **du** gâteau? Il est au chocolat! [1]
   f) Tu veux **des** raisins? Ils ne coûtent pas trop chers. [1]

4. J'habite avec **mon** [1] père, **ma** [1] mère et mes deux frères. Notre maison est assez moderne, mais **notre** [1] jardin est très petit. Je partage ma chambre avec mon frère cadet: mon lit est dans le coin et **son** [1] lit est devant la fenêtre. Mon frère aîné a la meilleure chambre: **sa** [1] chambre est plus grande que la mienne. Nous avons aussi deux chiens. **Nos** [1] chiens s'appellent Boule et Bill. **Mes** [1] parents travaillent pour la même entreprise. **Leur** [1] bureau n'est pas loin de notre maison. Et toi? Il y a combien de personnes dans **ta** famille? Où travaillent **tes** [1] parents?

Tip
The possessive adjectives **'notre / nos'** (our) and **'leur / leurs'** (their) are often forgotten and can trip people up in an exam. Learn them carefully.

5. a) C'est un **bon** film. [2]
   b) C'est une **jolie** fille. [2]
   c) C'est une voiture **noire**. [2]
   d) Ce sont des garçons **intelligents**. [2]
   e) Ce sont les **meilleures** baskets. [2]

6. a) Ta / Votre maison est plus belle que ma maison. [2]
   b) Mon chien est moins intelligent que ton / votre chien. [2]
   c) Elle est la plus grande fille du collège. [2]

Pages 170–171: Adverbs and the Present Tense

1. a) Je n'ai pas beaucoup d'argent. J'ai **seulement** trois euros! [1]
   b) **Malheureusement,** je ne peux pas venir à ta fête, parce que je suis malade. [1]
   c) Tu marches trop **lentement**! Le film commence dans cinq minutes! [1]
   d) Oh, merci! Des chocolats! C'est **vraiment** très gentil. [1]
   e) Tu connais mon frère? Ah, oui, je le connais très **bien**. [1]
   f) Hier, j'étais malade, mais aujourd'hui, je vais beaucoup **mieux**. [1]

Tip
Adverbs like **'malheureusement'**, **'vraiment'** and **'mieux'** can be hard to spell correctly, but if spoken and written correctly, they will impress an examiner, so learn them by heart.

2.

Regular –er verb	Regular –ir verb	Regular –re verb
donner (to give)	**choisir** (to choose)	**attendre** (to wait)
je donne (I give) [1] **tu donnes** (you give) [1] **il /elle / on donne** (he / she / one gives) [1] **nous donnons** (we give) [1] **vous donnez** (you give) [1] **ils / elles donnent** (they give) [1]	**je choisis** (I choose)[1] **tu choisis** (you choose) [1] **il / elle / on choisit** (he / she / one chooses) [1] **nous choisissons** (we choose) [1] **vous choisissez** (you choose) [1] **ils / elles choisissent** (they choose) [1]	**j'attends** (I wait) [1] **tu attends** (you wait) [1] **il / elle / on attend** (he / she / one waits) [1] **nous attendons** (we wait) [1] **vous attendez** (you wait) [1] **ils / elles attendent** (they wait) [1]

Tip
By learning the endings for regular –er, –ir and –re verbs, you can apply them to new verbs you come across. There are many, many verbs in French, so make sure you know how they work!

3. Verbs must be as shown. Rest of each sentence will vary. Example answers:
   a) Il **porte** un pantalon gris. [2]
   b) Nous **aidons** nos parents. [2]
   c) Elles **travaillent** dans un magasin de mode. [2]
   d) Tu **perds** souvent ton portable! [2]
   e) Je **réponds** à la question. [2]
   f) Vous **choisissez** quel dessert? [2]

4. a) Je *me* lève de bonne heure. (I get up early.) [2]

b) *Il* s'entend bien avec sa sœur. (He gets on well with his sister.) [2]

c) Mes parents *se* fâchent contre moi. (My parents get angry with me.) [2]

d) *Nous* nous amusons bien au parc. (We have fun in the park.) [2]

e) *Tu* te couches à quelle heure? (What time do you go to bed?) [2]

f) Vous *vous* ennuyez le dimanche? (Do you get bored on Sundays?) [2]

5. a) J'habite ici depuis cinq ans. [1]

b) Je fais du judo depuis deux ans. [1]

c) J'étudie le français depuis six ans. [1]

> **Tip**
> Remember, when translating, that you use **depuis** + the *present tense* to say how long something has been going on, even though we use a past tense (has / have been…), in English.

6. a) Écoute le professeur! [1]

b) Allez aux magasins! [1]

Grammar 2

Pages 172–173: Using Verbs in the Present Tense and Future Time-frame

1. a) Nous n'avons pas envie de rentrer. [1] b) Ils sont en train de tchatter en ligne. [1] c) Vous voulez sortir samedi soir? [1] d) Elles ne peuvent pas venir. [1] e) Vous me faites rigoler! [1] f) Nous allons passer des vacances à la plage. [1]

2.

+ Infinitive only		+ à + infinitive		+ de + infinitive	
adorer	[1]	apprendre	[1]	arrêter	[1]
aimer	[1]	commencer	[1]	décider	[1]
espérer	[1]	s'intéresser	[1]	essayer	[1]
préférer	[1]	réussir	[1]	éviter	[1]

3. a) Je vais passer le week-end à Paris. [1] b) Nous allons (On va) visiter la Tour Eiffel. [1] c) Nous allons (On va) manger dans un restaurant français renommé. [1] d) Les filles vont jouer au volley. [1] e) Vas-tu sortir ce soir? [1]

4. L'année prochaine **je vais rester / je resterai [1]** au collège. Si j'ai de bonnes notes, je vais **étudier / j'étudierai [1]** les sciences. **Ça va être / Ce sera [1]** plus amusant de choisir ce qu'on apprend! Après les examens, je **vais partir / je partirai [1]** en vacances avec mes copains. Nous **allons aller / nous irons [1]** à la campagne et nous **allons faire / nous ferons [1]** du camping sauvage. S'il fait beau, on **va (vouloir)/ on voudra [1]** essayer l'escalade et l'équitation. En fait, on **va (pouvoir) / on pourra [1]** faire tout ce qu'on veut! Quelle aventure!

5. If I were the Minister of the Environment, I would change a lot of things! Everyone would have to recycle (their) rubbish. Adults would not waste energy. Children would save water. The government would really want to protect endangered animals. It would be an ideal world. [7]

6. a) S'il pleuvait, nous ferions des achats en ville. [1]

b) S'il venait chez nous, on visiterait Paris. [1]

c) Si je réussissais à mon bac, je chercherais un emploi. [1]

d) Si j'avais plus d'argent, j'achèterais une voiture. [1]

e) Si je gagnais à la loterie, j'aiderais les sans-abris. [1]

Pages 174 and 175: Past Time-frame: Perfect Tense & Imperfect Tense and Pluperfect Tense

1. a) Nous **sommes** venus trop tard. [1] b) Je n'ai rien **bu**. [1] c) Ils /Elles n'ont pas vu le film. [1] d) Elles **ne** sont **pas** parties en vacances. [1] e) Ils ont **mangé** des escargots. [1]

2. Own answer. [10]

3. a) Après avoir entendu les nouvelles, il a téléphoné à son copain. [1] b) Après avoir fait une promenade, nous avons mangé un gâteau au café. [1] c) Après être arrivés au marché de Noël, nous avons acheté des cadeaux. [1] d) Après s'être levée très tôt le matin, elle est partie à l'étranger. [1]

4. a) Elle ne voulait pas sortir. = She didn't want to go out. [1] b) Il y avait trop de monde. = There were too many people. [1] c) C'était trop bruyant. = It was too noisy. [1] d) Il faisait trop chaud. = It was too hot. [1]

5. a) Pour fêter mon dernier anniversaire, ma famille <u>a organisé</u> une surprise partie. [1]

b) Mes parents <u>ont loué</u> une salle dans le centre-ville, mais je n'en <u>savais</u> rien. [2]

c) Tous mes amis <u>sont venus</u> vers sept heures et demie – ils <u>étaient</u> très excités! [2]

d) Quand je <u>suis arrivé(e)</u> à huit heures, tout le monde <u>se cachait</u> derrière un grand rideau! [2]

e) C'<u>était</u> une soirée inoubliable – nous <u>avons dansé</u> et (nous avons) <u>célébré</u> jusqu'à minuit. [3]

6.

Infinitive	Perfect tense	Imperfect tense	Pluperfect tense
avoir	j'ai eu – I had	j'avais – I was having	j'avais eu – I had had
mettre	j'ai mis – I put [1]	je mettais – I was putting [1]	j'avais mis – I had put [1]
devoir	j'ai dû – I had to [1]	je devais – I had to [1]	j'avais dû – I had had to [1]
sortir	je suis sorti(e) – I went out [1]	je sortais – I was going out [1]	j'étais sorti(e) – I had gone out [1]
se coucher	je me suis couché(e) – I went to bed [1]	je me couchais – I was going to bed [1]	je m'étais couché(e) – I had gone to bed [1]

Grammar 3

Pages 176–177: Pronouns and Questions

1. a) les [1]   b) la [1]   c) les [1]   d) l' [1]   e) la [1]

2. a) elle [1]

b) elle [1]

c) nous [1]

d) ils [1]

e) elles [1]

3. a) Je ne les aime pas. [1]
   b) Je suis d'accord avec elle. [1]
   c) Je ne suis pas d'accord avec eux. [1]
   d) Je suis resté(e) chez moi hier. [1]
   e) Je ne les gaspille pas. [1]

4. a) qui [1] b) où [1] c) combien de temps [1]
   d) quand [1] e) avec qui [1] f) comment [1]
   g) pourquoi [1] h) pour qui [1]

5. a) Est-ce que tu recycles? [1]
   b) Avec qui est-ce que tu vas en vacances normalement? [1]
   c) Pourquoi est-ce que tu gaspilles l'électricité? [1]
   d) Où est-ce que tu voudrais aller en vacances? [1]

6. Answers will vary. Suggested answers:
   Où es-tu allée en vacances? [1]
   Comment as-tu voyagé? Comment as-tu trouvé les vacances? [1]
   Pourquoi y es-tu allé(e)? [1]
   Quand as-tu voyagé? Quand es-tu parti(e)? Quand es-tu revenu(e)? [1]
   Avec qui es-tu allé(e) en vacances / avec qui as-tu passé tes vacances? [1]

Pages 178–179: Prepositions and Conjunctions & Subjunctive Mood and the Passive Voice

1. a) de [1]
   b) sans [1]
   c) pour [1]
   d) en [1]
   e) depuis [1]

2. a) selon ma mère [1]
   b) sans passer [1]
   c) pour protéger [1]
   d) parmi les problèmes [1]
   e) malgré mes efforts [1]

3. a) pourtant [1]
   b) alors [1]
   c) à cause de [1]
   d) donc [1]
   e) parce qu' [1]

4. a) comme = as [1] lorsque = when [1] si = if [1]
   puisque = since [1] tandis que = whereas [1]
   b) 1. si [1]
      2. comme [1]
      3. puisque [1]
      4. lorsque [1]
      5. tandis que [1]

5. The sentences in the subjunctive are a and c. [5]

6. a) soit: subjunctive [1]
   b) est [1]
   c) fasse: subjunctive [1]
   d) puisse: subjunctive [1]
   e) est [1]

7. a) Although my town is quite modern, there are a lot of problems with poverty. [1]
   b) I don't doubt that the hotel is quite disappointing. [1]
   c) I must do more to protect the environment. [1]
   d) I am happy that my friend is able to come with us on holiday this summer. [1]
   e) Even if it is sometimes difficult to recycle, we must do our best. [1]

8. The sentences in the passive voice are a, c and d. [5]

Pages 180–191

Higher Tier Paper 1 Listening – Mark Scheme

Section A Questions and answers in English

1. E [1]; 2. C [1]; 3. A [1]; 4. D [1]; 5. C [1]; 6. C [1]; 7. A [1]
8.1 A [1]; 8.2 C [1]; 9.1 C [1]; 9.2 A [1]; 10.1 B [1]; 10.2 C [1]
11. Advantage: it's practical (when you live a long way from shopping centres) [1]
Disadvantage: you / one can't try things on [1]
12. Advantage: compare prices (before buying) [1]
Disadvantage: (waiting for) delivery [1]
13. everything / necessary [1]; (more) (self-) confidence [1]
14. what they like / what they want [1]; all look the same / dress in the same way [1]
15.1 he hates team sports [1]; 15.2 he likes doing water sports (at the beach) / he would like to try wind-surfing / it will be more fun than football [any two for 2 marks]
16.1 C [1]; 16.2 11am / 11 o'clock [1]; 16.3 have dinner / cruise on the river [1]; go to one of the parks (with a great view of the Eiffel Tower) [1]
17.1 the supermarket will offer a wide range of cheaper items and more people will shop there [1];
17.2 the smaller shops may be forced to close as a result [1]
18.1 more people will visit the town [1]; 18.2 infrastructure (roads, public transport) will improve [1]
19.1 town should welcome new jobs and houses [1];
19.2 supermarket should give free advertising to local businesses [1]
20.1 A [1]; 20.2 C [1]
21.1 A [1]; 21.2 B [1]
22.1 A [1]; 22.2 C [1]

Section B Questions and answers in French

23. A [1], E [1]; 24. C [1], D [1]
25.1. importante [1]; 25.2. facile [1]; 25.3. parler [1]; 25.4. méchant [1]
26. (i) B [1] (ii) C [1]

Pages 192–194

Higher Tier Paper 2 Speaking – Mark Scheme

Role-play

Your teacher will start the role-play by saying an introductory text such as:
Introduction: Tu discutes avec ton ami français des problèmes d'environnement. Moi, je suis ton ami/e.
1. <u>Teacher</u>: **Quels sont les problèmes de l'environnement dans ta ville?**
   What are the environmental problems in your town?
   <u>Student</u>: **Dans ma ville il y a trop de circulation et il y a beaucoup de déchets par terre.**
   In my town there is too much traffic and there is a lot of rubbish on the ground.

> **Tip**
> Make sure you include two elements as required in the question.

2. Unprepared question
   <u>Teacher</u>: **Qu'est-ce que tu fais pour protéger l'environnement dans ta ville?**
   What do you do to protect the environment in your town?

Student: Suggested answers: any of:
Je marche. / Je trie mes déchets. / Je ne prends pas la voiture. / Je vais à l'école en vélo.
I walk. / I sort out my rubbish. / I don't use the car. / I cycle to school.
[anything that you do to help protect the environment in the present tense]

3. Teacher: **Qu'est-ce que tu as fait récemment?**
   What have you done recently?
   Student: **Hier je suis allée à l'école à pied et j'ai recyclé mes déchets.**
   Yesterday I walked to school and I recycled my rubbish.

4. Teacher: **À ton avis qu'est-ce qu'il faudrait changer dans ta ville pour améliorer la situation?**
   In your opinion what should be changed in your town to help protect the environment?
   Student: **Je pense qu'on devrait utiliser plus les transports en commun parce qu'il y a trop de voitures.**
   I think that we should use public transport more because there are too many cars.

5. Asking a question
   Student: **Est-ce que tu recycles chez toi?**
   Do you recycle at home?

Teacher: **Oui je fais attention à ma consommation d'énergie**
Yes, I pay attention to my energy consumption.

Preparation tips

When you are preparing for your role-play consider:
- How many elements you need to include in each of your answers
- Whether you need to use 'tu' or 'vous'
- The tense that is expected – the tense will be inferred. For example, in this role-play we have the past implied by récemment (recently).

For the question you need to ask, examine the tense of the question and whether you are going to say 'tu' or 'vous'.

Photo Card

Example answers:

1st question
Sur la photo, il y a un groupe de jeunes gens qui sont assis sur un lit. Je pense qu'ils sont chez un d'eux. Ils s'amusent bien et ils rient beaucoup. C'est peut-être à cause d'une

blague / une histoire drôle que quelqu'un a racontée. Il y a quatre filles et trois garçons et je crois qu'ils se connaissent bien et qu'ils sont très bons amis.

2nd question
À mon avis, il est très important d'avoir de bons amis, parce qu'il faut avoir quelqu'un avec qui on peut sortir, s'amuser et parler de ses problèmes. Pour moi, un bon ami est quelqu'un qui est toujours fidèle, qui n'est jamais de mauvaise humeur et avec qui on a beaucoup de choses en commun.

3rd question
D'habitude, je sors avec mes amis tous les week-ends. Normalement, on se retrouve en ville, on fait les magasins et ensuite on prend un casse-croûte quelque part. Samedi dernier, après avoir mangé une pizza, on est allés au cinéma ensemble. On a vu un film de science-fiction, mais je l'ai trouvé un peu ennuyeux. Le Samedi prochain, je pense qu'on va jouer au bowling. On va s'amuser bien!

You will be asked two further questions, on the same topic. Other questions you might be asked are:
- Décris-moi ton meilleur ami / ta meilleure amie. Il / Elle est comment?
- Pourquoi est-ce que tu t'entends bien avec lui / elle?
- Qu'est-ce que vous faites ensemble?
- Qu'est-ce que tu feras avec tes amis, le week-end prochain / pendant les vacances?
- À ton avis, quelles sont les qualités d'un(e) bon(ne) ami(e)?
- Comment est-ce qu'on peut se faire de nouveaux amis?

Prepare your answers to these questions, too!

General Conversation

Theme 2: Local, national, international and global areas of interest

Aimed at Foundation level candidate – 3–5 minutes

Comment est ta maison?

J'habite dans une grande maison jumelée en ville. Il y a neuf pièces et un petit jardin. Au rez-de-chaussée il y a le salon et la salle à manger, qui se trouve en face de la cuisine. À l'étage il y a trois chambres, un bureau et la salle de bains. Ma chambre se trouve en face de la chambre de mes parents. J'adore ma maison parce que c'est grand!

Tu aimes ta chambre?

Oui, j'adore ma chambre parce qu'elle est grande et toujours propre. Je nettoie ma chambre tous les week-ends. J'ai une grande armoire, une commode et beaucoup de posters au mur.

Qu'est-ce qu'il y a pour les jeunes dans ta ville?

Il y a un centre commercial avec beaucoup de magasins. J'adore y aller avec mes amis pour les soldes parce que tout est bon marché. Il y a un parc qui se trouve près de la gare, mais il n'y a pas de cinéma. En plus on a besoin d'un cinéma.

Quels sont les bienfaits et désavantages d'habiter en campagne?

Ici à la campagne il n'y a pas beaucoup de circulation et c'est calme et tranquille. C'est un endroit très propre et on voit les collines tous les matins. La ville est trop bruyante et chère. En revanche, on n'a pas de voisins et je dois me déplacer en voiture pour voir mes amis.

Qu'as tu fait le week-end dernier pour être en bonne santé?

Le week-end dernier j'ai fait beaucoup de sport. Samedi matin je suis allé(e) à la piscine avec mon ami, et l'après-midi nous avons fait du vélo. Dimanche j'ai joué au rugby pour mon club local. J'ai évité les produits gras et j'ai bu plein d'eau minérale.

As-tu des projets pour vivre plus sainement?

Oui, l'année prochaine je vais aller au gymnase pour faire de la musculation. Pour le moment je suis trop jeune. Je vais continuer à manger sainement. Par exemple je vais éviter les aliments gras et je vais arrêter de manger des gâteaux. C'est ma faiblesse.

Theme 3: Current and future study and employment

Aimed at Higher level candidate – 5–7 minutes

Qu'est-ce que tu n'aimes pas comme matières? Pourquoi ?

J'aime bien les sciences. Je suis très fort(e) en biologie et en chimie en particulière. En plus le prof de biologie est marrant. Ma matière préférée c'est l'histoire-géo parce que c'est intéressant et utile. Je n'aime pas le dessin parce que, à mon avis, c'est barbant. Je déteste la technologie car je suis nul(le) en toutes les matières pratiques.

Pourquoi as-tu choisi d'étudier le français?

J'ai choisi le français parce que c'est une matière que j'adore. C'est génial parce que je peux parler français quand je vais en France avec ma famille. J'ai l'intention de continuer mes études au lycée l'année prochaine, et j'irai peut-être à la fac. J'aimerais travailler à l'étranger.

Quelles sont les différences entre les écoles en France et en Angleterre?

> **Tip**
> Sometimes you may need to apply what you have learned to a slightly different angle on a topic. Here drawing a comparison allows for the use of comparative language, but also for you to talk about what you know about the system in France. If you have personal experience such as an exchange visit, talk about it!

En Angleterre on doit porter un uniforme scolaire, mais en France on peut porter n'importe quoi. J'ai fait un échange scolaire et j'ai remarqué qu'il y a moins de technologie dans les cours. Les journées scolaires sont plus longues en France. On commence à huit heures et on finit à dix-sept heures. C'est une longue journée, je préfère la journée scolaire ici!

À ton avis, quelles sont les pressions pour les élèves dans ton collège?

> **Tip**
> A question such as this allows for a range of structures as there is no tense or structured argument necessary. Take a point of view and stick to it. This candidate has used a modal verb (**devoir** – to have to) as well as structures such as '**il faut** – it is necessary'. These mean the same thing but demonstrate that this candidate has a good range of language.

Il faut faire trop de devoirs chaque nuit. Moi, je vais passer mes examens cette été donc si on va réussir on doit faire des longues heures de révision. Même le week-end! Je dois réussir parce que j'ai l'intention d'aller au lycée l'année prochaine.

Qu'est-ce que tu-vas étudier au lycée l'année prochaine? / As-tu l'intention d'aller au lycée l'année prochaine?

> **Tip**
> These questions are testing the future tense so this candidate has demonstrated a number of ways of indicating the future. Reasons for choices are given too, with 'car' replacing 'parce que' to demonstrate variety.

J'adore les langues donc j'aimerais étudier l'espagnol et le français. C'est important pour moi car après le lycée je voudrais prendre une année sabbatique. Je vais voyager donc je voudrais parler des langues étrangères. Je laisserai tomber mes autres matières sauf les maths.

Comment serait ton emploi idéal?

> **Tip**
> A question such as this opens up the possibility to be creative and a bit zany. This candidate has talked about the dream features as one would expect of a teenager. However, the candidate then comes back to what is important and what his or her own family does.

Mon emploi idéal sera évidemment bien payé! Je voudrais avoir une grande maison au bord de la mer et une voiture de luxe. Mais il est important que c'est un boulot varié et enrichissant. Ce que j'espère, c'est que je travaillerai à mon compte et que je voyagerai un peu. Mon père est patron de sa propre entreprise et j'espère faire quelque chose de semblable. J'aurai une famille et je ferai ce qui me rend heureux(euse).

Pages 195–211

Higher Tier Paper 3 Reading – Mark Scheme

Section A Questions and answers in English

1.1 C [1], D [1]; **1.2** B [1], D [1]
2.1 A + B [1]; **2.2** A [1]; **2.3** B [1]; **2.4** B [1]
3.1 she doesn't like it [1]; **3.2** he is annoyed [1]; **3.3** because children (accept we) grow up too fast [1]
4.1 B [1]; **4.2** One of: They want to laugh (at Nicolas) / have a laugh; Nicolas looks like a puppet / clown when he has been to the hairdresser's; they want to see how the hairdresser does it [1].
4.3 Rufus says he will tell / complain to his father, who is a policeman [1]; **4.4** C [1]
5.1 That his school is much cleaner [1]; **5.2** not very happy / they were a waste of money [1]; **5.3** there were already enough bins [1]; **5.4** they are lazy [1]
6.1 C [1]; **6.2** C [1]; **6.3** A [1]; **6.4** B [1]
7.1 She agrees with it. [1] **7.2** Internet access makes it easy to cheat (in class / in exams), because you can find information about everything (quickly). [1]
8.1 less than half [1]; **8.2** the difference between the sexes / boys and girls [1]; **8.3.** they have a negative image / opinion of physical activity [1]; **8.4.** B [1]
9.1

	Reason	Complaint
Mobile phones not allowed in class	A distraction [1]	Wants to look on the internet / use a calculator [1]

9.2

	Reason	Complaint
Pressures	Exams to pass [1]	Tired / long school days [1]

Section B Questions and answers in French

10. «Moi? Je [G] comme tout le monde moi…Tu promets de rentrer un peu plus [B] [1] que d'habitude?» «Oui», accepta Sébastien, «je rentrerai aussitôt que [H] [1] commencera à tomber. Pour Angelina et aussi parce que Belle doit manger son lard. Tu sais, je crois que maintenant elle ne chasse plus, elle préfère la soupe qu'Angelina lui [A] [1]! Je la pose tous les soirs au pied de l'escalier et [E] [1] il n'y a plus rien. Il n'y a pas longtemps de ça, tu sais, deux ou trois jours seulement. Avant elle [C] [1] mais elle ne touchait pas à la soupe.»

11.1 Il évite les produits qui sont plein de sucre. [1]
11.2 Fruits et légumes [1]; poisson [1]
11.3 C'est ennuyeux [1]
11.4 Il va jouer au foot [1]; il va nager un peu [1]
12.1 B [2]
12.2 A [2]
13.1 (2 from) Le bruit [1]; la circulation [1]; le loyer cher [1]; les rues sales [1]
13.2 (1 from) Transport moins fréquent [1]; besoin de voyager en voiture [1]

Section C Translation into English

Nous allons de temps en temps	From time to time / sometimes / now and then we go [1]
aux grands concerts à Paris,	to large / big concerts in Paris [1]
parce qu'on peut toujours voir	because we / you / one / people can always see [1]
les groupes les plus populaires.	the most popular groups. [1]
La dernière fois que j'y suis allé,	The last time that I went there [1]
on a utilisé les transports en commun	we / I used public transport [1]
pour arriver au stade.	to get to the stadium [1]
Même si c'est pire pour l'environnement,	Even if it's worse for the environment, [1]
mes amis préfèreraient prendre un taxi à l'avenir!	my friends would prefer to take a / go by taxi in future! [1]

Pages 212–215

Higher Tier Paper 4 Writing – Mark Scheme

Question 1

> **Tip**
> This type of question asks for a lot of information in comparatively few words. It does not matter if you go a little over but do not spend time counting words. Get a feel for what 90 words looks like in advance. Then, when completing the question stick to the point.

It is vital that you answer each part of the question, even if only to give an opinion or fact. The bullet points will guide you into doing things that the examiner wants to see. For example, here the last two points are looking for the use of tenses. This will often be the case.

Example answer:

Ma matière préférée à l'école est la chimie parce que je suis fort en sciences et que c'est pratique et intéressant. J'aime aussi l'espagnol parce que mon prof est super marrant! L'école est grande et il y a neuf cents élèves. Les profs sont habiles et agréables mais le proviseur est très sévère. Hier j'ai commencé à neuf heures par deux heures de sciences. Après la récré on a eu un cours de maths puis d'anglais. Après avoir mangé j'ai eu une heure de musique.
L'année prochaine je vais continuer mes études au lycée où je ferai des sciences et du français. [16]

Question 2

Example answer:

Mes vacances
Ce que j'aime le plus (1) c'est me promener **en plein air (2)** <u>surtout</u> **si (3) nous allons (4)** à la montagne. **Ce qui me plaît (5)** aussi c'est de découvrir la région **où (6)** nous sommes, <u>alors</u> je visite <u>souvent</u> des sites historiques **comme (7)** les églises ou les châteaux. **Je ne pourrais pas (8)** passer mes vacances à **ne rien faire (9)** <u>car pour moi</u> les vacances c'est pour découvrir! Je ne comprends pas les gens **qui (10)** passent des heures sur la plage. Moi, **je trouverais (11)** ça très ennuyeux. J'adore <u>aussi</u> **goûter (12)** aux spécialités de la région. Par exemple l'année dernière **nous avons passé (13)** nos vacances dans le sud de la France à Carcassonne et **j'ai voulu goûter (14)** au cassoulet. Alors <u>nous sommes allés</u> dans **le meilleur (15)** restaurant de la ville **mais malheureusement (16) la soirée (17) a été (18)** un désastre! **J'ai commencé à (19)** <u>en</u> manger <u>mais aussitôt</u> **j'ai eu envie de vomir (20)**! **Nous avons dû (21)** quitter le restaurant très vite <u>car j'étais vraiment</u> malade! **Je ne mangerai plus jamais (22)** de cassoulet! [32]

Highlighted words = complex language

1 **Ce que j'aime le plus**   what I like the most
2 **en plein air**   outdoors
3 **si**   if
4 **nous allons**   'we' form
5 **Ce qui me plaît**   what I like
6 **où**   where
7 **comme**   like / such as
8 **Je ne pourrais pas**   I couldn't – modal verb in the conditional tense
9 **ne rien faire**   a negative with an infinitive
10 **qui**   who, subordinate clause
11 **je trouverais**   conditional tense to express an opinion
12 **goûter**   to taste – original verb
13 **nous avons passé**   perfect tense in the 'we' form
14 **j'ai voulu goûter**   2 verbs together – I wanted to try
15 **le meilleur**   the best — superlative
16 **malheureusement**   unfortunately
17 **la soirée**   original vocabulary — the evening
18 **a été**   perfect – was
19 **J'ai commencé à**   a verb followed by a preposition – I started to
20 **j'ai eu envie de vomir**   I felt sick – with <u>avoir envie de</u> + infinitive
21 **Nous avons dû**   modal verb in the perfect tense in the 'we' form – we had to
22 **Je ne mangerai plus jamais**   future tense with negative

Can you spot any other good language?
What can you say about the words or phrases that are underlined?
Are there any underlined words that you could improve?

Question 3

Example answer:

J'utilise les réseaux sociaux pour rester en contact avec mes ami(e)s / copains (copines). C'est très utile, parce qu'on peut (parce que tu peux / vous pouvez) envoyer des messages, ou partager des photos. Le week-end dernier, j'ai acheté une tablette qui est plus rapide que mon ordinateur et j'ai fait des recherches pour mes devoirs. Demain, je vais faire des achats en ligne et je voudrais / j'aimerais télécharger de la musique. [12]

Collins

GCSE
FRENCH

Higher Tier Paper 1 Listening Test Transcript

Section A	Questions and answers in **English**

01   **F1**   On vient de confirmer que le nombre de personnes qui sont sans emploi dans la région a augmenté le mois dernier et que ce sont surtout les jeunes qui ne trouvent pas de travail.

02   **F1**   Cette nuit un groupe de jeunes a cassé une fenêtre au premier étage de l'hôtel de la Place et a volé une somme d'argent importante. Ils ont été aperçus par des clients de l'hôtel.

03   **F1**   Cette semaine il va falloir être plus écolo et essayer de prendre les transports en commun ou marcher plus car un rapport nous montre que nous utilisons trop la voiture et que ce n'est pas bien pour notre ville et la planète!

04   **F1**   Finalement, n'oubliez pas d'envoyer vos noms et prénoms par e-mail pour essayer de gagner un séjour d'une semaine au Futuroscope pour quatre personnes. Vous avez jusqu'à ce soir minuit! Bonne chance.

05   **M1**   N'oubliez pas de vous inscrire à nos croisières sur le fleuve. Elles se déroulent chaque jour du mardi au dimanche, départ à dix heures.

06   **M1**   Vous pouvez réserver votre place en ligne ou à notre réception. Si vous le faites ici aujourd'hui vous aurez droit à une réduction de deux euros par adulte pour une croisière cette semaine.

07	M1	À bord, si vous ne voulez pas apporter votre propre nourriture, nous vous proposons une grande sélection de menus à tous les prix.
08	M1	Le Vélo'v permet aux personnes de louer un vélo en libre-service 24 heures sur 24 et 7 jours sur 7 depuis maintenant plus de 300 stations dans la ville de Lyon et le Vélo'v est de plus en plus apprécié, non seulement par les habitants mais aussi par ceux qui visitent la ville.
09	M1	Émeline, que pensez-vous du Vélo'v?
	F2	Je pense que le Vélo'v est un moyen efficace pour réduire la pollution et que c'est le moyen de transport le plus pratique puisqu'on peut le prendre où on veut et quand on veut. Mes amis pensent le contraire mais ils l'utilisent quand même de temps en temps.
10	M1	Mais beaucoup disent que c'est un système qui est assez cher et qui est dangereux.
	F2	Cher? Je ne suis pas d'accord. Il ne coûte presque rien comparé au prix des autres moyens de transport qui eux peuvent coûter une fortune aux utilisateurs. Dangereux…oui, on ne peut pas ignorer les problèmes de circulation. Pour encourager les gens à utiliser le vélo au lieu de la voiture, la ville a construit plus de pistes cyclables mais des collisions ont lieu le plus souvent dans les rues qui ne sont pas assez larges. Il est vrai que certaines pistes cyclables sont assez dangereuses.
11	M1	Le shopping en ligne devient très populaire. Pensez-vous que les achats en ligne pourraient remplacer le shopping en ville, Françoise?
	F2	Il est pratique d'acheter des choses en ligne (quand on habite loin des centres commerciaux), mais on ne peut pas les essayer.
12	M1	Et vous, Didier, qu'en pensez-vous?
	M2	Je trouve que c'est bien de pouvoir comparer les prix avant d'acheter quelque chose, mais ce que je n'apprécie pas, c'est quand il faut rester des heures à la maison à attendre la livraison!
13	F2	À mon avis la mode c'est la vie. Pour la plupart des ados, avoir un style, un look, c'est vraiment nécessaire. Ça donne plus de confiance en soi.

14	F3	La mode est une chose inutile pour moi, car chacun devrait s'habiller comme il le souhaite et non pas en suivant une mode. Et si tout le monde suivait la mode, nous serions tous vêtus de la même façon, ce qui serait comme un uniforme scolaire!
15	M1	Êtes-vous sportif, Pierre?
	M2	Au collège, je ne suis pas très sportif, car j'ai horreur des sports d'équipe. Pendant les grandes vacances, cependant, j'aime bien faire des sports nautiques. Cet été je voudrais essayer la planche à voile. Ce sera beaucoup plus amusant que le foot!
16	F1	Le 14 juillet, la fête nationale bat son plein à Paris. Du matin au soir, si vous êtes visiteur ou parisien, jeune ou pas si jeune, il y aura un programme varié pour tous les âges et tous les goûts à ne pas manquer!
		Le matin, le défilé militaire commencera à onze heures, après l'arrivée du président à 10h 20.
		Le soir, pour admirer le feu d'artifice dès 23h, on propose un dîner-croisière à bord d'un bateau sur la Seine. Ou, sans dépenser d'argent, la meilleure solution sera d'aller à l'un des parcs publics qui offre une vue magnifique sur la tour Eiffel.
17	F2	Les habitants de Neuvic sont inquiets à cause d'un projet proposé par la chaîne de supermarchés Leclerc qui veut construire un grand centre commercial, c'est-à-dire une grande surface à côté de la ville. Les habitants croient que les petits commerces vont souffrir.
	F2	Je suis avec Monsieur David, boulanger dans la ville et représentant des commerces locaux. Alors, Monsieur David, de quoi avez-vous peur?
	M1	Il est clair que le supermarché va offrir un grand choix de produits bon marché et que la plupart des gens y feront leurs courses. Ce qui n'est pas clair, c'est que ces produits ne seront probablement pas de la même qualité. En conséquence les petits commerces et les boutiques en ville finiront par fermer.
18	F2	Madame Félix, vous êtes employée chez Leclerc et chargée de faire construire ce centre. Vous pensez que la ville en bénéficiera?

	F1	Oui, à long terme, la ville deviendra plus forte. Écoutez, les centres commerciaux apportent avec eux de grands avantages. Plus de gens visitent la ville en passant et ils iront dans les petits commerces et les cafés. En plus, Leclerc va améliorer les routes et les transports en commun.
19	F2	Danny, tu viens de Neuvic et tu es étudiant dans un lycée de Périgueux. Qu'en penses-tu?
	M2	Pour moi c'est un compromis dont on a besoin parce que les habitudes envers le shopping ont changé. La ville doit souhaiter la bienvenue aux grandes surfaces parce que cela va apporter des emplois et de nouvelles maisons. Mais en même temps le supermarché doit encourager ses clients à venir ici, dans la vieille ville, grâce à de la publicité gratuite.
20	F3	Vous êtes tenté par les cigarettes? C'est cool, hé? Vos amis achètent des cigarettes électroniques? «Ah» disent-ils, «Ce n'est pas dangereux. Mon grand-père fume depuis toujours… Mon père a renoncé au tabac mais a choisi la cigarette électronique pour avoir toujours l'impression de fumer!» Ne les écoutez pas! Le tabac provoque des cancers. La cigarette électronique…qui sait? Soyez-en certains. Évitez de fumer. Électrique ou pas.
21	M2	Vous savez combien de tasses de sucres il y a dans cette cannette de soda?
	M3	Oui, mais ce n'est pas grave, je fais du sport, moi.
	M2	Vous savez que plus de jeunes sont obèses que jamais?
	M3	Non, ce n'est pas vrai!
	M2	Si! Et en plus, ce n'est pas du tout bon pour les dents…
	M3	Et alors…?
	M2	Essayez/Buvez de l'eau minérale. C'est bon pour la santé…et c'est français!
	M3	Oh là là, ben oui…
22	F1	Lucas, que fais-tu ici en Côte d'Ivoire?
	M1	En ce moment je fais une année sabbatique. Je suis en train d'étudier pour devenir médecin et j'ai décidé de venir ici avant de commencer mes deux dernières années parce que j'ai vu à la télé des images qui m'ont choqué. Ces gens ont besoin d'aide médicale, donc je suis venu ici comme bénévole. C'est une mission organisée par une association caritative.

Section B   Questions and answers in **French**

23   **F1**   Maxime, tes rapports avec tes parents, ils sont comment?

   M2   Ils ne sont pas toujours faciles. Mes parents sont divorcés et j'habite chez ma mère. Mon père s'est remarié il y a deux ans et depuis, je ne le vois que rarement. Il s'intéresse plus à sa nouvelle famille, car il a eu un enfant avec ma belle-mère. Quand on se voit, mon père n'a pratiquement rien à me dire. Je trouve ça triste, puisqu'avant le divorce, on avait beaucoup de choses en commun.

24   **F1**   Et les relations avec ta mère, elles sont comment?

   M2   Je m'entends mieux avec elle qu'avec mon père. Le problème, c'est que, depuis le divorce, elle doit gagner plus d'argent, donc ses horaires de travail sont plutôt longs et elle est souvent fatiguée. En général, on s'entend bien ensemble et je sais que je peux me confier à elle. Mais de temps en temps elle se fâche contre moi, par exemple à cause des tâches ménagères que je n'ai pas faites, ou parfois si je n'ai pas assez bien travaillé au collège.

25   **M3**   Nabila, que penses-tu des réseaux sociaux?

   F3   Pour mes amis et moi, Facebook, c'est l'invention la plus importante du siècle! On peut tenir ses amis au courant de ce qu'on fait en envoyant des messages et en partageant des photos ou des vidéos. Je l'utilise pour rester en contact avec les autres, puisqu'il est si facile de se retrouver en ligne à tout moment. C'est vraiment le meilleur moyen de communication pour moi.

   Et toi, Malik, qu'est-ce que tu en penses?

   M3   Il est évident que les réseaux sociaux sont très populaires, et pas seulement chez les jeunes. Mais je pense que les gens y passent trop de temps, au lieu de se retrouver en personne et de parler face-à-face. De plus, ça devient trop souvent un concours de popularité – «Tu as combien d'amis sur Facebook?», «Moi, j'en ai trente, quarante, cinquante», etc. Et le cyberharcèlement est un gros problème de nos jours, parce qu'il est trop facile d'écrire quelque chose de méchant en ligne et de rester anonyme.

26   **F1**   Il ne faut jamais partager son mot de passe avec les autres, même avec ses amis. Il est très important aussi de ne pas garder trop longtemps le même mot de passe, parce qu'il peut être découvert. Changez-le une fois par mois.

           M1   Il faut toujours savoir avec qui on parle en ligne et refuser le contact si on ne reconnaît pas le nom ou l'adresse e-mail de l'envoyeur. Si vous recevez un document en ligne d'une source inconnue, surtout ne pas l'ouvrir, car il peut contenir un virus dangereux pour votre ordinateur.

END OF TEST

Revision Tips

Rethink Revision

Have you ever taken part in a quiz and thought *'I know this!'* but, despite frantically racking your brain, you just couldn't come up with the answer?

It's very frustrating when this happens but, in a fun situation, it doesn't really matter. However, in your GCSE exams, it will be essential that you can recall the relevant information quickly when you need to.

Most students think that revision is about making sure you **know** stuff. Of course, this is important, but it is also about becoming confident that you can **retain** that *stuff* over time and **recall** it quickly when needed.

Revision That Really Works

Experts have discovered that there are two techniques that help with all of these things and consistently produce better results in exams compared to other revision techniques.

Applying these techniques to your GCSE revision will ensure you get better results in your exams and will have all the relevant knowledge at your fingertips when you start studying for further qualifications, like AS and A Levels, or begin work.

It really isn't rocket science either – you simply need to:

- **test yourself** on each topic as many times as possible
- **leave a gap** between the test sessions.

Three Essential Revision Tips

1. **Use Your Time Wisely**

   - Allow yourself plenty of time.
   - Try to start revising at least six months before your exams – it's more effective and less stressful.
   - Your revision time is precious so use it wisely – using the techniques described on this page will ensure you revise effectively and efficiently and get the best results.
   - Don't waste time re-reading the same information over and over again – it's time-consuming and not effective!

2. **Make a Plan**

   - Identify all the topics you need to revise (this All-in-One Revision & Practice book will help you).
   - Plan at least five sessions for each topic.
   - One hour should be ample time to test yourself on the key ideas for a topic.
   - Spread out the practice sessions for each topic – the optimum time to leave between each session is about one month but, if this isn't possible, just make the gaps as big as realistically possible.

3. **Test Yourself**

   - Methods for testing yourself include: quizzes, practice questions, flashcards, past papers, explaining a topic to someone else, etc.
   - This All-in-One Revision & Practice book provides seven practice opportunities per topic.
   - Don't worry if you get an answer wrong – provided you check what the correct answer is, you are more likely to get the same or similar questions right in future!

Visit our website to download your free flashcards, for more information about the benefits of these techniques, and for further guidance on how to plan ahead and make them work for you.

www.collins.co.uk/collinsGCSErevision